Latifa Echakhch

jrp|ringier

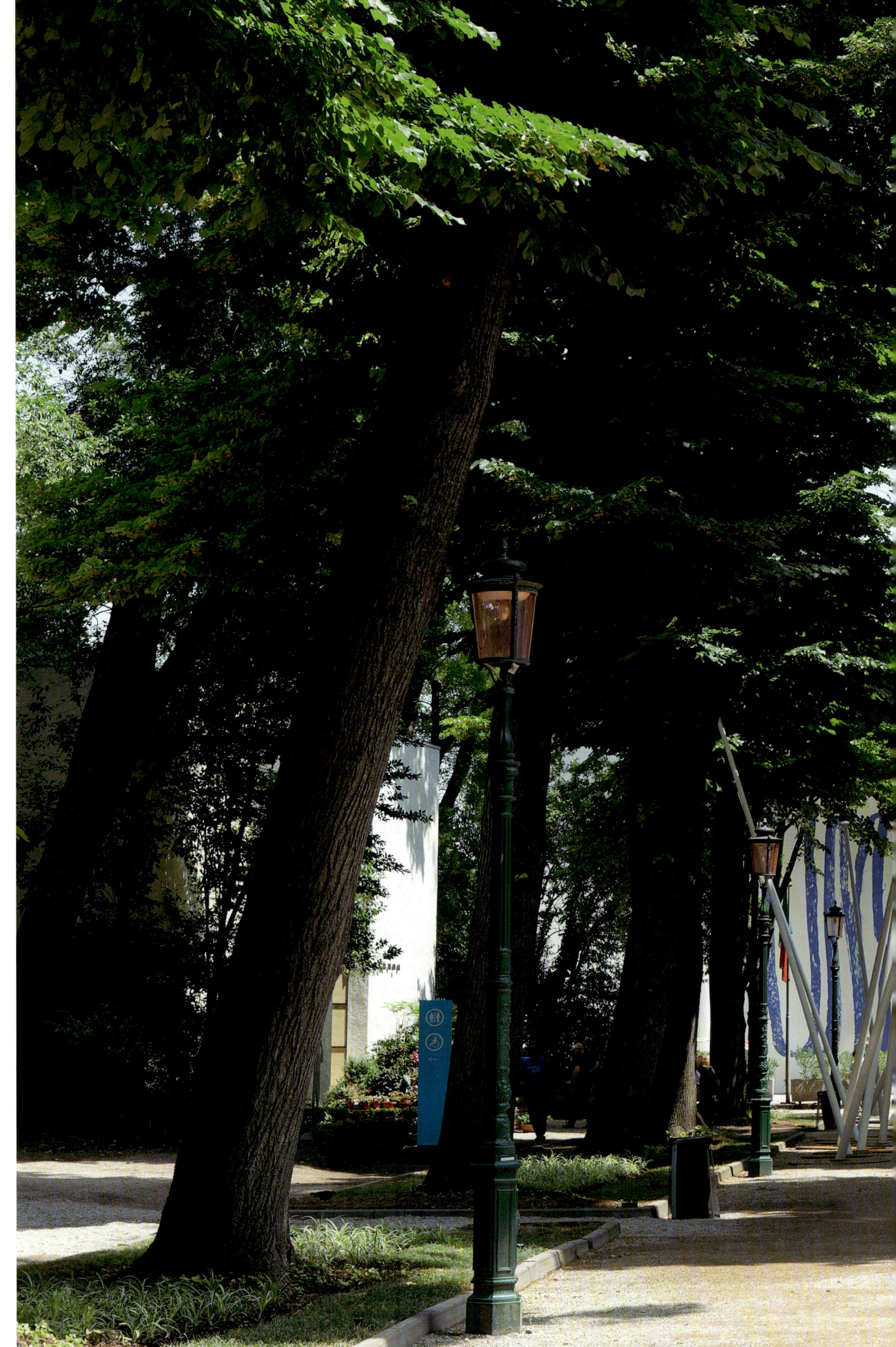

Fantasia (Empty Flag), 2011
Exhibition view, ILLUMInations, 54th Venice Biennale, Venice, 2011
Fiberglass flagpoles and steel bases, dimensions variable, max. height: 10 m

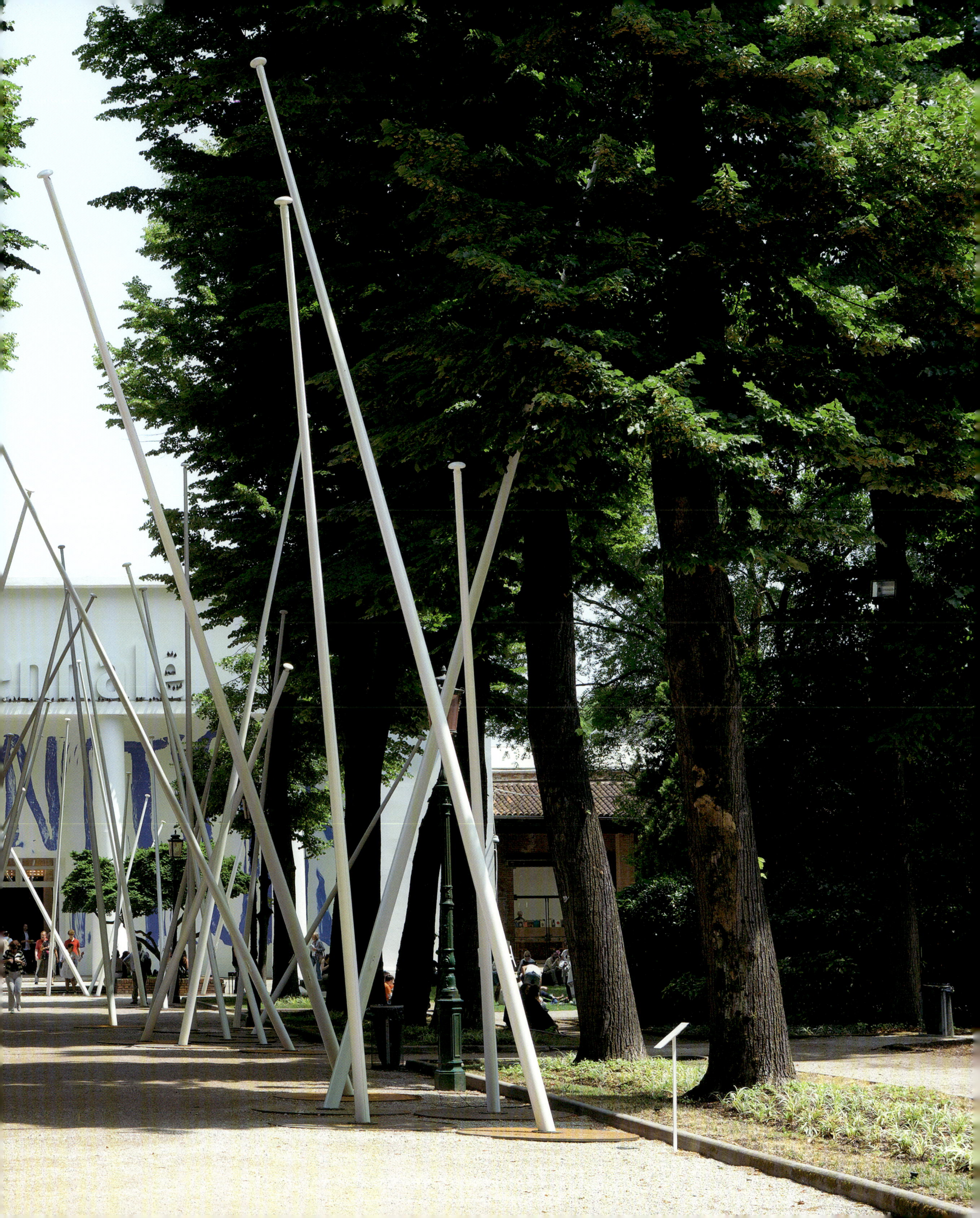

Plainte, 2009
Exhibition view, Movement and Complication, Swiss Institute, New York, 2009
Charcoal on walls, dimensions variable, different heights (according to Le Corbusier's Modulor dimensions):
27 cm, 43 cm, 70 cm, 86 cm, 113 cm, 140 cm, 183 cm, and 226 cm

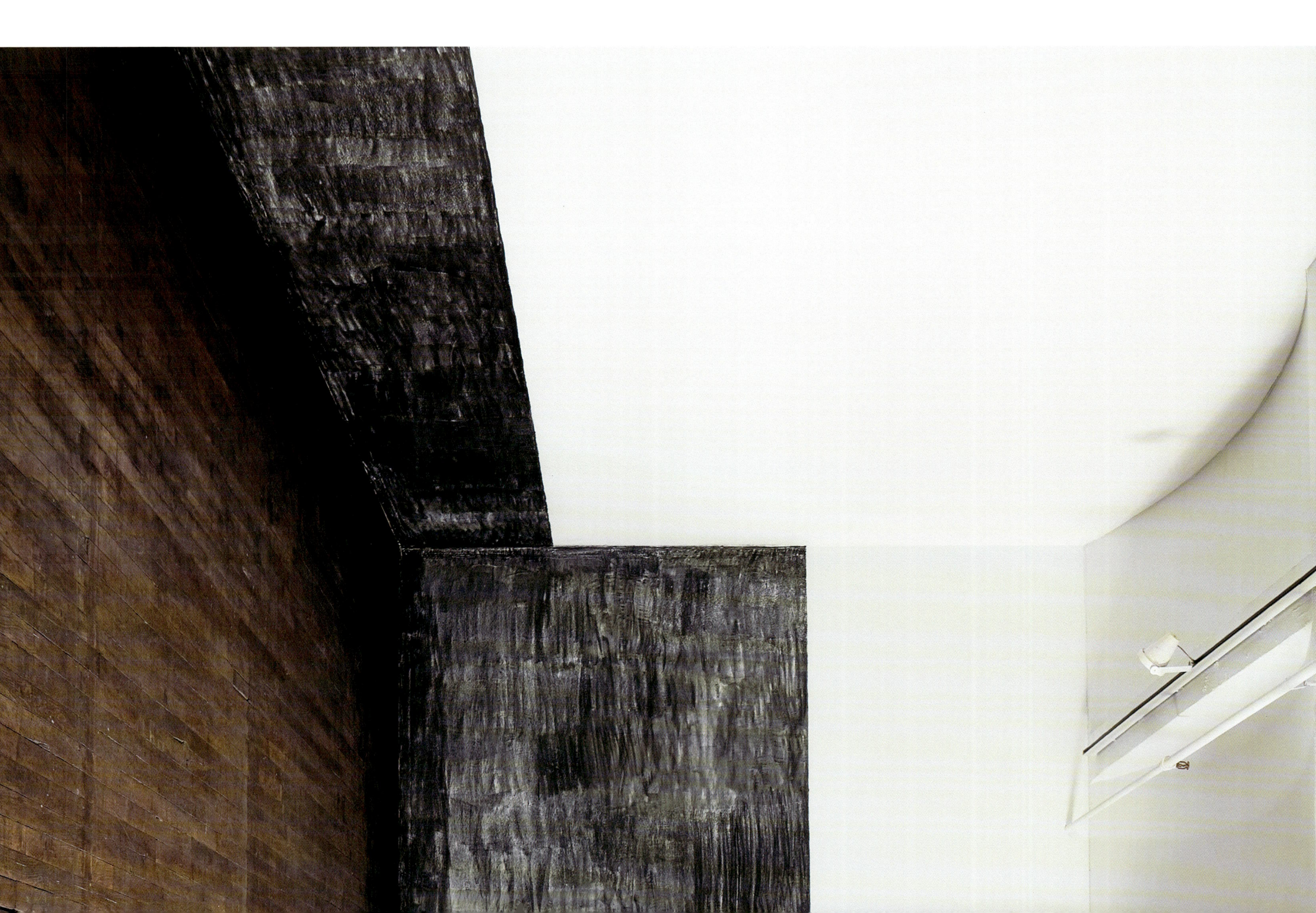

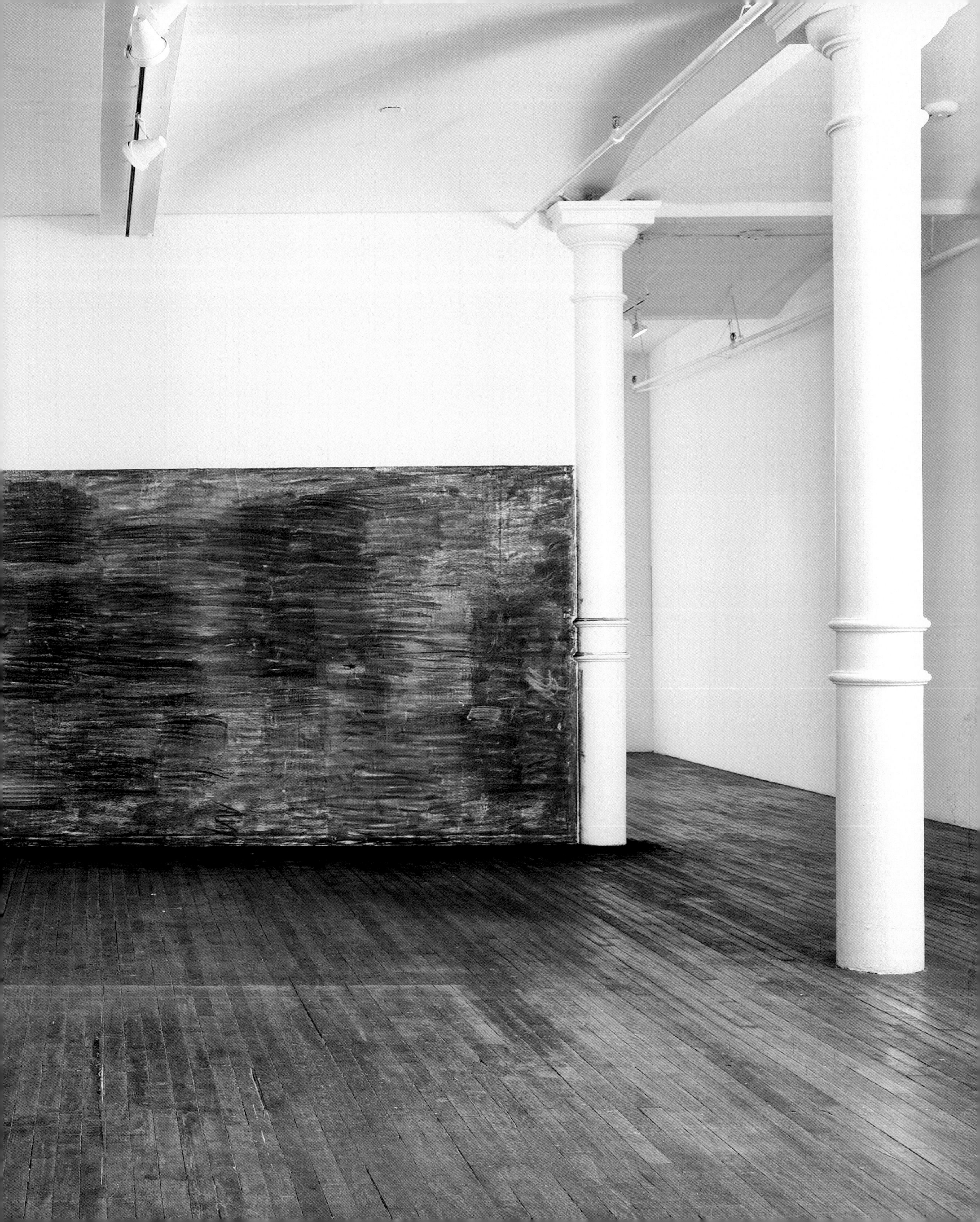

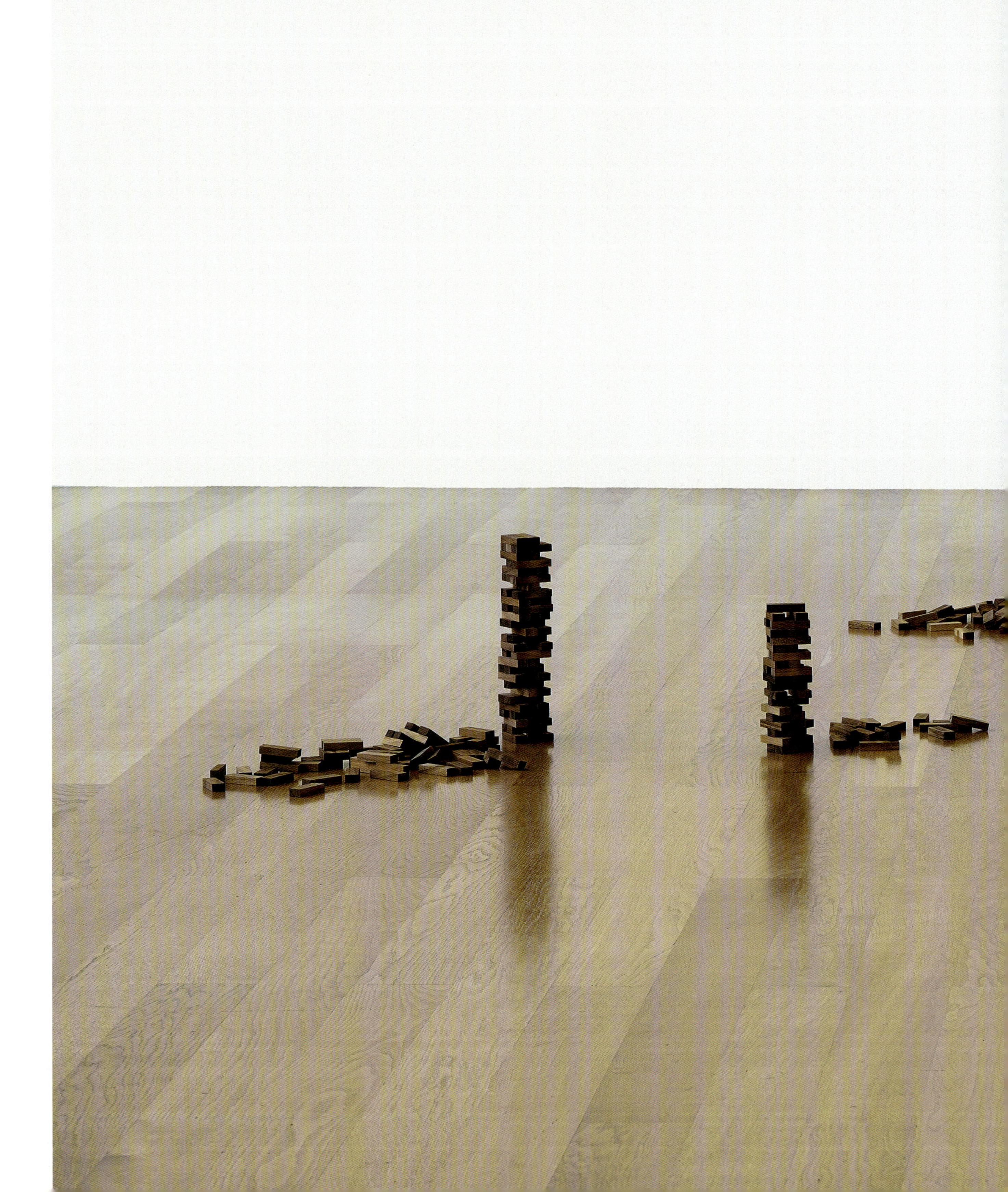

Tour de Babel, 2010–2011
Exhibition view, Dialogue: Latifa Echakhch, Kunstmuseum Liechtenstein, Vaduz, 2012
Wood, dimensions variable, height: c. 40 cm

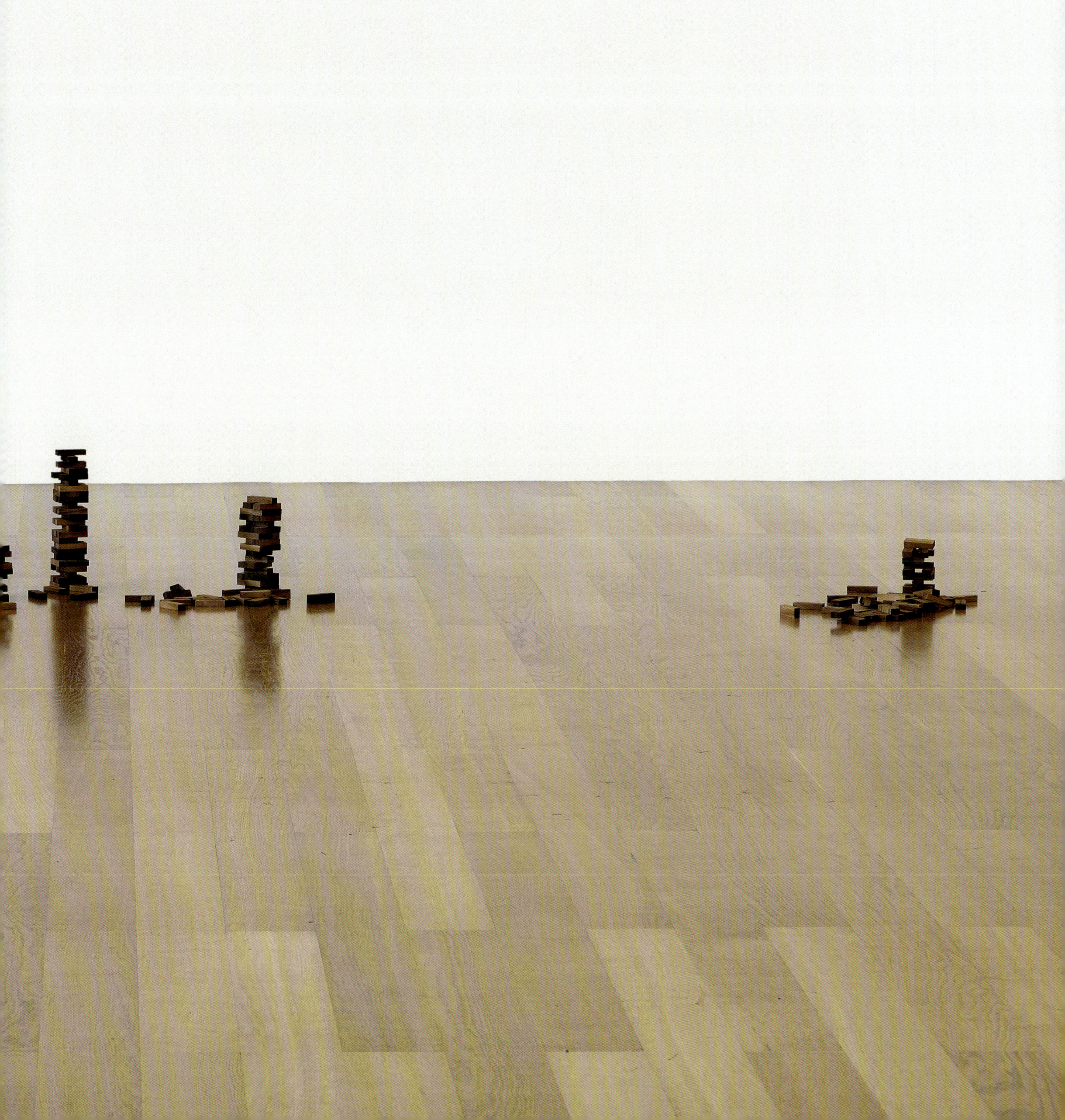

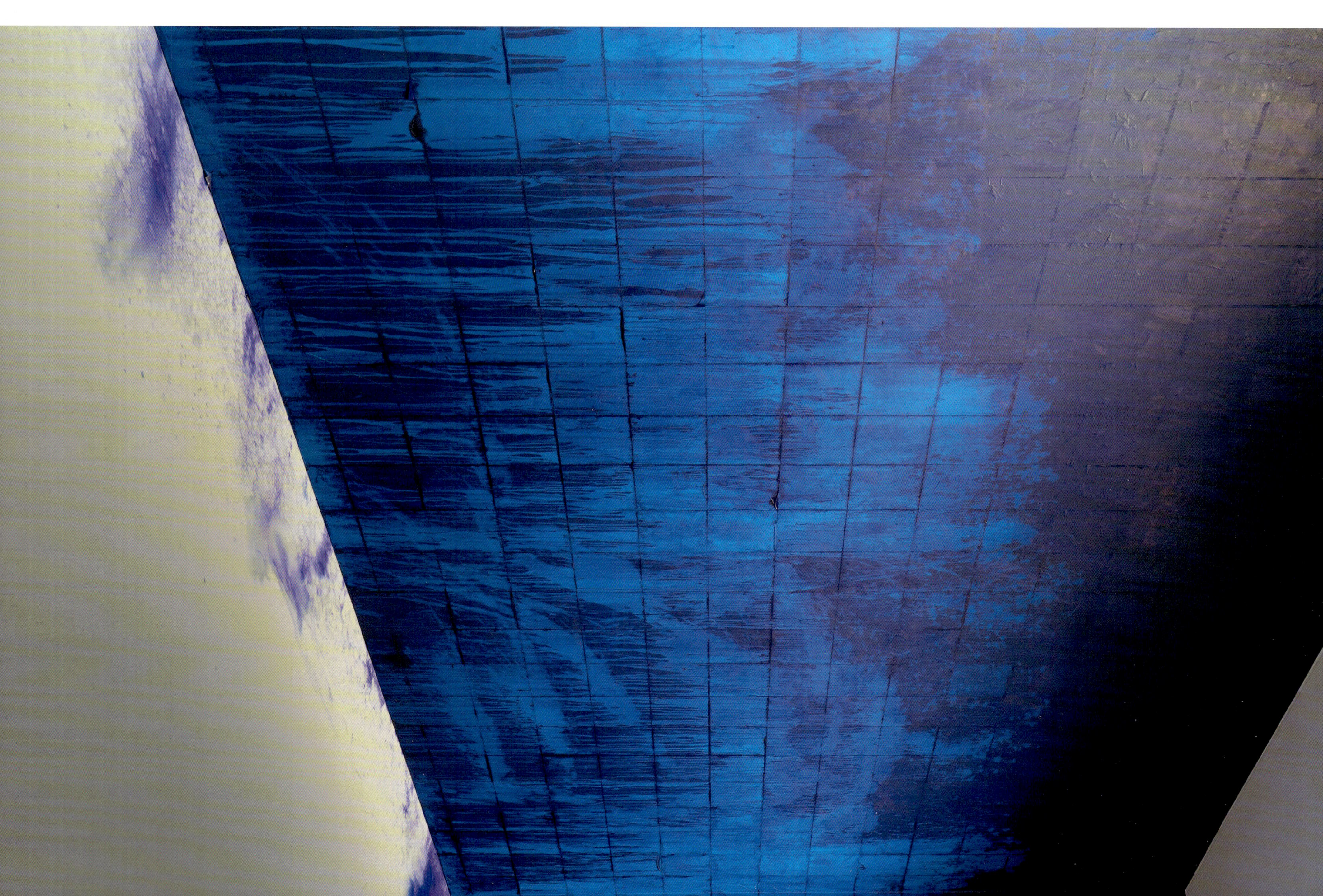

À chaque stencil une révolution, 2007
Exhibition view, Volume!, MACBA, Barcelona, 2011
Wall installation; A4 carbon paper, glue, methylated alcohol, dimensions variable
Collection MACBA-Museu d'Art Contemporani, Barcelona

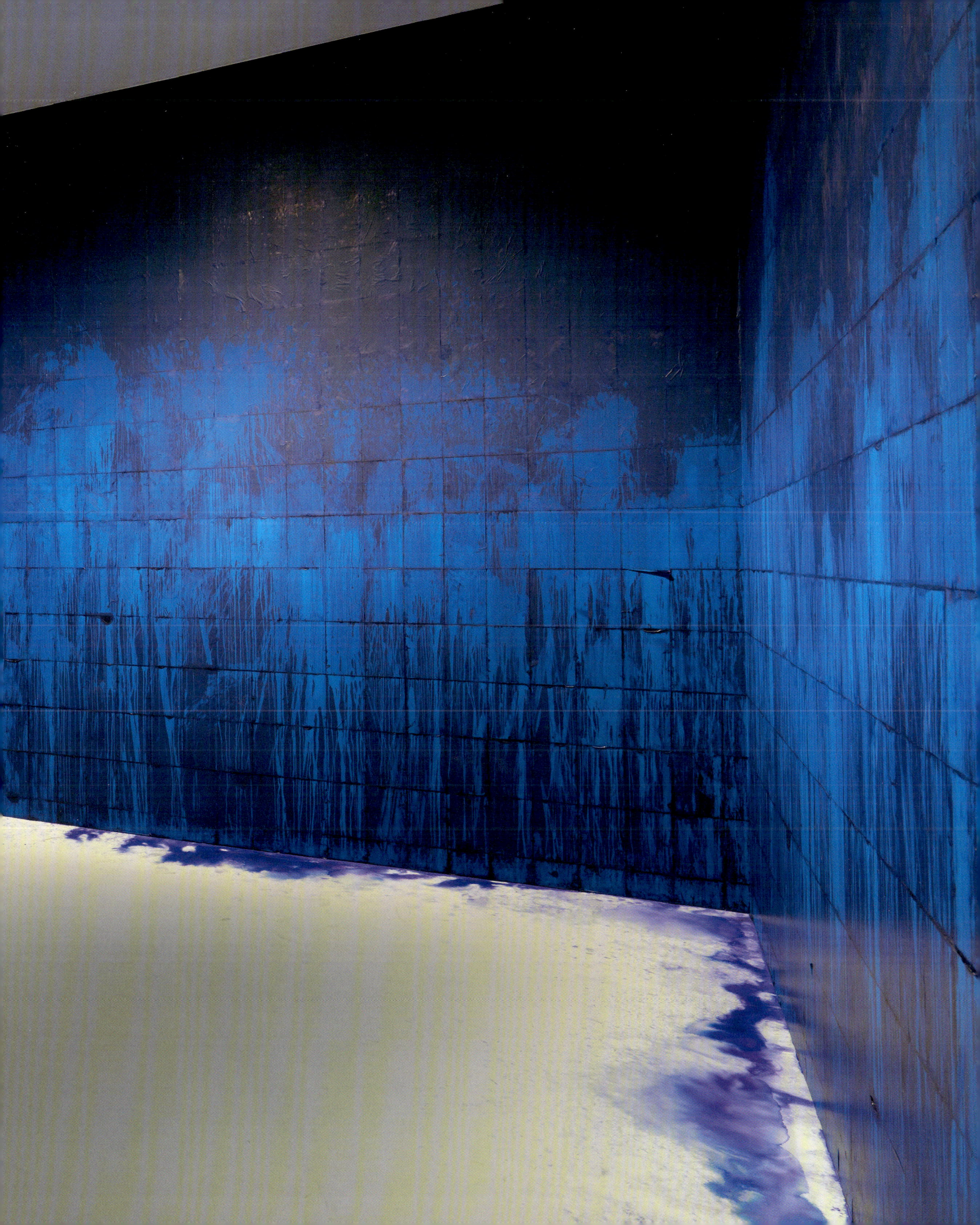

Gaya (E102) Horizon, 2010
Exhibition view, Le rappel des oiseaux, GAMeC, Bergamo, 2010
E102 synthetic food dye, water, dimensions variable, height: 166 cm (artist's eyes level)
Collection FRAC Lorraine, Metz
With a detail of Le thé de Saïd, 2010

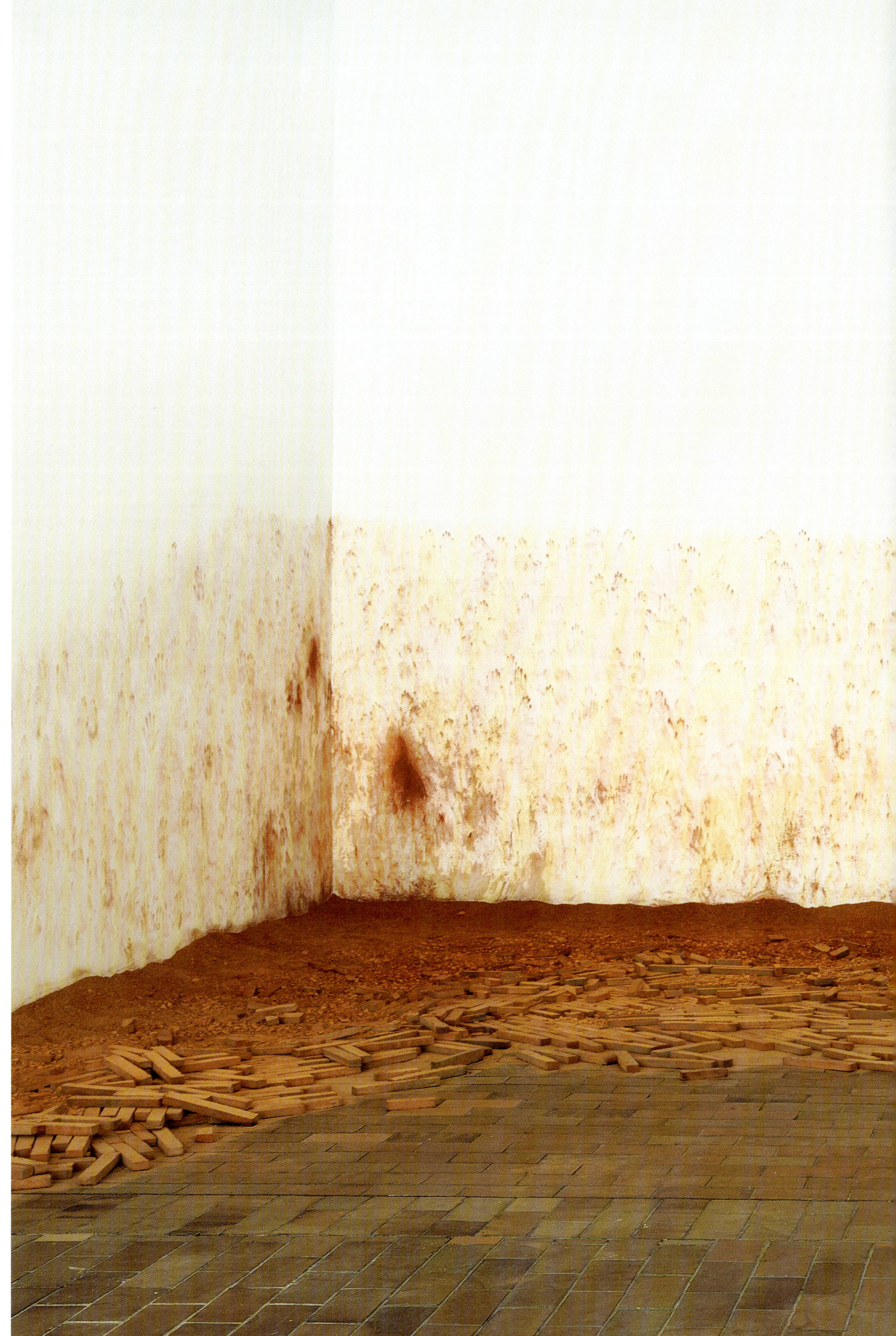

Tkaf, 2011
Exhibition view, You Are Not Alone, Fundació Miró, Barcelona, 2011
Bricks and sanguine pigment, max. height: 2 m

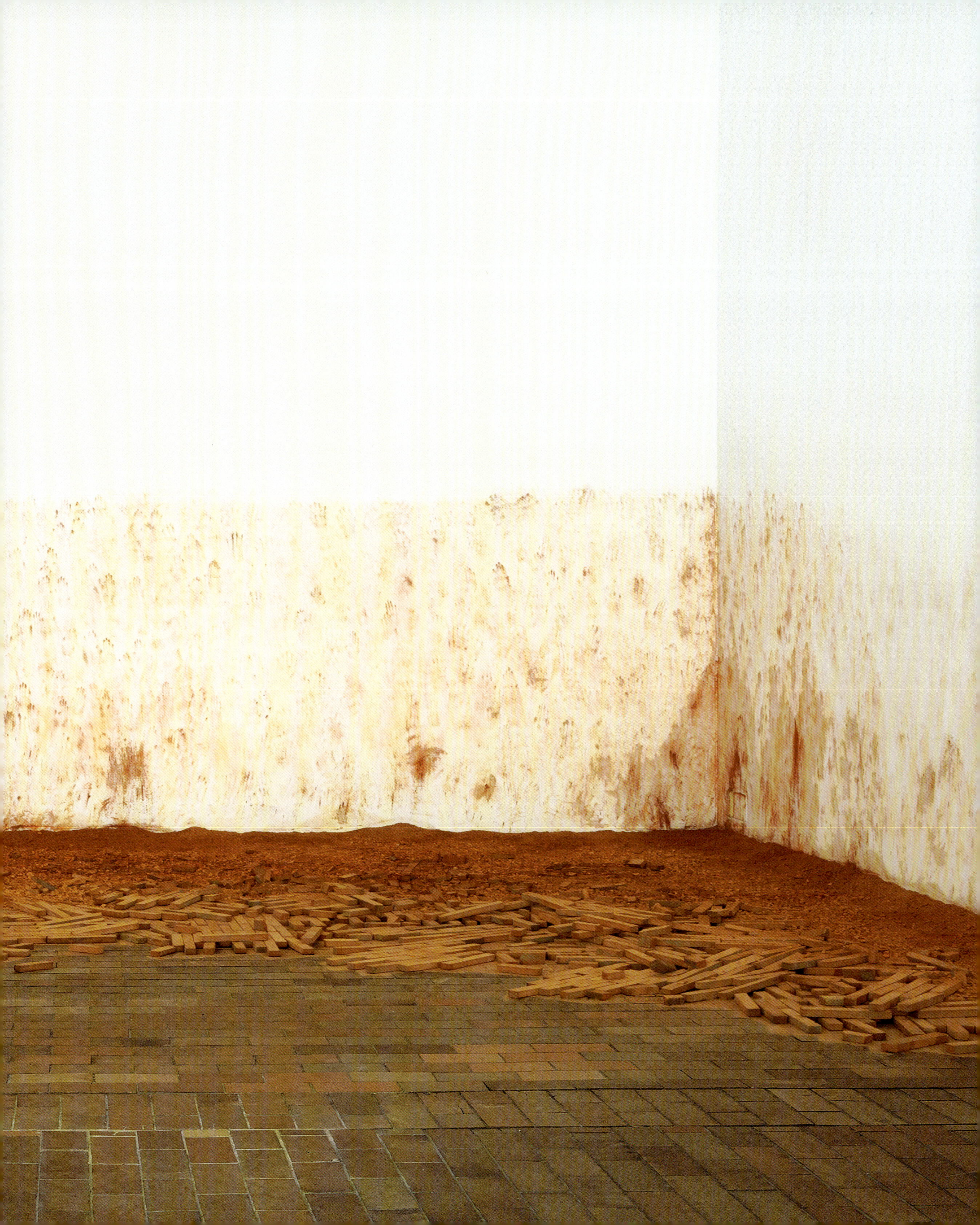

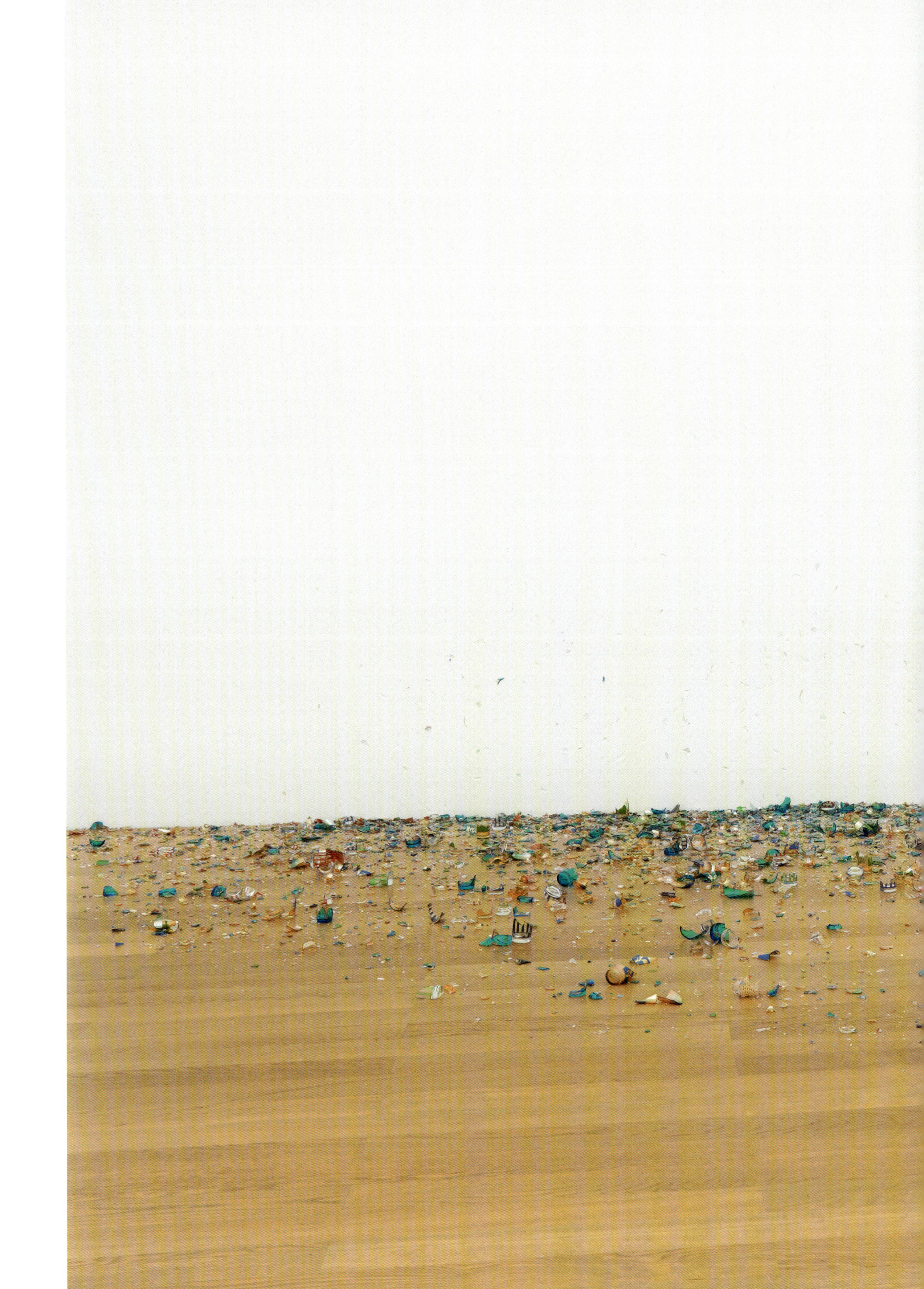

Erratum, 2009
Exhibition view, Example Switzerland, Kunstmuseum Liechtenstein, Vaduz, 2011
Tea glasses smashed on site, dimensions variable according to the walls
Collection Kunstmuseum Liechtenstein, Vaduz

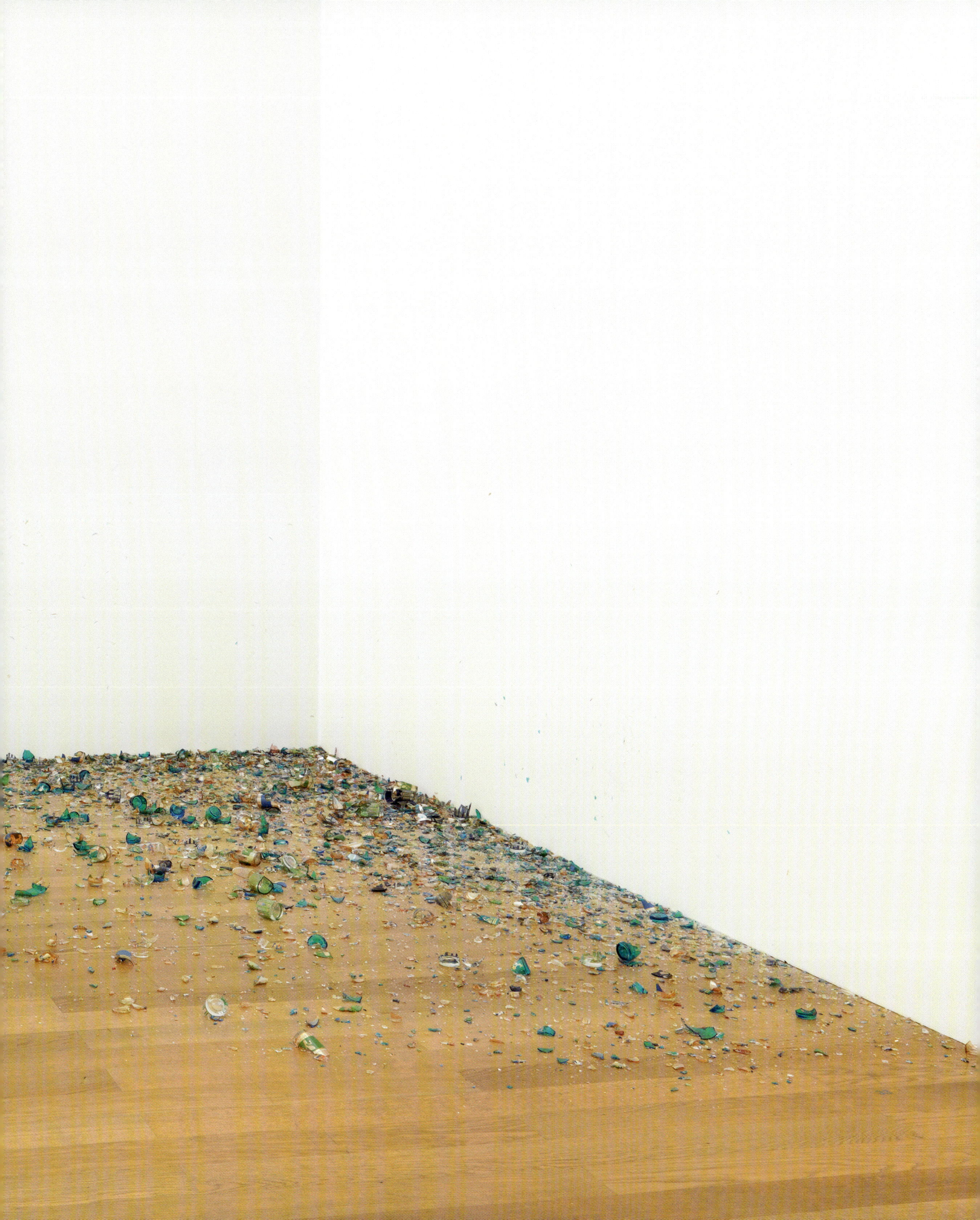

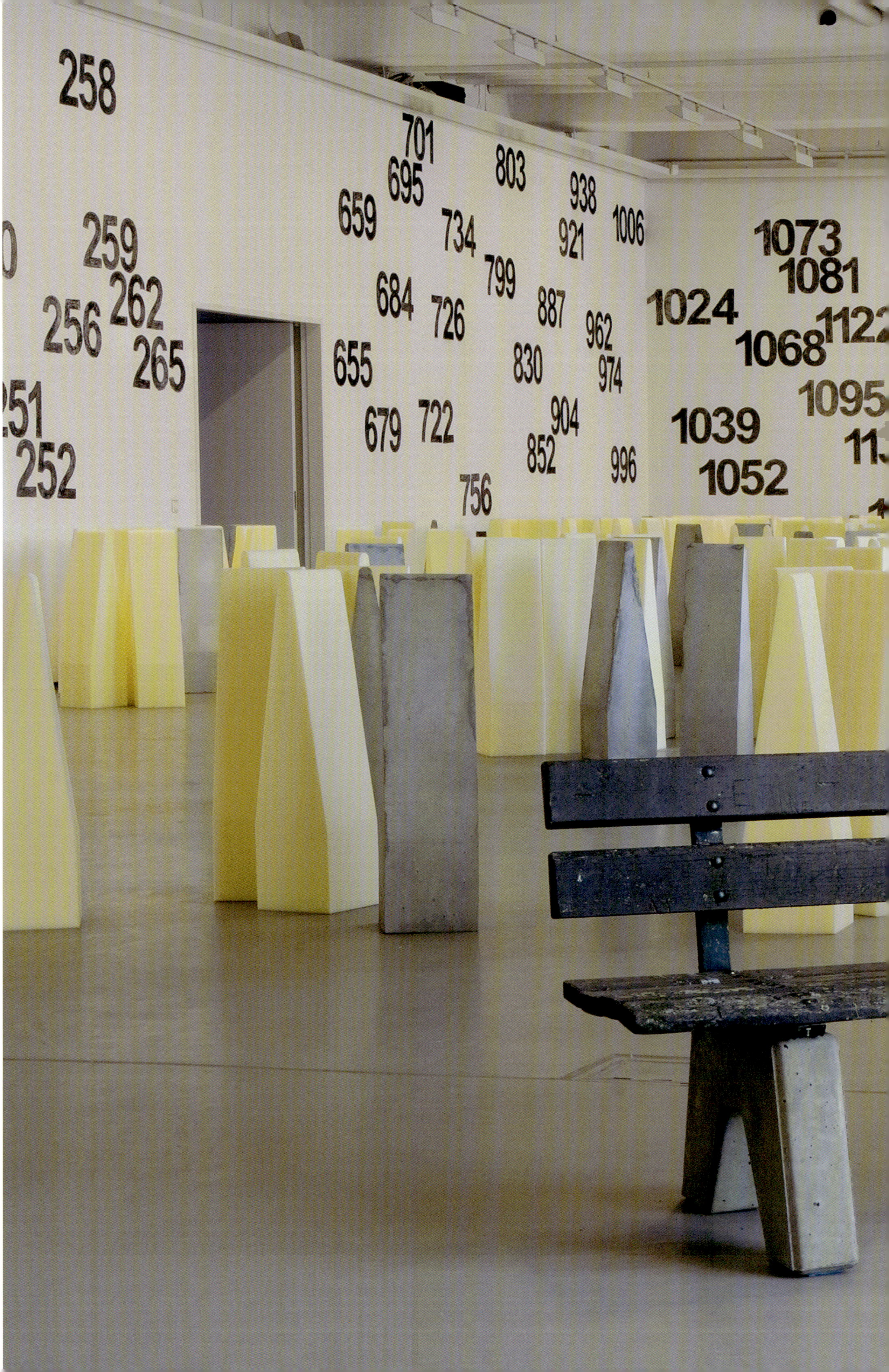

Exhibition view, Les sanglots longs, Kunsthalle Fridericianum, Kassel, 2009
With the works Kasseler Parkbänke, 2009; Chambre, 2009; Résolutions, 2009–in progress

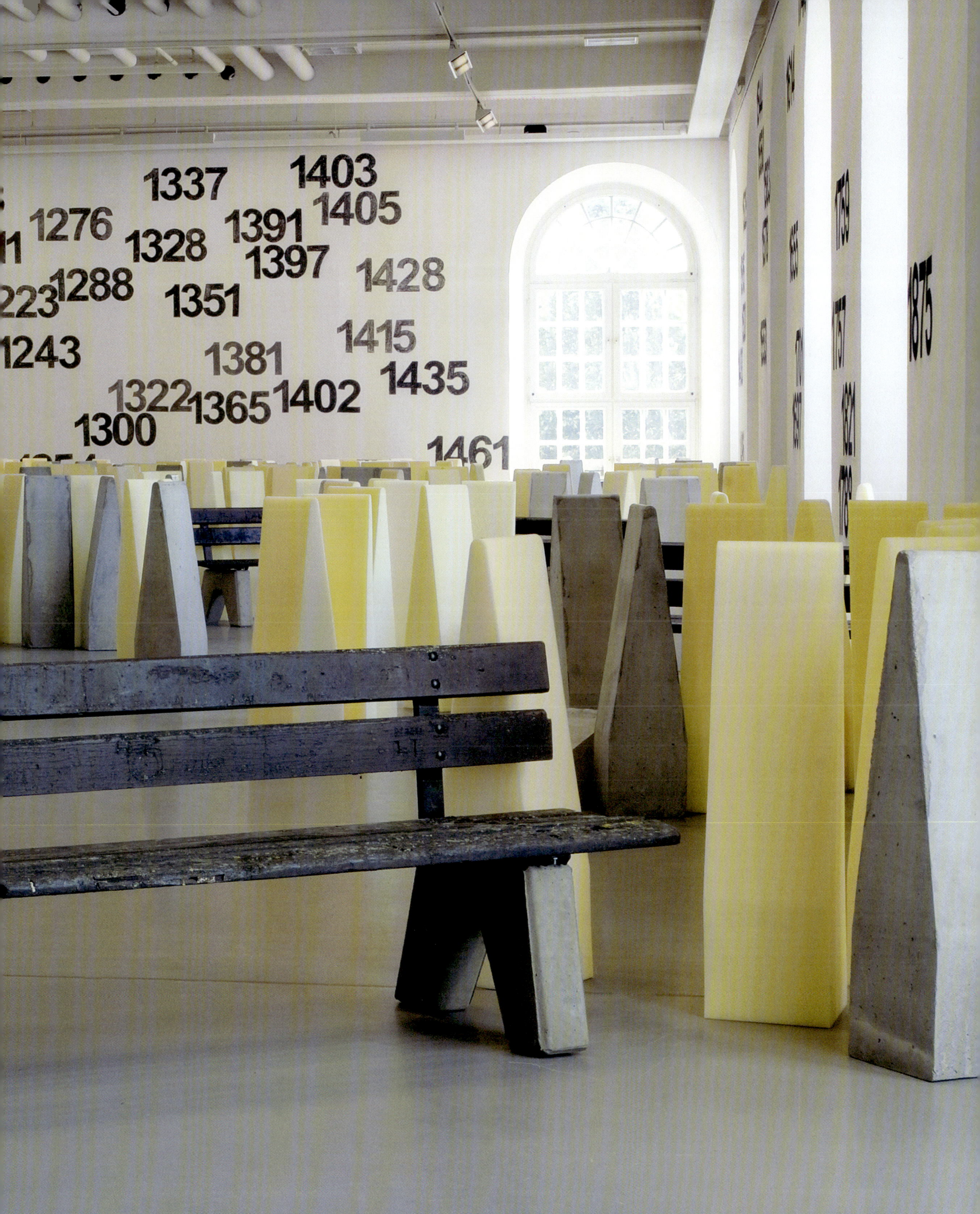
1337
1403
1405
1276
1391
1328
1397
1428
1288
1351
1415
1243
1381
1435
1322
1365
1402
1300
1461
1769
1875
1757
1821

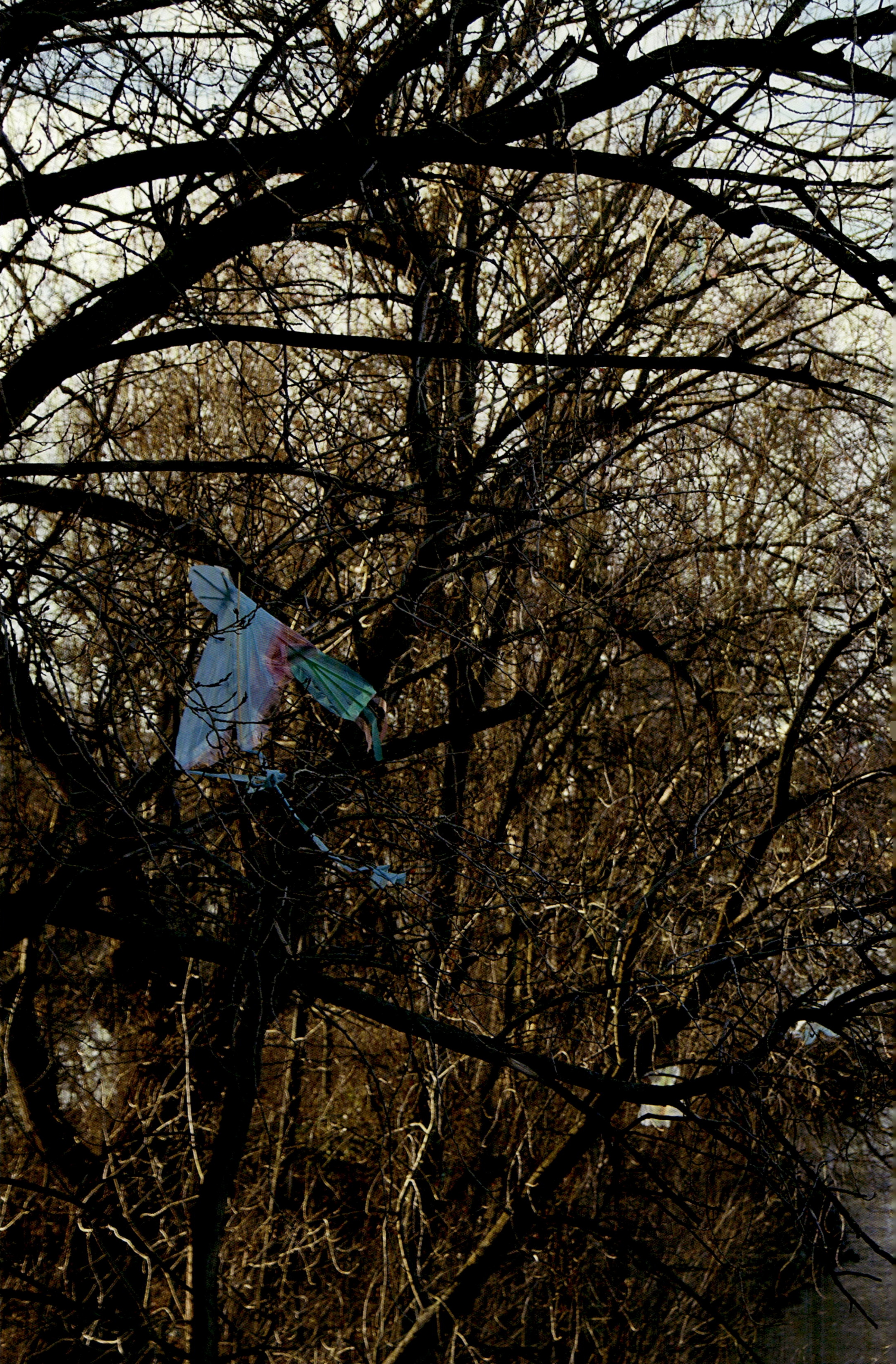

Die Vögel, 2012
Exhibition view, Die Vögel, Portikus, Frankfurt, 2012
Plastic bag kite, wood, tape, staples, ties, dimensions variable

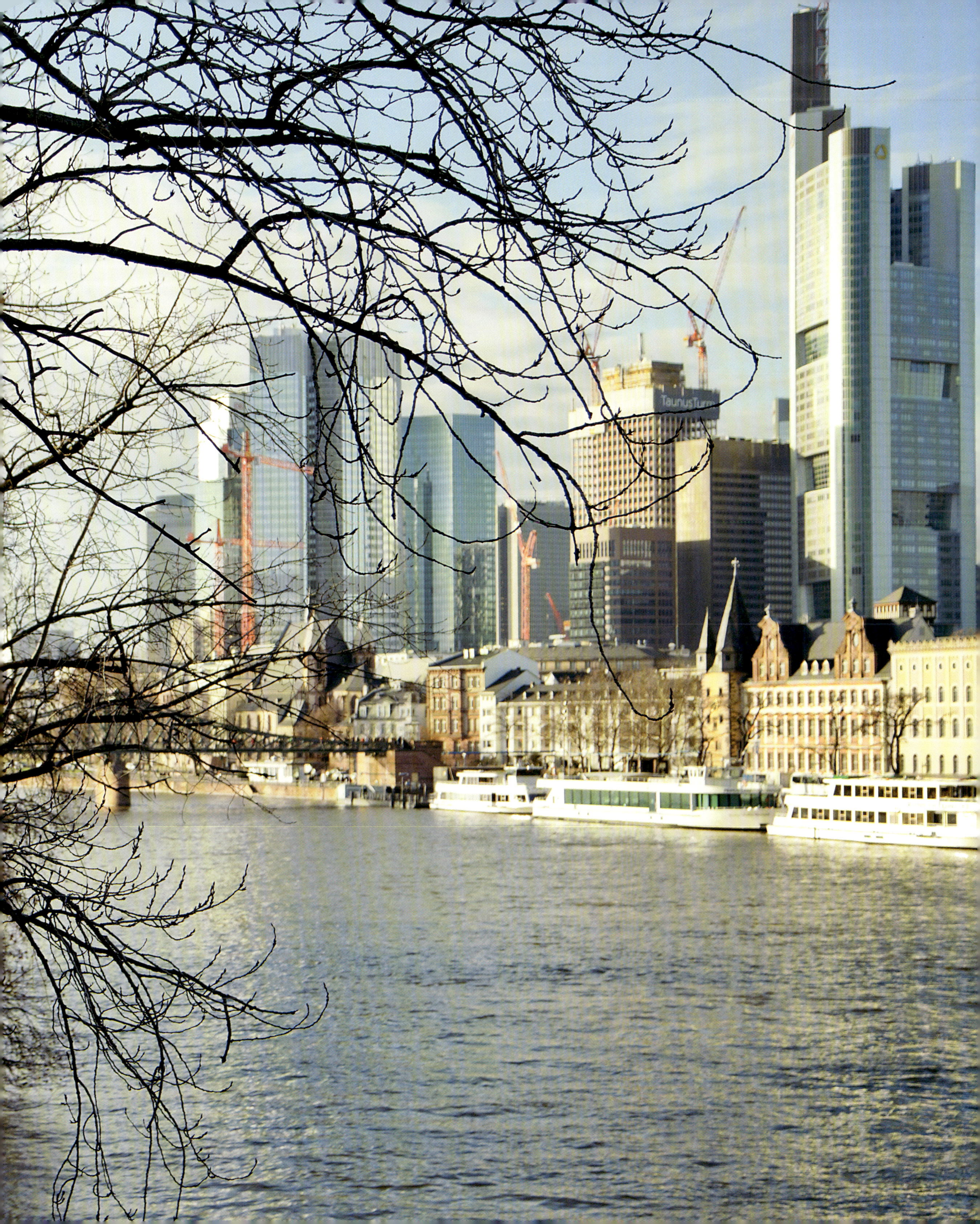
TaunusTurm

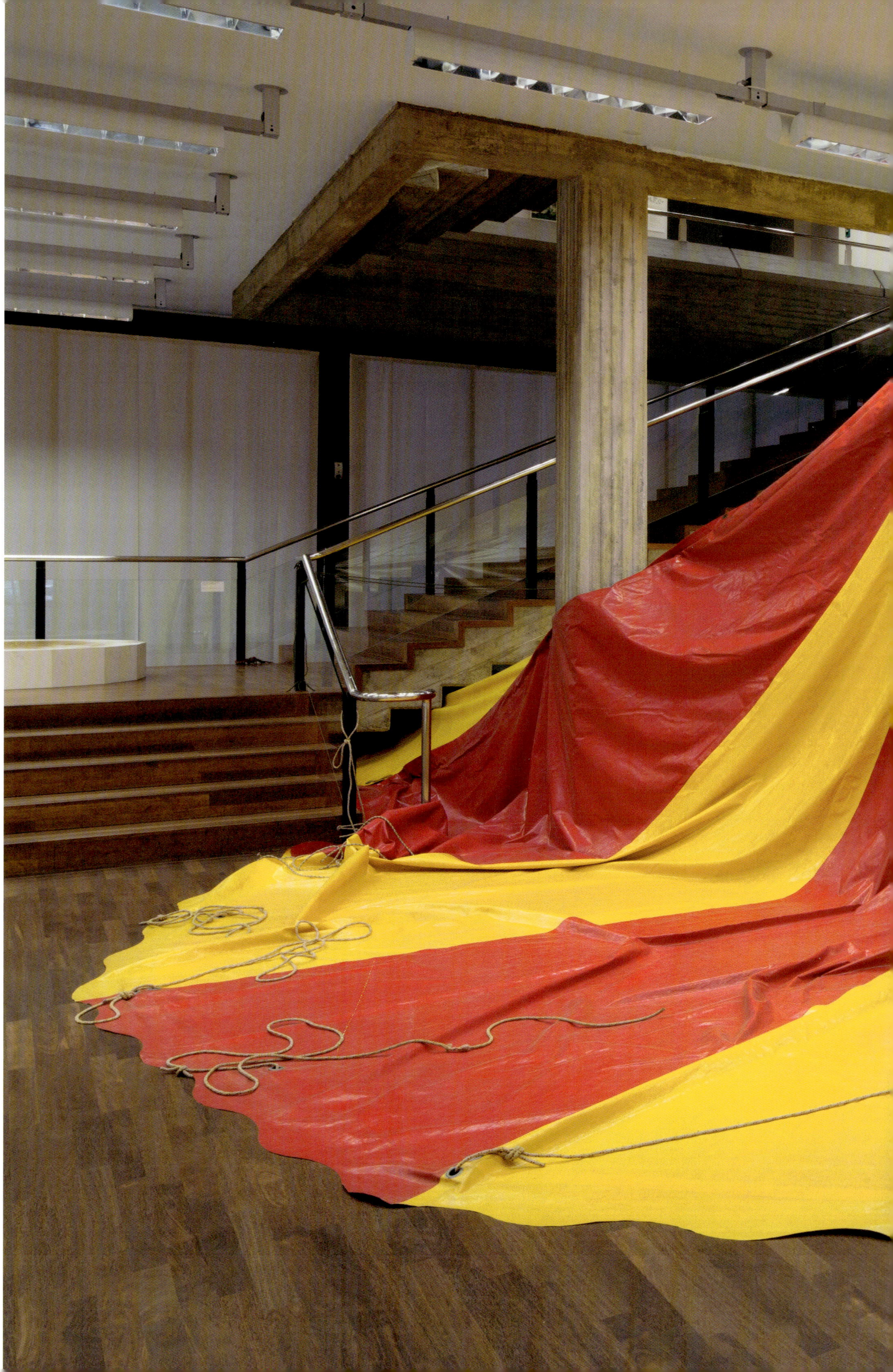

Exhibition view, Goodbye Horses, Kunsthaus Zürich, Zurich, 2012
With the works Untitled (Circus Tent), 2012; Untitled (One Figure and a Ball), 2012

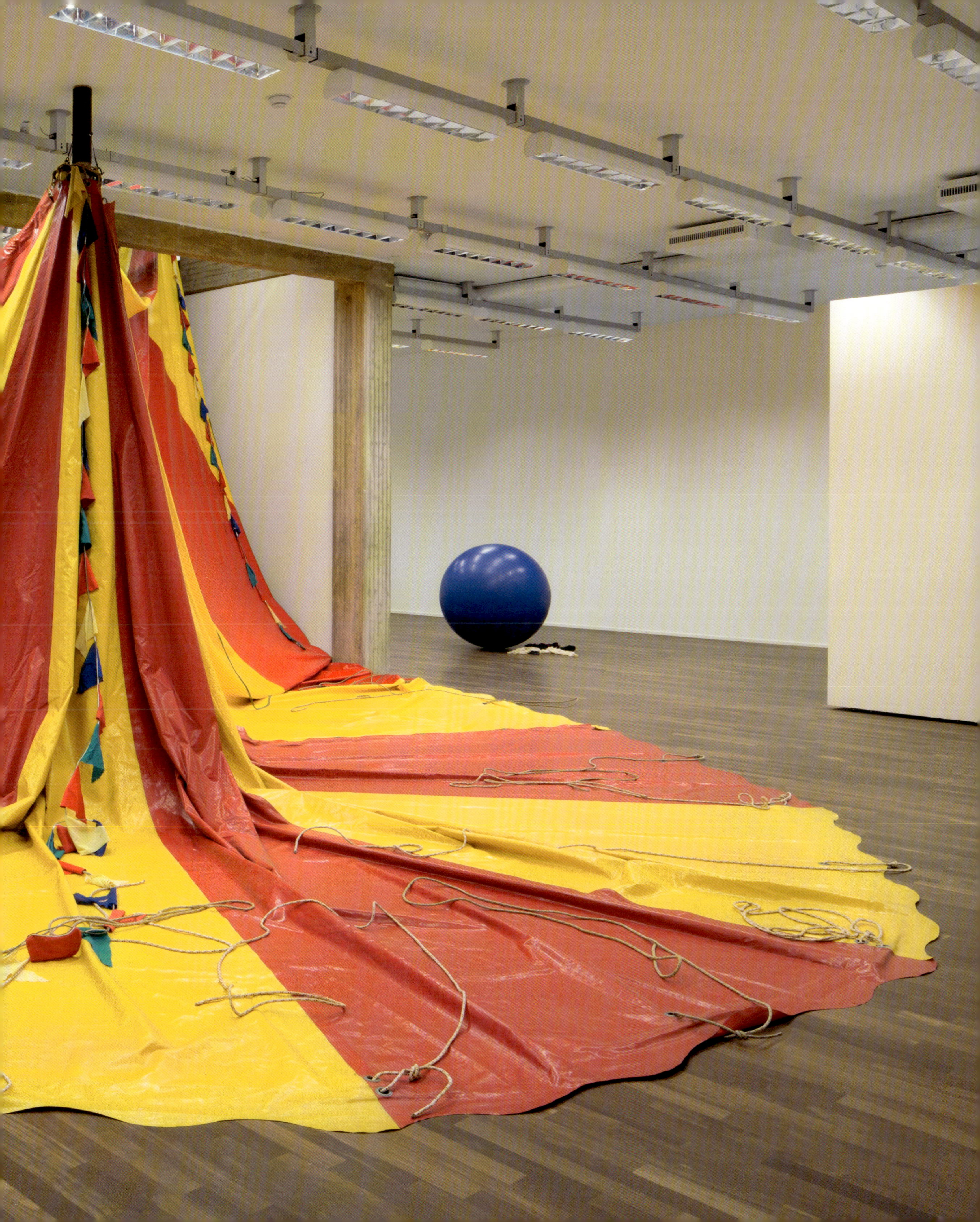

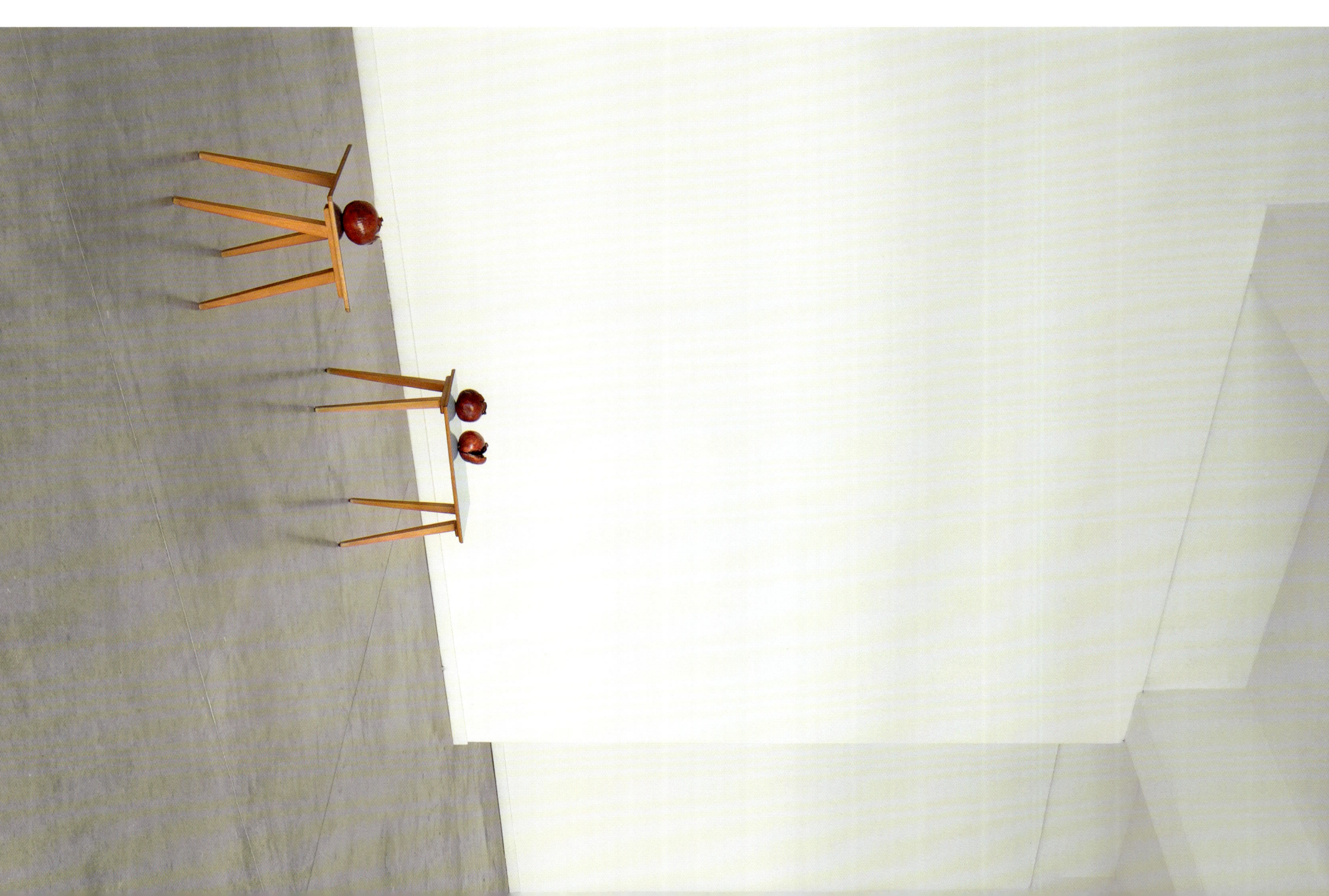

Exhibition view, Bait, Dvir Gallery, Tel Aviv, 2013
With the works Les fruits de mon ami, 2013; Untitled (The Keys), 2013;
Untitled (Well-Tempered Balance), 2013; Untitled (The Self), 2013

→ → Stoning, 2010
Exhibition view, Le rappel des oiseaux, FRAC Champagne-Ardenne, Reims, 2010
Dressed stones from the former Boulingrin Halles market, Reims, dimensions variable
Collection FRAC Champagne-Ardenne, Reims

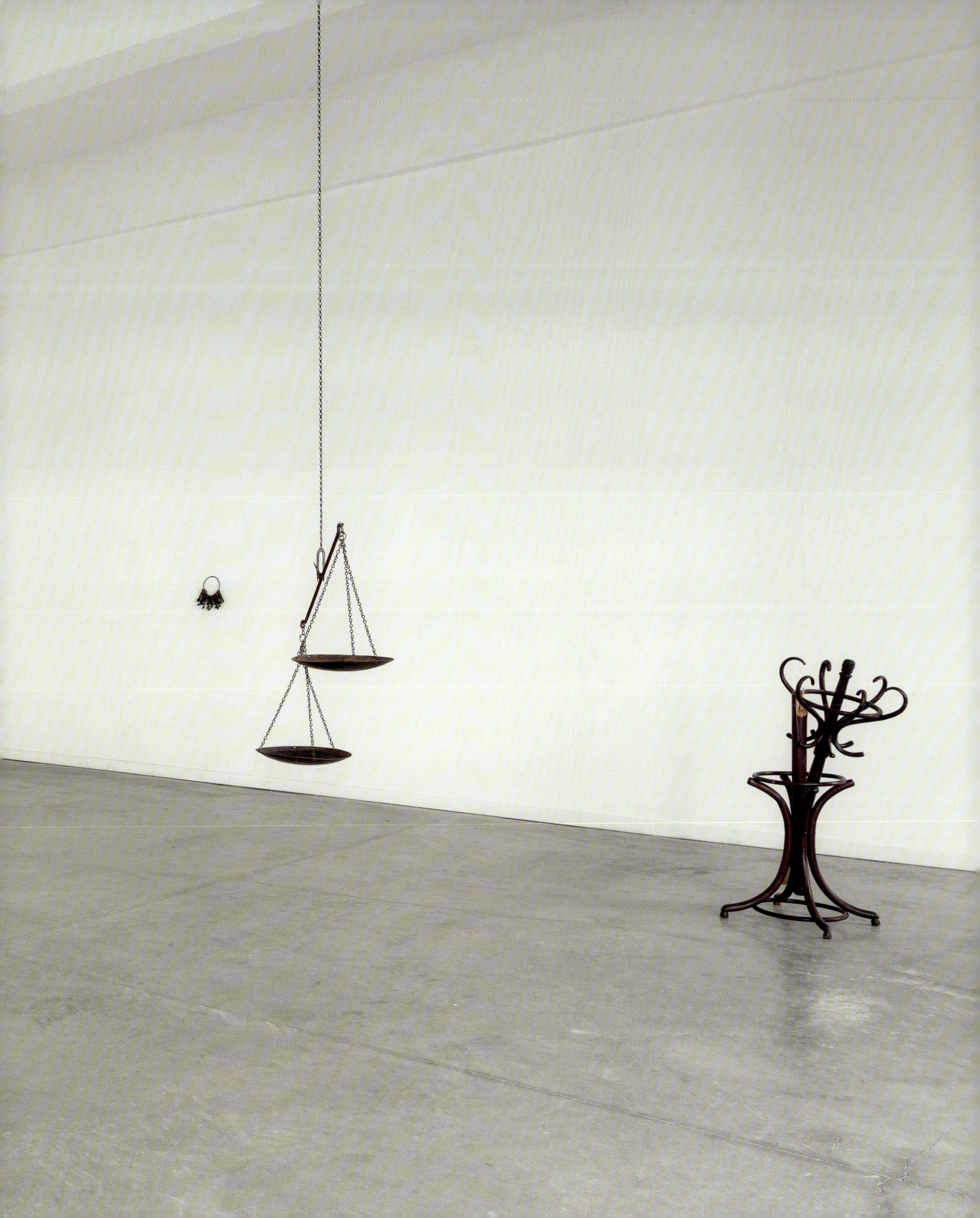

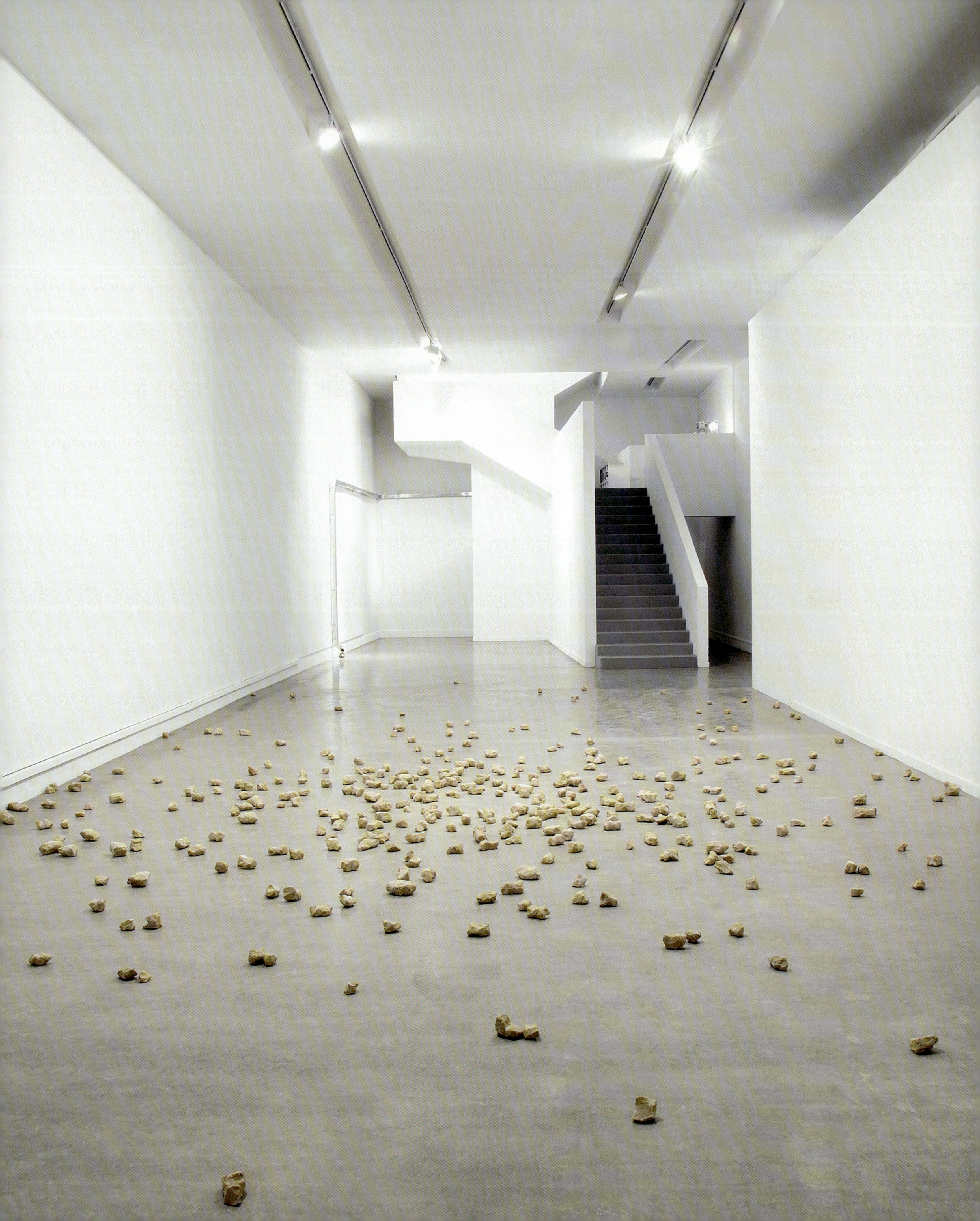

Table of Contents

Foreword

Latifa Echakhch was born in 1974 in El Khnansa, Morocco, arrived in France at the age of three, and now lives in Switzerland. In barely a decade she has managed to find a place in the international art scene as one of the most important artists of her generation.

What makes her oeuvre so significant is above all the remarkable conceptual and formal coherence of her work, the sobriety of her vocabulary, the simplicity of her gestures, and, at the same time, the modesty of the materials and the universality of the elements that she uses. Her research, which explores both private and public spheres and encompasses different cultures, identities, and languages, also makes her an especially distinctive figure by virtue of its eminently contemporary nature.

We are particularly pleased and proud to have hosted solo exhibitions by Latifa Echakhch between 2009 and 2010 in Kassel (Les sanglots longs), Bielefeld (Partitas), Reims (Le rappel des oiseaux), and Bergamo (Le rappel des oiseaux). These exhibitions all profoundly marked the history of the institutions we represent; the traces of these exhibitions will long be preserved, if only in our memories. This publication illustrates our ongoing commitment to the artist and her work. Through it, we express our heartfelt thanks to her dedication and generosity in the production of these projects.

This publication exists today thanks to the involvement of the following institutions: Kunsthalle Fridericianum, Kassel; Bielefelder Kunstverein, Bielefeld; FRAC Champagne-Ardenne, Reims; GAMeC, Bergamo. It has been made possible by the generous support of the Galerie kamel mennour in Paris, kaufman repetto in Milan, Dvir Gallery in Tel Aviv, and the Galerie Eva Presenhuber in Zurich, for which we thank them, as well as for their valuable collaboration. The authors of the hitherto unpublished essays published here, Ben Borthwick and Alessandro Rabottini, have managed to perfectly describe Latifa Echakhch's oeuvre, for which we are deeply grateful.

Florence Derieux, Director, FRAC Champagne-Ardenne, Reims
Giacinto Di Pietrantonio, Director, GAMeC, Bergamo
Thomas Thiel, Director, Bielefelder Kunstverein, Bielefeld
Rein Wolfs, Artistic Director, Kunsthalle Fridericianum, Kassel

Introduction
Florence Derieux

Latifa Echakhch creates systems. Her works are actually complex sets of signs, symbols, references, clues, and remnants. In most cases, the exhibitions she devises give rise to a novel rearrangement of entities coming from her different bodies of work, based on this new setting. Whether the works are new or older, whether they are site specific or reenacted elsewhere, and whether they have already been shown or not, the only thing that matters is this new situation, the specific narrative that the artist has wanted to create, and the experience engendered. All sets are determined by the nature of their component parts, by the interactions existing between them, and by the criterion of belonging to the system itself and/or its environment. This definition helps define the oeuvre of this artist insofar as it eliminates any consideration connected with the novel and original character of the work. For the artist, this type of distinction is now obsolete. And if she does indeed work in situ, the notions traditionally associated with this term have been dispensed with once and for all. For if the context informs, it also transforms by making semantic shifts and broader meanings for the works. So there are more possible readings, and interpretations seem unlimited. For the artist, her works are so many tools that enable her to explore the different fields of experience and knowledge in order to try and make sense of the world around us.

Latifa Echakhch has a special interest in the concept of history and its processes of development. She explores the norms inherent in our societies while making reference to a system of membership and cultural attribution, within which she herself evolves as Other, as woman, and as artist. If her installations are produced in direct association with the space and context in which they are presented, they are also fueled by personal and common histories, as well as different references mainly associated with literature, philosophy, and music. The artist questions notions of identity, belonging, and origin, exploring both private and public spheres, and revealing what often appear to be discrepancies between desires, realities, and individual and collective necessities. She underscores the everyday, recurrent character of societal practices of determination, and is forever challenging the clichés, generalizations, and prejudices that result from them. She uses, all at once, objects, images, and texts taken from given situations, which she moves and disturbs, calling into question their appearance and meaning. Through her interest in language it is indeed the very ideas of power, authority, and negation intrinsic to it that she reveals and tries to upset.

Latifa Echakhch's works form sets through which she expresses the complexity and contradictions of her research, which is sometimes akin to a quest for identity. For many years she has striven to deconstruct the processes that constitute culture and identity. So when she makes use of objects, materials, motifs, words, and themes that are foreign or even unknown to her, she simply tries to deconstruct what she is being constantly drawn to and confronted by. She manipulates elements which are meant to be oriental, and which are thus supposed to define her culturally, like the tea glasses that nevertheless seem as exotic to her "as to any Westerner." In reality, these elements are just ersatz substitutes, cheaply manufactured objects that reflect internationalization and globalization, which she tries to ruin, destroy, and empty of their meaning–or more exactly of their absence of meaning. Latifa Echakhch empties, hollows, cuts around, cuts out. At the same time she defines, hems, delimits, retains, and frames; she tries to provide meaning. She has a powerful need to question stereotypes and deconstruct them in order to make room for something else.

What might be perceived as a heterogeneous practice stems, on the contrary, from a remarkable conceptual and formal coherence. The history of art, and first and foremost the art of the 1960s and 1970s, is the source from which Latifa Echakhch has, from the outset, put together her aesthetic vocabulary. At the beginning of her career the formal strategies she set up did not really belong to her, but were appropriated. Some of her early works in fact drew inspiration freely and deliberately from Minimal and Conceptual art, such as Seuils (2004), an installation that delimits an area on the ground with the help of metal door thresholds, and removes the fitted carpet, which seems to refer as much to Lawrence Weiner's A 36" × 36" REMOVAL TO THE LATHING OR SUPPORT WALL OF PLASTER OR WALL-BOARD FROM A WALL (1968) as to Gino de Dominicis' Cubo Invisibile (1969). Also in 2004, for the first time, Echakhch produced Erratum by throwing oriental mint tea glasses, as colorful as they were inexpensive, at the corner of the wall and floor of the exhibition venue in the manner of a Richard Serra Splash Piece (1968–1970)–here lead was replaced by cultural matter. In 2005 she quite literally "borrowed" crates used for transporting works from Marcel Broodthaers' Musée d'Art Moderne/Département des Aigles (1968) to make Les Caisses, while one of his films (La Pluie, 1969) was the inspiration for her famous video, Sans titre, 11 mars 2005, which comprised static shots of a demonstration in Paris. Later on, it was Situationist psychogeographical strategies–and with them the principles of experimentation, anarchy, and games that are attached to them–that would make their appearance by way of the series Dérive (2009), those abstract pictorial arabesques initially developed on the walls of the exhibition venues, and subsequently organized on canvases. Recently, as we look at some of her mural works, we think of Mario Merz's pieces incorporating the Fibonacci sequence, and Sol LeWitt's wall drawings. The examples seem to be able to be developed ad infinitum.

Le rappel des oiseaux, the exhibition she produced at the FRAC Champagne-Ardenne in Reims, seems to have marked nothing less than a turning point in Latifa Echakhch's career. Ushering in the year 2010 in Reims, the artist then chose to close it with the same show at the GAMeC–Galleria d'Arte Moderna e Contemporanea in Bergamo, thus marking the end of a cycle. The main installation on view in that exhibition, titled Stoning, made direct reference to the Land art works of the 1970s, but above all to a major work by the American artist Jimmie Durham, produced in 1996 in the courtyard of the former College of Jesuits housing the FRAC (Stoning the Refrigerator). The ideas usually associated with Durham's work–origin, removal, language, negativity, etc.–are enough to explain Echakhch's choice, as is the fact that his work is systematically brought back to his Cherokee "origins." This reference nevertheless enabled her above all to anchor the whole of her project within the recent history of art and within the history of the institution itself. The exhibition was incorporated in the space and time of art, while casting a very particular and personal eye on contemporary political, socio-economic, and cultural realities. Produced with stones used for the construction of an architecture representative of the period of reconstruction in France after the First World War [The Boulingrin Halles market], Stoning seems to introduce a constant seesaw-like motion between modernity and what threatens it. Like this large installation, a muffled violence emanated from all the works on view in a proportion that was still novel in the artist's work. On the borderline between game and punishment, she put the viewer in an ambivalent, voyeuristic, and uncomfortable position.

It is also the appearance of Surrealist-inspired works that marked this pivotal moment. The Grand Jeu literary and artistic group created in Reims in 1922, which developed research parallel to that of the Surrealists, seems to have inspired Latifa Echakhch to come up with more poetic and image-rich propositions, kinds of contemporary still lifes which have found their way since into her oeuvre. So oriental glasses, rugs, semolina, sugarloaves, and false saffron have recently given way to objects that are removed from identity-related and authoritarian themes, to make more room for poetry. Mirrors, hats, costumes, furniture, and musical instruments, which manage to more powerfully incarnate feelings, lead us toward the world of spectacle, fiction, dreams, and games. Paradoxically, however, these works, which have become so musical, resound all the more loudly with the artist's silent viewpoint about the bankruptcy of utopias and the current state of the world. In this sense, in recent years, her work has determinedly taken a new turn. The thinking of the Reims-born philosopher Jean Baudrillard, his reflection about everyday objects, needless to say, but even more so his demonstration that within a henceforth dematerialized reality no positive alternative can be envisaged, seems to shed light on many aspects of the artist's work. Like Baudrillard, the artist seems to have reached an awareness that only "singularities," conveying otherness rather than identity, can now cause the system to fail–if the engagement is real.

The strength of Latifa Echakhch's works resides in their relation to the space in which they are exhibited. Matter, space, and their arrangement remain in effect an unchanging principle. The interplay of confrontation and resonance between the different works exhibited offers nothing less than an exhibition narrative, where each element is inspired by the previous one, and responds to the following one. "A slight discrepancy is sometimes enough to open up another field," she reminds us. The visual intensity created by the combinations that she makes, between minimalism and romanticism, between politics and poetics, offers the visitor a unique and poignant experience. By upsetting the relation between the work and its exhibition space, she resolutely places the spectator as the central factor of the content of her works. But having seemingly herself also reached the conclusion of a collective impossibility, it is now a question for the artist of quite simply seeking to rematerialize the artistic experience.

Remaining, Seized, Matter
Ben Borthwick

Large numbers scatter across the walls with an orderly randomness. Each number is stenciled using a uniform typeface and size. It is drawn and filled in with charcoal, the outline precise while the interior is loosely handled and sketchy, sometimes over-spilling the outline, drawing out the rough grain of what seemed to be a pristine and smooth white wall. There is a discernible rhythm that flows in their distribution: spaces open up as individual numbers drift, then intensify into constellations before dissipating once more. They are roughly in sequence but there are gaps in the sequence, sometimes leaps of 50 or more, before dense clusters of numbers, some consecutive, cascade down the wall. At first glance the numbers appear to follow a pattern, as if there is an underlying code that will, at some point, manifest into something legible like a gigantic connect-the-dots drawing. Yet conclusions are constantly disrupted: the numbers simultaneously read on a left to right as well as up and down axis; there are glitches in sequences that end up being arranged in non-linear order; there are dashes, sometimes a host of them marking a blankness, then none for an extended run before the next lone dash crops up. The harder one tries to resolve the logic and identify a formula, the more the numbers refuse to comply, merely pointing to greater randomness. The overwhelming impulse to rationalize could be read as an invitation from the artist, as if to say "have a go, see if you can make sense of it."

The numbers, and the title Résolutions (2009–in progress), refer to all of the United Nations resolutions relating to the Israeli-Palestinian conflict. It is a grim reminder of the history of the 20th century, in which the utopian vision of the UN as an all encompassing, self-regulating organization that would foster international unity was immediately beset by new conflicts arising from the radical realignment of post-1945 geopolitics. The Israeli-Palestinian conflict was one of these, created by the exit of a colonial power, which, as a parting gift, imposed a seemingly irresolvable situation.

Consistent with many of Echakhch's other pieces, the formal language of this work draws on a broad swath of 20th-century avant-garde movements, across time periods, geography, and cultural and philosophical traditions. Within this, the 1960s and 1970s are particularly evident: the implied infinite variation of Donald Judd's objects that so irked Michael Fried; the coded logic of Fibonacci prime numbers that so fascinated Mario Merz; the absurdist geometry of Sol LeWitt's open cubes are just a few examples. Within these legacies there are the local dialects she shares with other artists, particularly from France, where there is a tendency toward minimal interventions into a material or formal language that opens up the space of poetic allusion. Yet she also retains a parallel distance from this mode of practice, and infuses such philosophical gestures with formally understated, but highly charged political references in the manner of an artist like Doris Salcedo. The actual references are often cryptic or hidden, but at a phenomenological level it is usually clear that something socially and politically significant is at stake.

There has always been a strong linguistic turn to Echakhch's work. The titles of many works play a crucial role in informing the materials and spatial arrangements, language itself is frequently used, and references to literature and poetry abound. But she also treats works she has made in the past as a personal lexicon that can be used as a kind of shorthand by which previous and new meanings are combined. Her 2009 exhibition Les sanglots longs [The Long Sobs] at the Fridericianum, Kassel, takes its title from Paul Verlaine's iconic poem written in 1866. Taught in every French classroom, its melancholic onomatopoeia has a repetitive quality in which there is vast variation. The poem was also the code broadcast by the British forces in 1944 to alert the French Resistance to the details of the D-Day landings. The exhibition drew together a number of works into a single display across two rooms. Different tiers of scale were combined and presented with Résolutions acting as a framing device by covering all the walls of both rooms. The foam and concrete "wedge" sculptures of Chambre (2009) dominated the floor space of one room, while the other was cast in the blue light from Plexiglas panels filtering light from the windows. Among these installations were individual pieces, such as the recent Kasseler Parkbänke (2009), or Trotteuse (1999) made ten years earlier. In both rooms a piano composition played, commissioned by the artist from composer Qin Huang.

Aspects of Qin Huang's composition resemble an Arnold Schoenberg piece with deconstructed melodies and rhythms, or Erik Satie's works for solo piano, in which the spatiality of the compositions is an aural equivalent of architecture. The piece was composed for, and performed on, the quarter tone piano system invented by Abdallah Chahine, the Lebanese composer and musician. Chahine was responding to the question of how to fully represent the aesthetic complexity of Arab musical traditions that are based on quarter tones, on the piano, the dominant technology of Western musical culture, which is based on half tones. The lack of an effective mode of translation that allows Occidental and Arab musical cultures to "speak" in the same language immediately excludes significant works of Arab music culture. The interplay of the place of an Arab voice within Western cultural discourses is at the heart of Echakhch's practice, making Chahine's piano a fascinating historical point of reference. Chahine presented his piano in 1952 in Damascus, then in Beirut at the UNESCO Palace in 1954. Its association with UNESCO–the United Nations Educational, Scientific, and Cultural Organization to give its full title–makes it even more prescient for its geographical and historical proximity to the Israeli and Palestinian issue.

Aside from the sound element of the installation, the exhibition had many musical references that traverse history. The concrete and foam wedges of Chambre refer to IRCAM's famous anechoic chambers, rooms of the kind where John Cage famously went in search of silence, and discovered, instead, the cacophonous sound of his own circulatory system. In addition to Satie and Schoenberg, Johann Sebastian Bach is the most audible reference. Through the choice of instrument for this piece, there are nods to Cornelius Cardew and Frederic Rzewski who also adopted the quarter tone piano as a political gesture. The historical genesis of the composition is Bach's Goldberg Variations, commissioned by the 4th Count Kaiserling, an insomniac who wanted a suite of repetitive, harmonic, harpsichord pieces that could be played to him through the night. His pianist, Johann Gottlieb Goldberg, would perform in an antechamber while the Count rested in the adjoining room. The blue light in one of Echakhch's rooms evokes the insomniac hours between night and dawn, while also making reference to the immersive blue environment of one of Echakhch's most well-known works, À chaque stencil une révolution (For Each Stencil a Revolution, 2007). The Kasseler Parkbänke benches occupied both spaces, placed in relation to the speakers, which were louder in the daylight room than the blue room.

Echakhch's first major solo exhibition in 2007 at Le Magasin in Grenoble was titled Il m'a fallu tant de chemins pour parvenir jusqu'à toi [I had to take so many paths to reach you].[1] As in the Fridericianum exhibition, a number of small individual works were repeated at intervals throughout the exhibition, linked by a series of large-scale projects that acted as framing devices for the whole. From this installation it is possible to track two key strands of subsequent evolution in Echakhch's practice. First, is that a single idea may have a number of different appropriate forms, and that if a new form is required she will adapt the idea to it. Beyond the basic level of "variable dimensions," she has taken a number of ideas and reconfigured them using different materials to fit a new context. For example, it is possible to track the evolution of Dérives (2007) from a small charcoal wall drawing at Interface in Dijon, which uses charcoal to play on its contextual proximity to the fireplace while deconstructing the classical geometry of Islamic pattern design into something that it simultaneously signifies and refuses. This idea was vastly scaled-up for Le Magasin into Dérives (Goudron) (2007), in which large rolls of sandpaper mapped the floor of the space in an ambitious transposition of scale, materials, and surface. The same set of principles has subsequently been applied to acrylic on canvas in 2009 (the Dérive series).

More interesting still is the way the spider lines of this two-dimensional work have been transposed from two to three dimensions in a series of other, seemingly unrelated, pieces. Closest at a visual level is the sculptural series Fantasia (2007–2011), in which flagpoles crowd in on an interior space, creating a claustrophobic web that, like the three-dimensional Dérives (Goudron), shifts and reconfigures as one moves about the room. There is a powerful political resonance between Fantasia and Résolutions, each visualizing the constantly shifting complexities of international relations through an extreme economy of means. These works build on the artist's long-held investigation of the surreal language of international law and national identity through works like 0-1 Visa (Alien of Extraordinary Ability) (2005), Hospitalité (2006), and Résolution (2003). The strangeness of the language invests it with a mythical power, like an incantation the literal meaning of which is hard to understand, but its symbolic function is absolutely clear. The texts used in each are, respectively, "Alien of extraordinary ability," "Space to be filled-in by the foreigner,"[2] and "Decides to remain seized of the matter."[3] The first two relate to the language of the state and draw on the experience of the artist who, as the holder of a non-Western passport, must regularly fill in the visa forms from which these lines are quoted. The third is an awkward phrase that gives little away. It is actually the term used to conclude an inconclusive resolution at the United Nations, the kind of language that is both noncommittal yet almost bodily in its intimacy. The kind signified by a dash in Résolutions.

At the level of materials and form, the closest relative of Dérives is Plainte (2009), a charcoal wall drawing that rises from the floor as a scratched block of color, as if a geological process had flattened all the geometrical intricacies into a single strata. The spectrum opened up by these various works is among many that can be used to trace the artist's negotiation of her family background in Morocco, and her own upbringing and education in France. While Dérives speaks of a fundamental dialogue with centuries of a prescribed, symbolic geometry of lines that dance like a lattice of thoughts across space, Plainte summons a different geometry–the absolute weight of minimal forms, rising from the floor like a symmetrical Serra slab. The movement across this historical, geographical, and intellectual spectrum signifies the bodies of equivalent knowledge that co-exist within the artist.

1 The artist quotes the Robert Bresson film Pickpocket (1959) from memory. The actual quote is, "Oh Jeanne, pour aller jusqu'à toi, quel drôle de chemin il m'a fallu prendre … "
2 Originally in French: "Espace à remplir par l'étranger."
3 Originally in French: "Décide de demeurer saisi de la question."

It is important to remember that Echakhch's choice of charcoal as the material that links these pieces was originally a formal decision responding directly to site-specific conditions for a wall drawing. Charcoal has since taken on an internal logic within Echakhch's practice. In addition to migrating across pieces as demonstrated above, the formal and handling qualities of charcoal have also been carried over to other materials such as brick dust in another site-specific installation, entitled *Tkaf*, for the exhibition, *From Threshold to Threshold* (2011), at the Mies van der Rohe Haus der Esters.

A crucial element of these wall-based works is the "remainder," the charcoal that does not adhere to the wall but falls onto the gallery floor like the unusable number fragment left over from a calculation. This dust is, inevitably, disturbed by footprints, and it is the introduction of human action that provides the key that both unlocks the enigma and points to the complexity of its subject. From very early on in Echakhch's practice, the remainder has played an important formal and political role. It signifies the edge, the border, the frame, the limit, those parts that are often seen as merely functional or extraneous, but refuse to disappear. In this respect the remainder becomes the thing that gives meaning to the content it produces or, at the very least, defines. *Frames* (2000–2012) is an extraordinary series of prayer mats and carpets with their centers removed, leaving just the bound edges and tasseled ends. It explores the limits as a cultural, philosophical, and religious symbol by eliminating the content. The cultural references move in both directions: as an icon of Islamic culture the carpet represents the idealized space of the garden, but on a more quotidian level the prayer mat is a cheap everyday object made from synthetic fibers, sold in any street market or bazaar. It is both a hallowed object and completely disposable. *Frames* is also in dialogue with the tendency of "relational" artists such as Dominique Gonzalez-Foerster who, in the 1990s and early 2000s, often used a piece of carpet on the ground–perhaps next to a shelf of books–as an architectural gesture that supposedly creates theoretical "social spaces" or "platforms." In this context *Frames*–or the related work *Seuils* (2004)–with its rectangular space cut out of the carpet, both negates the overdetermined history of the Persian carpet, and marks the relational strategy as an empty gesture.

The exploration of the limit as potential has been developed in a number of subsequent installations where the boundaries are blurred or contested. In the case of the installations, it is the border between wall and floor, but the cultural implications of the works explore the intersection of different aspects of society. *Erratum* (from 2004) is a room-sized installation with nothing on the walls, just the shattered remains of thousands of Moroccan tea glasses that have been hurled against the wall. There is a contradiction between the title's reference to correcting an accidental error, and the determined commitment to such a physical act of endurance. The violence of this gesture leaves small pits in the surface of the wall. Silence in the installation follows the cacophonous act of smashing thousands of glasses individually. *À chaque stencil une révolution* similarly leaves one to imagine the act of creating the installation, in which blue carbon paper has been sapped of its color by having highly flammable solvents poured over it. The title is a quote from Yasser Arafat, which already gives a context that links this work to *Résolutions* and Chahine's Lebanon, while the absent gesture brings to mind acts of civil disobedience, such as the riots that wracked Paris in 2005 following tensions between the police and North African youths. In *À chaque stencil une révolution* the remainder is the deep blue solution that forms in puddles on the floor, a formless ink that refuses to conform to any organized expression of political position. It is the unconscious of the carbon paper's bureaucratic or strategic potential that coalesces into chaos.

One of the key qualities of the installations with a "remainder" is the contingent element that is opened up by the potential for transformation and reconfiguration. The perfection of the remainder only usually lasts until the moment the artwork is exposed to the public. This is the moment it shifts from being the idealized form that has been tested only in the studio, to being subject to the unpredictability of social forces. Although the artwork on the walls will seemingly remain the same, the highly visible remainder is where the incursions into the floor inflect any reading of what is on the walls. The continual change throughout the course of the exhibition to the charcoal works like Plainte and Résolutions, or the ink pools in À chaque stencil une révolution, are arbitrary, and dependent on the way visitors negotiate the works' boundaries.

Echakhch has integrated this mutability into the internal logic of other aspects of particular works. À chaque stencil une révolution is an early iteration of this dynamic where the solvent keeps bleaching the walls throughout the course of the exhibition. When exhibited at Tate Modern, over three months it changed from a rich spectrum of blues at the opening to a much starker contrast between the untouched carbon paper's dark blue and a sun bleached pallor where the solvent continued to affect the materials. This poetics of transformation is dependent on the mutability of materials used and may change from one exhibition to the next, as well as with the duration of each installation. Résolutions takes a much more rigorously conceptual approach to mutability, leaving less to the chance operations of materials and other external factors by making the work itself an algorithm of change. The current state of the piece is, to quote its genealogical relative Résolution, that it "decides to remain seized of the matter": until there is a resolution of the Israeli-Palestinian conflict the work will continue to evolve, as will the piano composition that uses the resolution numbers as a score. There is no knowing if perpetual accumulation is its final form as more and more UN resolutions are passed, or if at some point in the future there will be a conclusion to the conflict meaning a definitive version of Résolutions. But even then, the underlying algorithm of the piece is that it will include all resolutions relating to the conflict, which necessarily means it includes the possibility of future conflict. Even if there is a peace that lasts ten, 20, or 100 years or more, there is always the specter that it will need to be revised once more. The only way in which the work will find a definitive form is if the United Nations itself ceases to exist.

This work alludes to the rhetoric of mathematics by which irrefutable truths are established. But in order to make things equal, mathematics must, at times, exclude a fragment from the equation, an inconvenient residue that cannot be accounted for. By giving the remainder an active role, Echakhch destabilizes this rhetoric and instead questions the values that make up the equation. There are clearly different qualities between what is on the wall and what is on the floor: the charcoal dust on the floor has literally been shaped by actions on the ground, while the calculations of world powers dominate the wall, but neither are given primacy. These are two different planes of knowledge, culture, history: each stubbornly clings to its own beautiful formula–a utopia–that simultaneously produces the other in a form that makes it hard to imagine resolution.

Soiling History Alessandro Rabottini

We leave a stain, we leave a trail, we leave our imprint. Impurity, cruelty, abuse, error, excrement, semen–there's no other way to be here. Nothing to do with disobedience. Nothing to do with grace or salvation or redemption. It's in everyone. Indwelling. Inherent. Defining.
–Philip Roth, The Human Stain[1]

I don't want to be the enemy anymore. The enemy is too easy to dismiss and attack. The thing that I want to do sometimes with one of these pieces about homosexual desire is to be more inclusive. Every time they see a clock or a stack of paper or a curtain, I want people to think twice. I want them to be like the protagonist in Repulsion by Polanski where everything to her becomes a threat to her virginity. Everything has a sexual mission, the walls, the pavement, everything.
–Felix Gonzalez-Torres[2]

In a conversation between Felix Gonzalez-Torres and Robert Storr published in 1995, the Cuban artist used an anecdote to explain his artistic strategy of appropriation and his desire for "inclusion," a desire within which the profoundly political nature of his work is linked to his aesthetic ambition. In the artist's words:

> There is a great quote by the director of the Christian Coalition, who said that he wanted to be a spy. "I want to be invisible," he said, "I do guerrilla warfare, I paint myself and travel at night. You don't know until election night." This is good! This is brilliant ... I want to be a spy, too. I do want to be the one who resembles something else.[3]

Gonzalez-Torres' desire to transform homosexual desire from object "against" to the subject of a policy of sharing is not based on the radical opposition between "system" and "otherness," but rather on a principle of infiltration, a strategy we can define as "homeopathic," one capable of dissolving the social and moral dichotomies of Reagan's America by corrupting them from within.

This concept draws on two main formal and conceptual strategies. On the one hand, there is the appropriation of forms of recent but already historicized traditions such as Minimalism, Conceptual art, and the anti-form movements, and on the other we have the visually modest, anti-monumental, and "mimetic" nature of most of his works, composed chiefly of ordinary materials–sheets of paper, candies, lightbulbs–or things that already seem to be there as a natural part of the environment hosting them, such as curtains, clocks, mirrors. They are things we

1 Philip Roth, The Human Stain, Houghton-Mifflin, Boston 2000, p. 242.
2 Robert Storr, "Felix Gonzalez-Torres: Being a Spy," Art Press, no. 198 (January 1995), p. 24–32.
3 Ibid.

don't immediately recognize as works of art, but that enter our perceptual field subtly, revealing themselves only later as the objects of a symbolic transformation. Gonzalez-Torres establishes a very precise relationship between architecture and tradition, between the normative forms of history and the forms of contingency and contamination, emphasizing time and again the need for a rapport with power based on the metaphor of infiltration and contagion:

> In our case, we should not be afraid of using such formal references, since they represent authority and history. Why not take them? When we insert our own discourse into these forms, we soil them. We make them dark. We make them our own and that is our final revenge. We became part of the language of the authority, part of history.[4]

In this essay I will refer to these aspects in the work of Gonzalez-Torres in order to investigate two fundamental–and mutually complementary–elements in the work of Latifa Echakhch: the relationship with the forms of history as the terrain for the critical analysis of the concept of cultural identity, and the relationship with architecture and exhibition space based on the principle of infiltration and contamination. First, however, it would be helpful to examine certain aspects of Echakhch's life before we move on to the formal analysis of some of the works that rapidly brought her to the attention of international critics.

Born in Morocco, Echakhch was raised in France as part of a family in which contact with the traditional Moroccan culture seems to have been limited. What we might define as the encounter with her "culture of provenance"–as problematic as this concept might be–actually occurred rather late, when she attended the École des Beaux-Arts in Lyon. For her, however, the traditional attributes that many immigrants–even second- and third-generation–normally claim as the basis for recognizing and sharing an identity, are instead the signs of a condition of continuous shifting and even friction between her culture of provenance and her acquired culture. And this is precisely the point: which one, French or Moroccan, is Echakhch's original culture and which is the acquired one?

For her, the symbols of the traditional Moroccan culture thus become instruments expressing a critical investigation of concepts such as "appurtenance," "authenticity," and "origin." I am not providing this biographical information for anecdotal purposes, but because I find it necessary to emphasize how careful, sensitive, and precise the process of the deconstruction of the mythology of identity is in Echakhch's artistic practice.

After nearly two decades, the principle of affective, sexual, and social identity that Gonzalez-Torres felt he had to "filter" within the official structures of politics and economics has become–for an artist like Echakhch–something difficult to place in time and space, something to which it is exceedingly difficult to attribute qualities that can be defined as "essential." Consequently, it is not only architecture as a symbolic space of social and cultural recognizability that is attacked and dissolved in her work. She investigates the very instruments striving to occupy the "official" social and cultural space–the materials and objects of the cultural tradition–until they finally reveal their nature, which is not "essential" by any means, but absolutely transitory, spurious, and hybrid. Gaya (E102) Horizon is emblematic of this process, which curator Mirjam Varadinis has defined as a "method of critical hybridity."[5] The work was created in 2010 for the artist's show at GAMeC. It consists of a horizon line drawn on all the walls of the exhibition space at the artist's eye level, using what is commonly referred to as "poor man's saffron," a coloring agent that looks like saffron but does not have its flavor; in the regions of North Africa it is added to give food a visual "dignity" of sorts. Echakhch sprayed a few drops of water on this very fine line of orange dust, in order to create yellowish drippings on the walls, doors, and spaces between the windows, drops

4 Nancy Spector, Felix Gonzalez-Torres, exh. cat., Guggenheim Museum, New York 2007, p. 15.
5 Shifting Identities: (Swiss) Art Now, JRP|Ringier, Zurich 2008, p. 92–95.

so pale that they almost fade into the architecture. Gaya (E102) Horizon does not limit itself to evoking the image of infiltration. The work is literally an infiltration, because even when the walls are repainted at the end of the exhibition, those few grams of a coloring agent imitating a prized spice, but without rivaling its culinary qualities, will remain in the skin of the building, impregnating its bearing structure. I have often been tempted to view this form of permanent infestation that conceals itself even from sight, as a discreet but immensely powerful metaphor for poverty, because–like poverty–Gaya (E102) Horizon is there above all when you cannot see it, because it innervates the structure of the museum in precisely the same way that poverty permeates society, despite the cosmetic measures we use on our cities and our consciences. I have always viewed Gaya (E102) Horizon as an insignia honoring the invisible, a tribute in the form of decoration that inverts the order of monumentality and attains permanence by following a negative path, through disappearance rather than affirmation and ostentation.

On numerous other occasions Echakhch has used modest materials for interventions in spaces where the walls, floor, and windows bear the evident signs of infiltration, soiling, or violation that, while temporary, manifest a careful choreography of violence and randomness, composition and disorder. For example, we can consider Plainte and À chaque stencil une révolution (For Each Stencil a Revolution), both of which were executed at several exhibitions, the former starting in 2009 and the latter in 2007. Plainte also takes up the motif of the wall as the support for the artwork, fusing decoration, setting, and vandalism. The heights of the modules Le Corbusier proposed in the mid-1920s, which he used to build his Unités d'Habitation, completed in Marseille in 1952, are sketched out on several walls of the exhibition space. The humanistic principle that inspired the Swiss-French architect–the human body as the measurement generating the division of living space and function as the organizing principle of architectural proportions–literally explodes in Echakhch's installation. Using black charcoal to saturate the wall portion corresponding to each module, Echakhch creates a landscape of delicate ruin by leaving on the floor the powder resulting from rubbing the charcoal on the walls. While Gaya (E102) Horizon achieves literal infiltration, Plainte constitutes an equally literal crumbling of a cornerstone of modernity, the dissolution of which is reinforced by the very title of the work. In fact, the French word "plainte" means "complaint," but it is also a homophone for a word meaning baseboards. It is within this ambiguity, this oscillation between a prosaic meaning tied to a minor architectural element and a critical meaning, that Echakhch opens up room to negotiate, not only between high and low, between utopia and the quotidian, between order and entropy, but also–and above all–between the image of history as a unitary and ideal project and the reality of history as a disjointed ensemble of individual stories and voices that resist coherent narration.

The title À chaque stencil une révolution, une après l'autre (2009) alludes to the words the Palestinian leader Yasser Arafat used to describe the turbulent sequence of political and social claims that distinguished the late 1960s. Echakhch takes up the reference to the daily and pervasive aspect of political struggle by using sheets of carbon paper, which were widely employed to publicize protests in the years before the Internet arose as a means for spreading ideas. In the different versions of this installation–executed in Grenoble, London, Basel, Paris, Milan, and Turin–the artist glued a grid of carbon paper onto the walls to form a sort of wallpaper, and then sprayed it with ethyl alcohol so the blue ink would drip onto the floor, creating large blotches of color. Here as well, it is in the corner–the space where the verticality of the wall and the horizontality of the floor meet–that a sort of collapse or disintegration takes place. Observing this work, I think it is legitimate to emphasize that the act of destruction–and the ensuing damage wrought by this destruction on the architecture of the exhibition space–is not only a positive and even generative gesture, but is chiefly a gesture that can problematize the artist's poetic and political position. What is dissolving and what are the consequences? Should

À chaque stencil une révolution be interpreted as a declaration on the dissolution of an era, on the end of collective participation in political commitment, or is it instead a statement about the ability of certain ideas to seep permanently into architecture and minds alike? Echakhch seems to suggest that, within history, certain ideas act like natural materials, shifting from a solid state to a liquid or gaseous one and then recrystallizing, and that the survival and vitality of the principle of freedom lies in its ability to become discreet and fleeting–and thus permanent for this very reason.

It is no accident that the corner where the wall meets the floor is the space for this dialectic between the shattering of the unity of things and the possibility that they will exist once more in a form that, while fragmented, is still just as effective. Indeed, the corner is where we temporarily shove what we have removed. More simply, it is where we heap the things we want to sweep away, as we do with dust and waste when we want to put things in order.

It is against a corner that the glasses composing the installation Erratum (from 2004) are shattered. In what is a rather direct citation of Richard Serra's Splashing (1968), Echakhch reactivates the American sculptor's performative gesture of hurling molten lead against a corner of the exhibition space. Nevertheless, while it is important to note that Echakhch evokes a work such as Splashing–which broke away from the orthogonality of American Minimalism to turn to freer performativity connected with the materials themselves–I think it is even more interesting to explore the idea that, whereas Serra's work follows the movement of a material from a liquid to a solid state, effectively invoking the principle of permanence, Echakhch's work reverses this trajectory, bringing the solid state of an object to the condition of debris, of something best swept away or that, in any case, echoes a profound state of instability and temporariness.

But this is not Echakhch's only act of inversion. While Gonzalez-Torres wanted to sexualize elements of architecture or everyday life that were not immediately identifiable with homosexuality–to activate a policy of dispersion, non-recognizability, and in the final analysis, sharing and participation–Echakhch actually does the opposite: she presents an object that, in the observer's mind, triggers an immediate association with Moroccan culture, only to destabilize this identity-based association. The glasses she breaks in Erratum are the traditional ones made of colored glass with gilt decorations that are used to drink mint tea. The difference is that the ones the artist uses are industrially produced and very cheap, probably made in an "elsewhere" of the world's economic geography and without any craftsmanship. They are mass-produced and widely used objects that absorb the dimension of globalization, rejecting the presumed dimension of authenticity. While in the final analysis Gonzalez-Torres' work imbues even the most common furnishings with homosexual desire, nostalgia, and a sense of loss, Echakhch's instead shatters and dissolves the very idea that an essential and original identity is conceivable.

For Echakhch, the ability of a material or object to absorb and articulate a symbolic and cultural function, to become something in which we can recognize ourselves, share, and replicate, continues to be a weak and arbitrary process against which we should somehow fling ourselves.

What underlies her work is an initially deconstructive impulse followed by a generative beat, an impulse she herself explains in these words:

> Perhaps violence is inherent in a lot of art practice. To sculpt marble, for example, is not an easy action, to cut paper for collage, to break ceramics for mosaic. Violence in my work deals more with the result of a radical and irreversible action. It's the simplest way to free an object from its use, to deconstruct it ... Sometimes one has to "kill" the object to make possible a different reading.[6]

6 Milovan Farronato, "Nature Morte" (interview), Mousse Magazine, no. 19 (June 2009), p. 104–106.

À chaque stencil une révolution

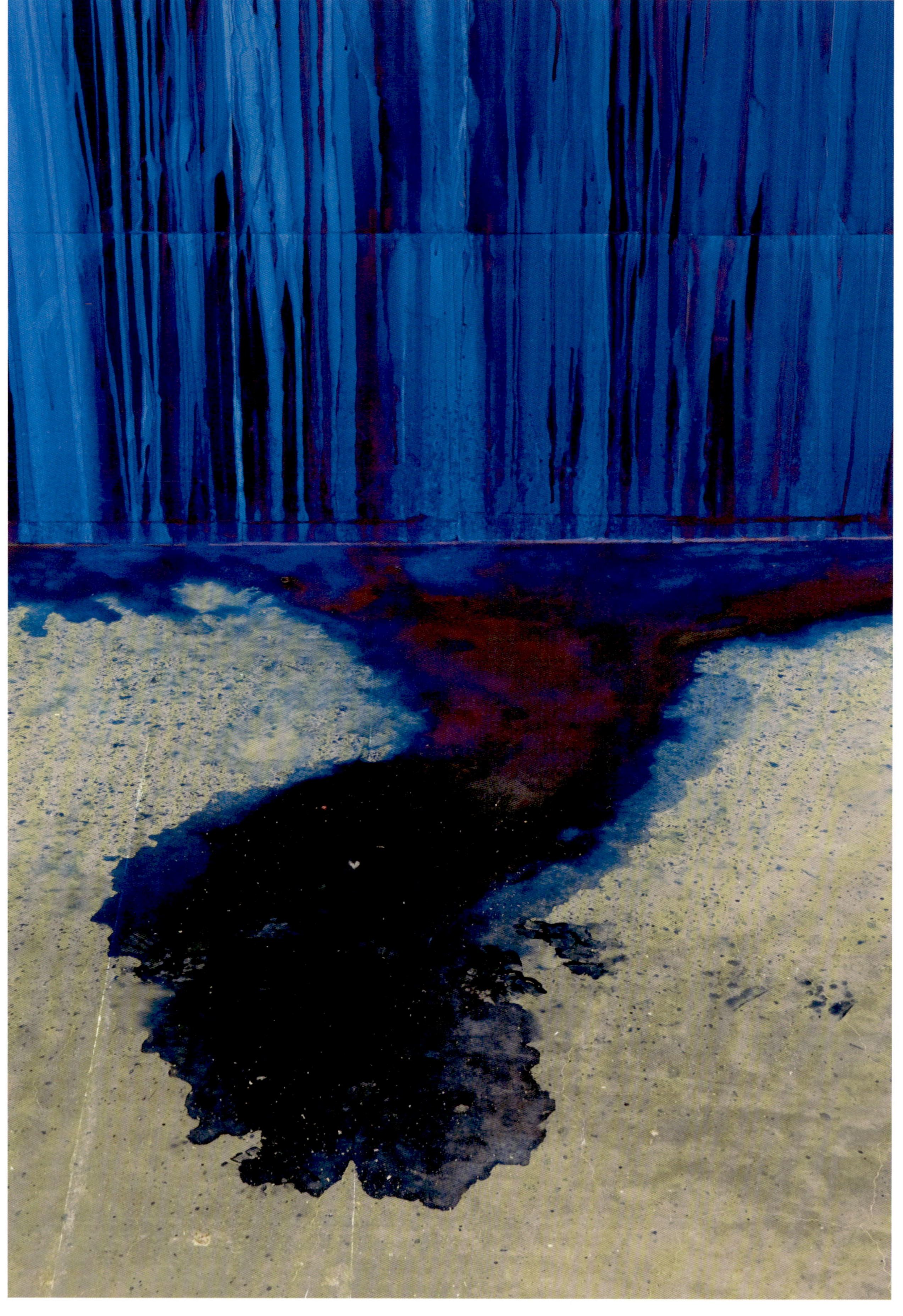

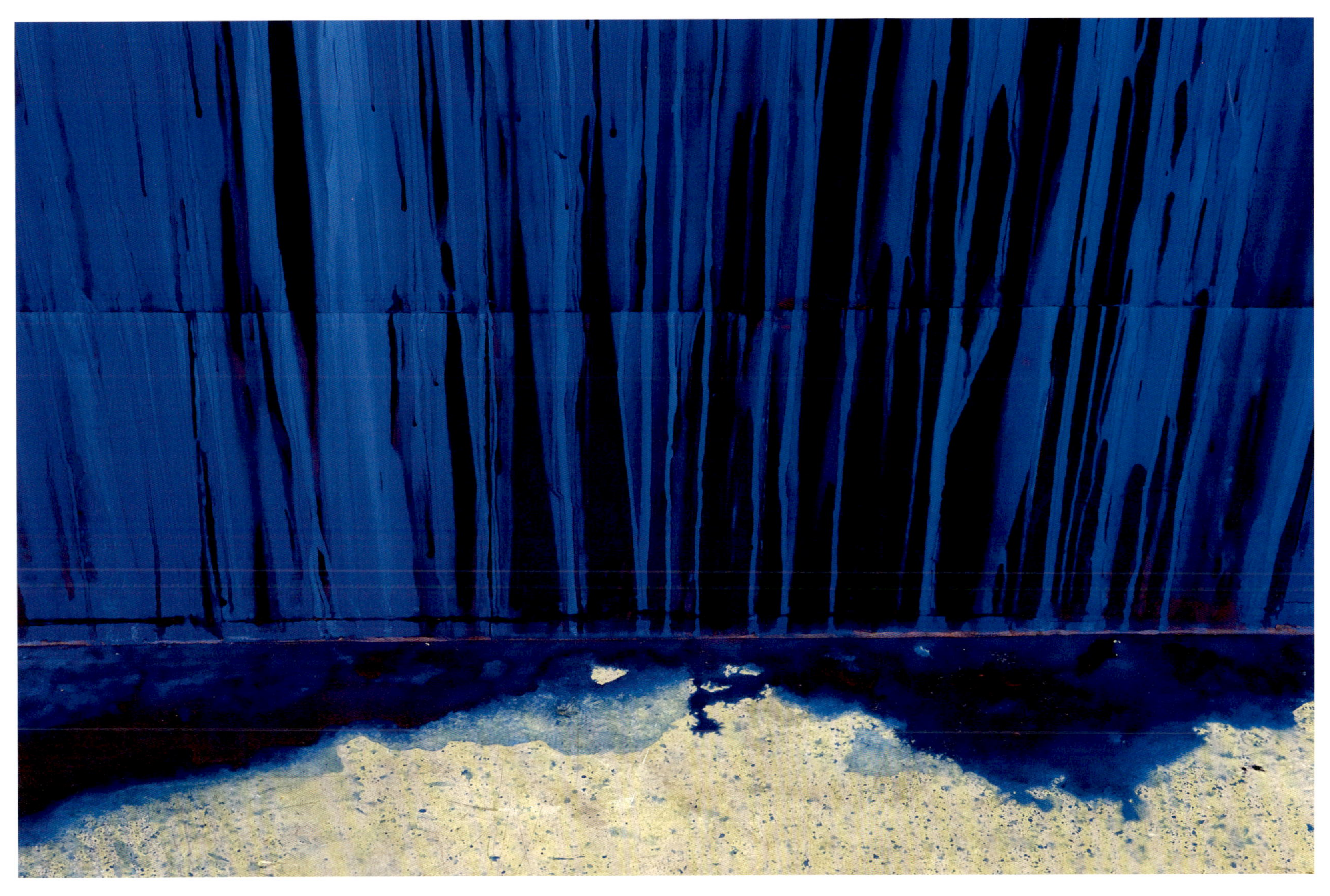

À chaque stencil une révolution, 2007
Wall installation; A4 carbon paper, glue, methylated alcohol, dimensions variable

Collections FRAC Nord-Pas de Calais, Dunkerque; MACBA–Museu d'Art Contemporani, Barcelona;
Fiorucci Art Trust, Roma; La Gaia, Busca;
Queensland Art Gallery, Queensland

À chaque stencil une révolution, une après l'autre

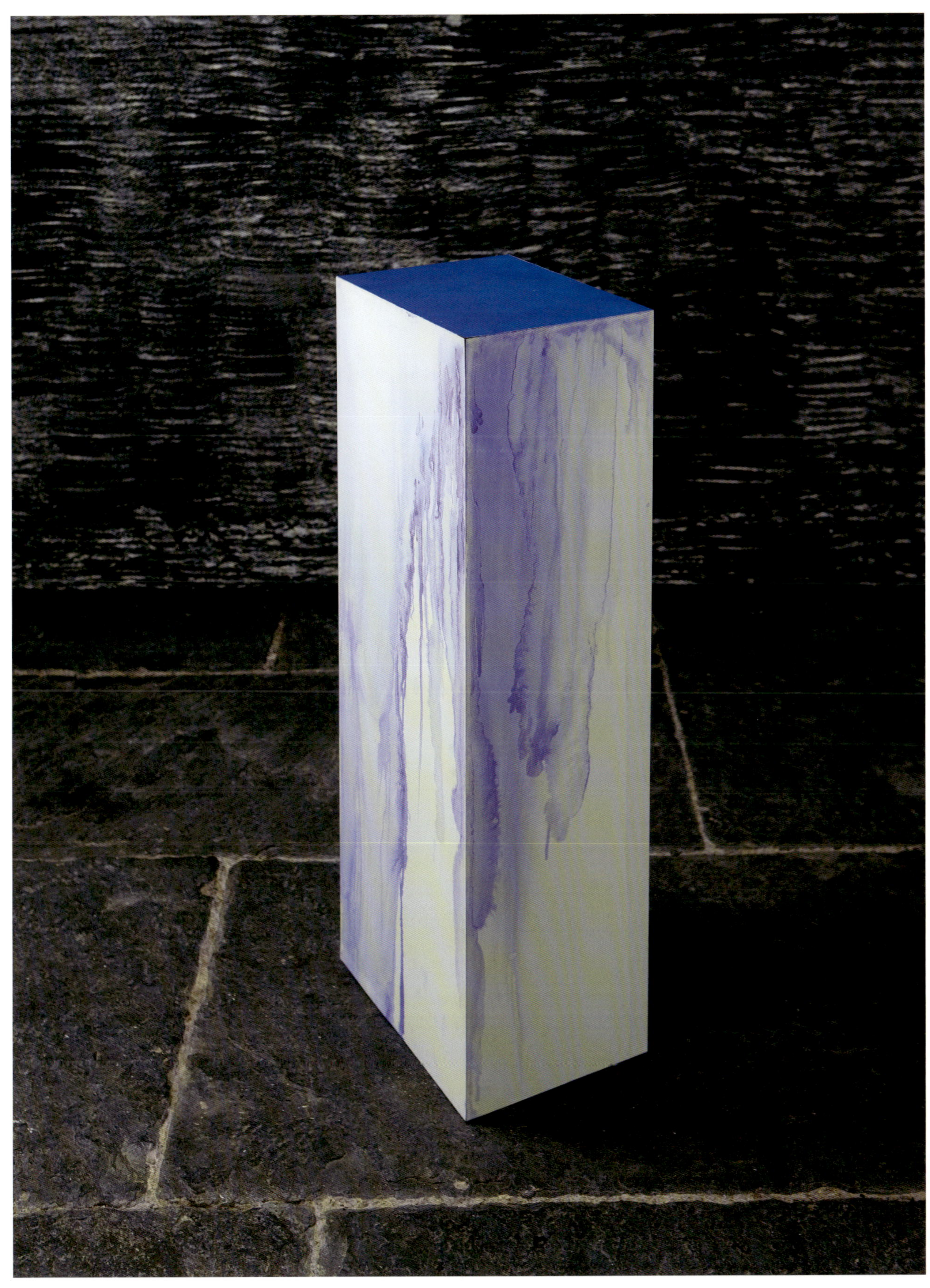

À chaque stencil une révolution, une après l'autre, 2009 (detail)
Installation of 9 elements; A4 carbon paper, methylated alcohol, mdf pedestals, 21 × 29.7 × 86 cm each
Exhibition view, kaufmann repetto, Milan, 2009

Chapeau d’encre

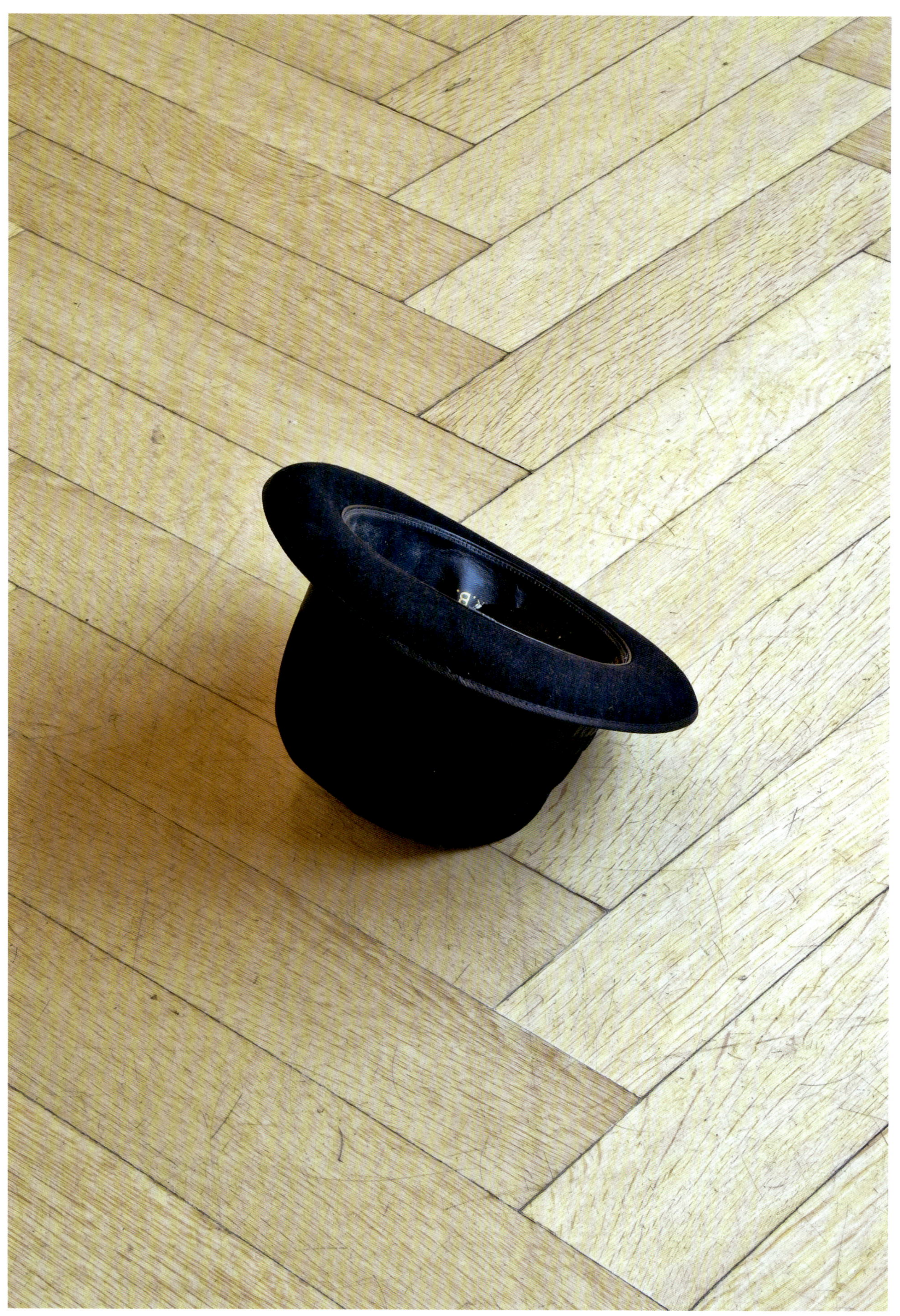

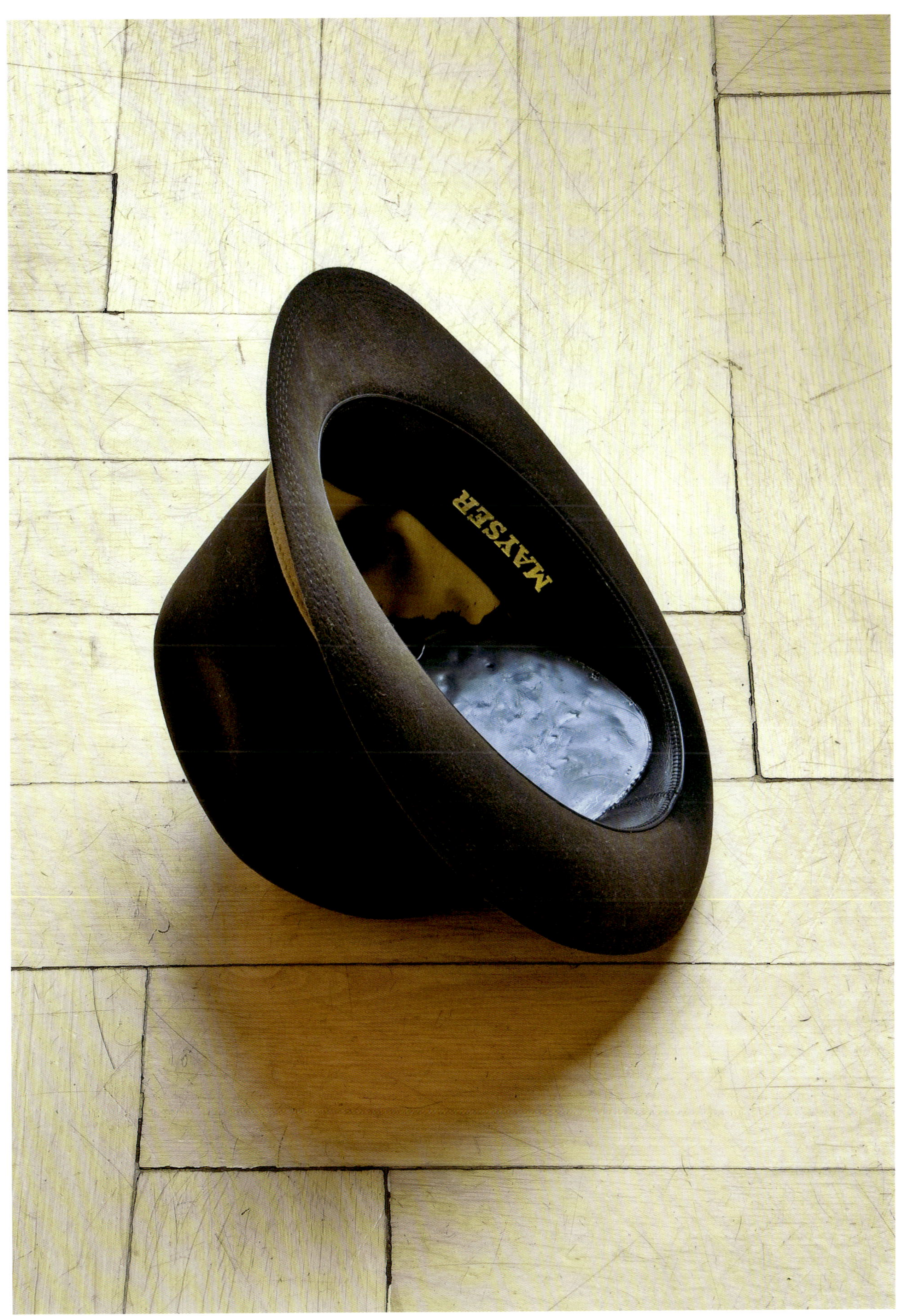

Chapeau d'encre, 2011
Mayser hats, polyester resin, India ink, dimensions variable
Exhibition view, From Threshold to Threshold, Mies van der Rohe Haus der Esters, Kunstmuseen, Krefeld, 2011

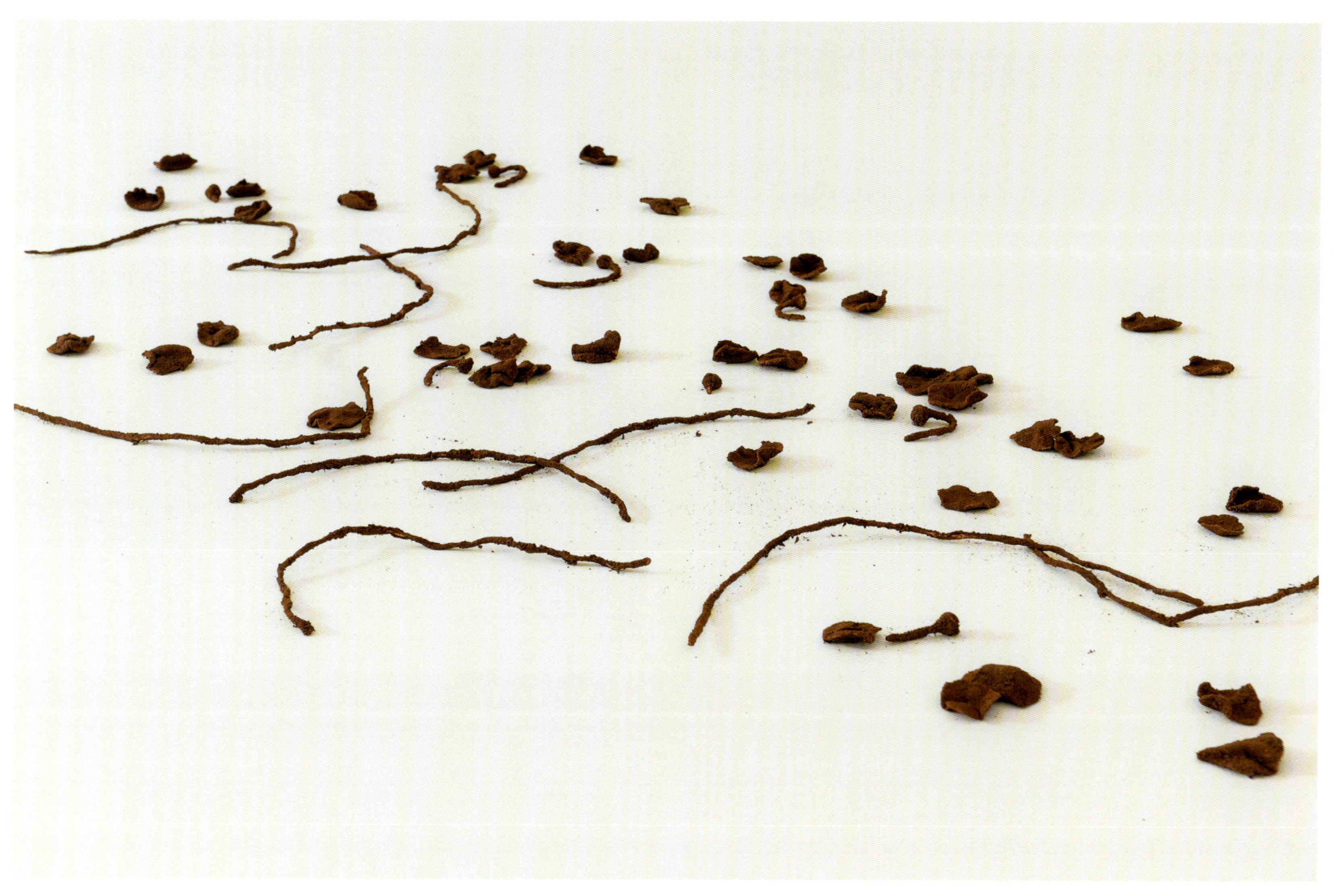

Charlie Brown's Poppies, 2011
Red soil and clay from Beirut,
dimensions variable
Exhibition view, The Beirut Experience,
Beirut Art Center, Beirut, 2011

Danse macabre

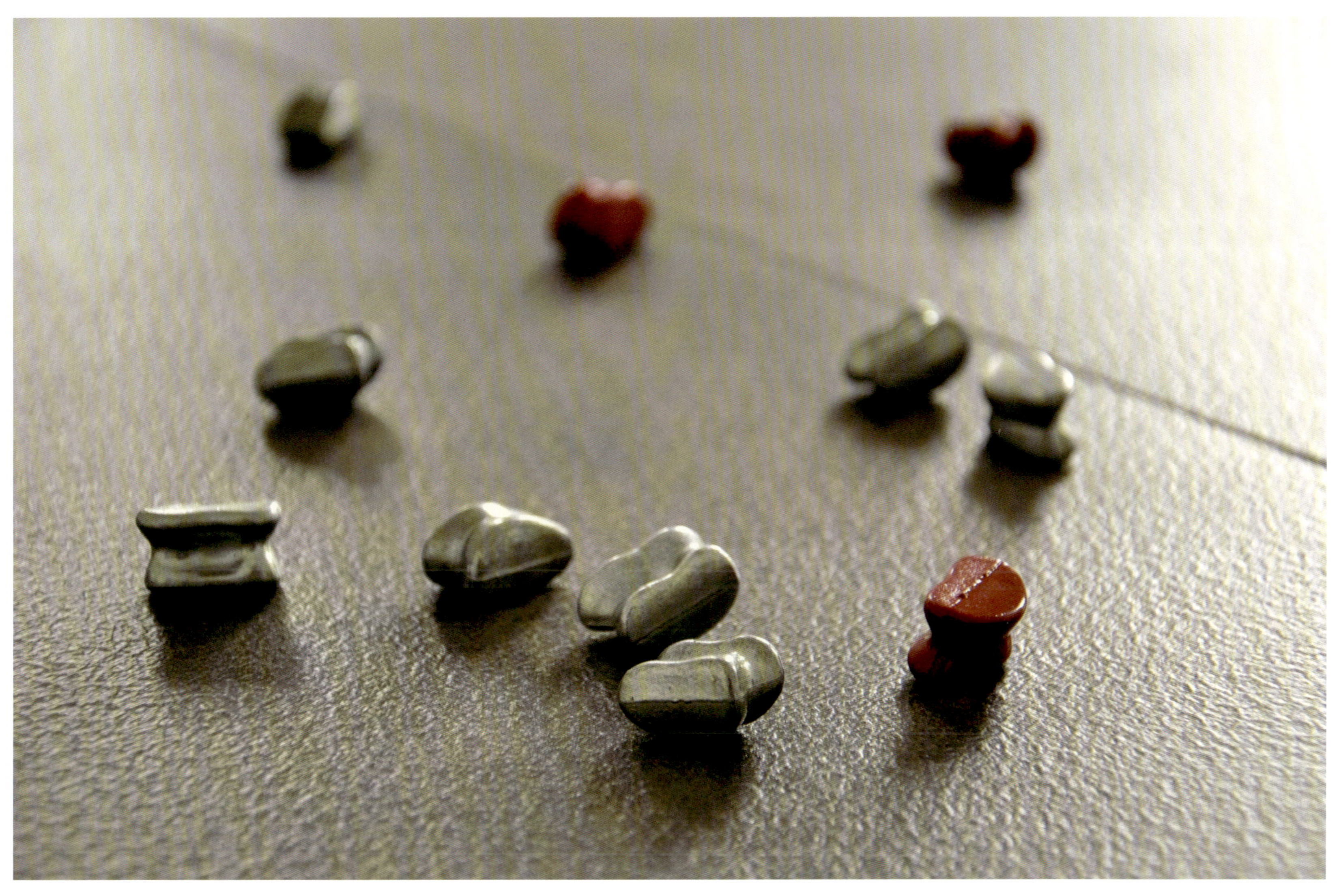

Danse macabre, 2010
15 jacks, pedestal, linoleum,
installation dimensions: 27 × 113 × 70 cm

Death of a Spanish Child (M.R.)

Death of a Spanish Child (M.R.), 2012
Lithographic stone, printing ink, varnish, steel angles, 30.8 × 25.4 × 4.1 cm

Dérive

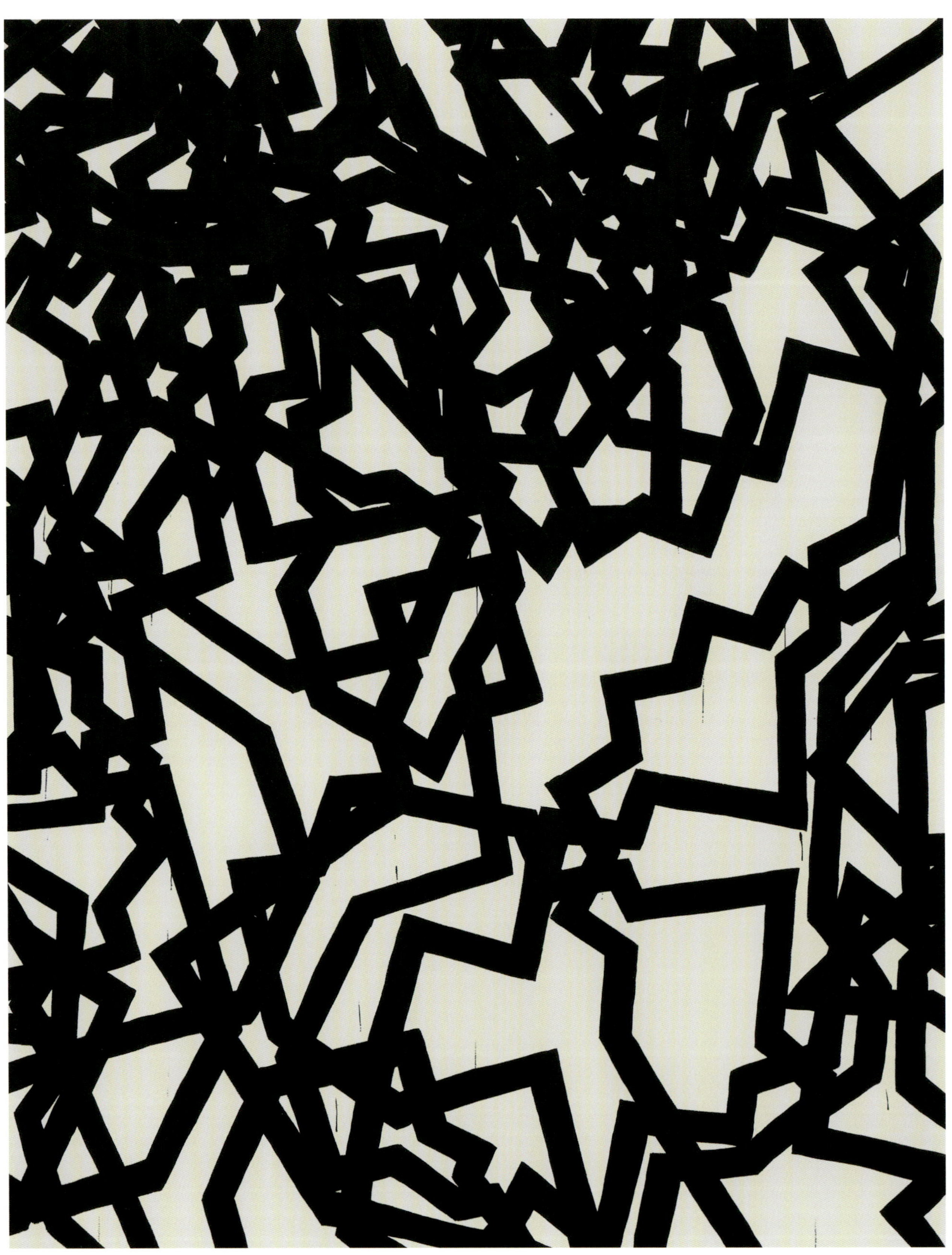

Dérive 15, 2009
Acrylic paint on canvas, 200 × 150 cm

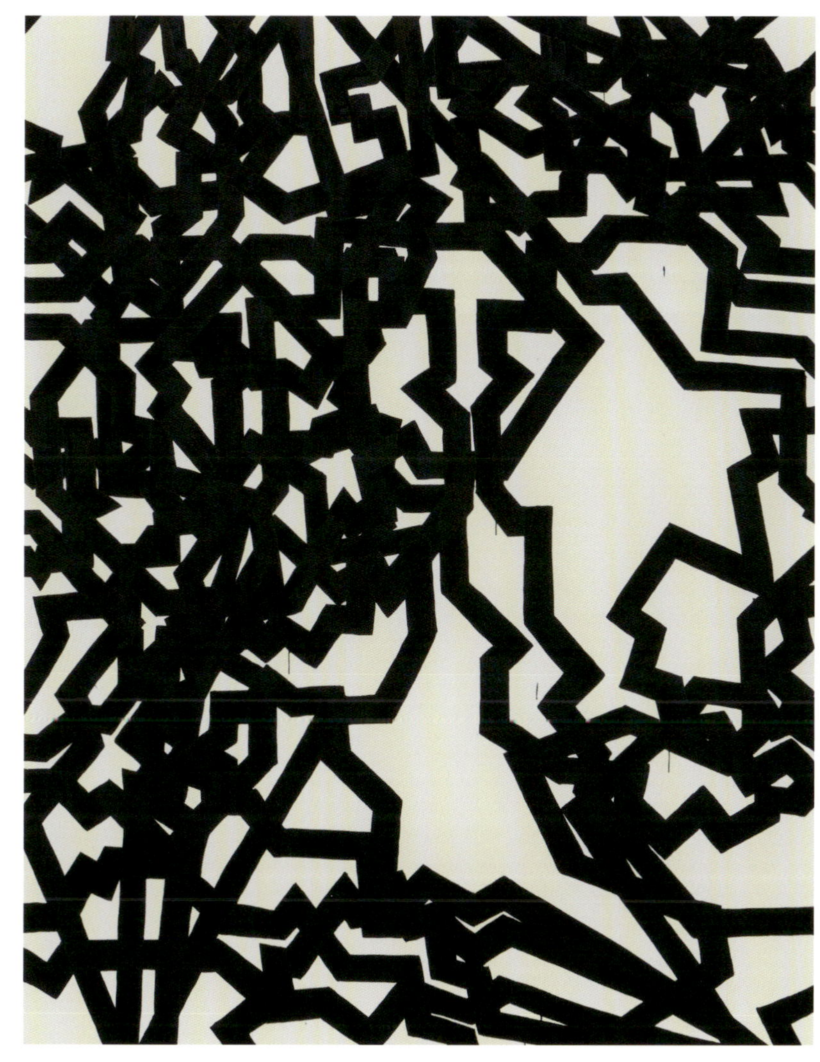

Dérive 12, 2009
Acrylic paint on canvas, 200 × 150 cm

Dérive 11, 2009
Acrylic paint on canvas, 200 × 150 cm

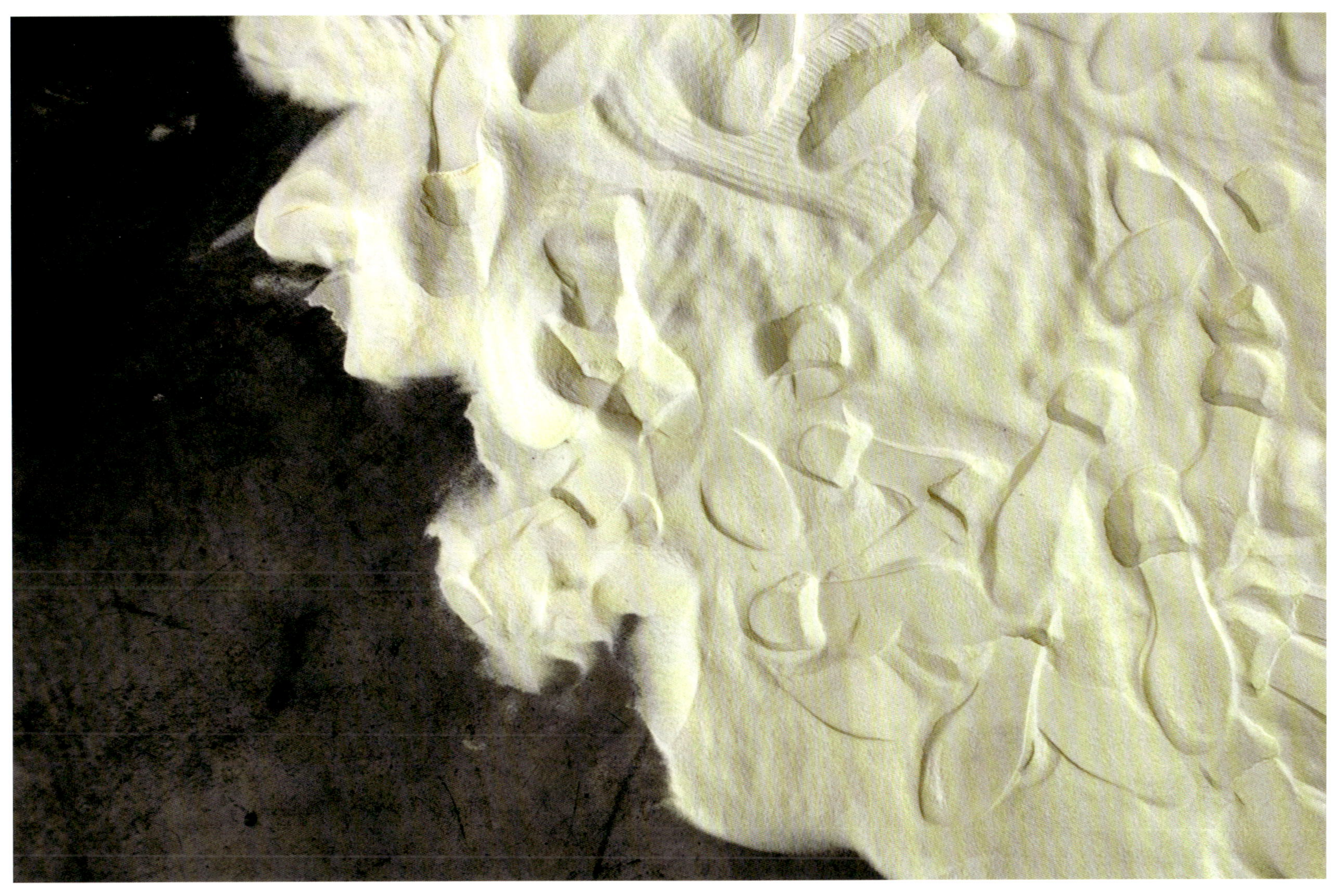

Désert, 2005
Semolina, dimensions variable
Exhibition view, The Pursuit of Pleasure,
Barriera, Turin

Die Vögel

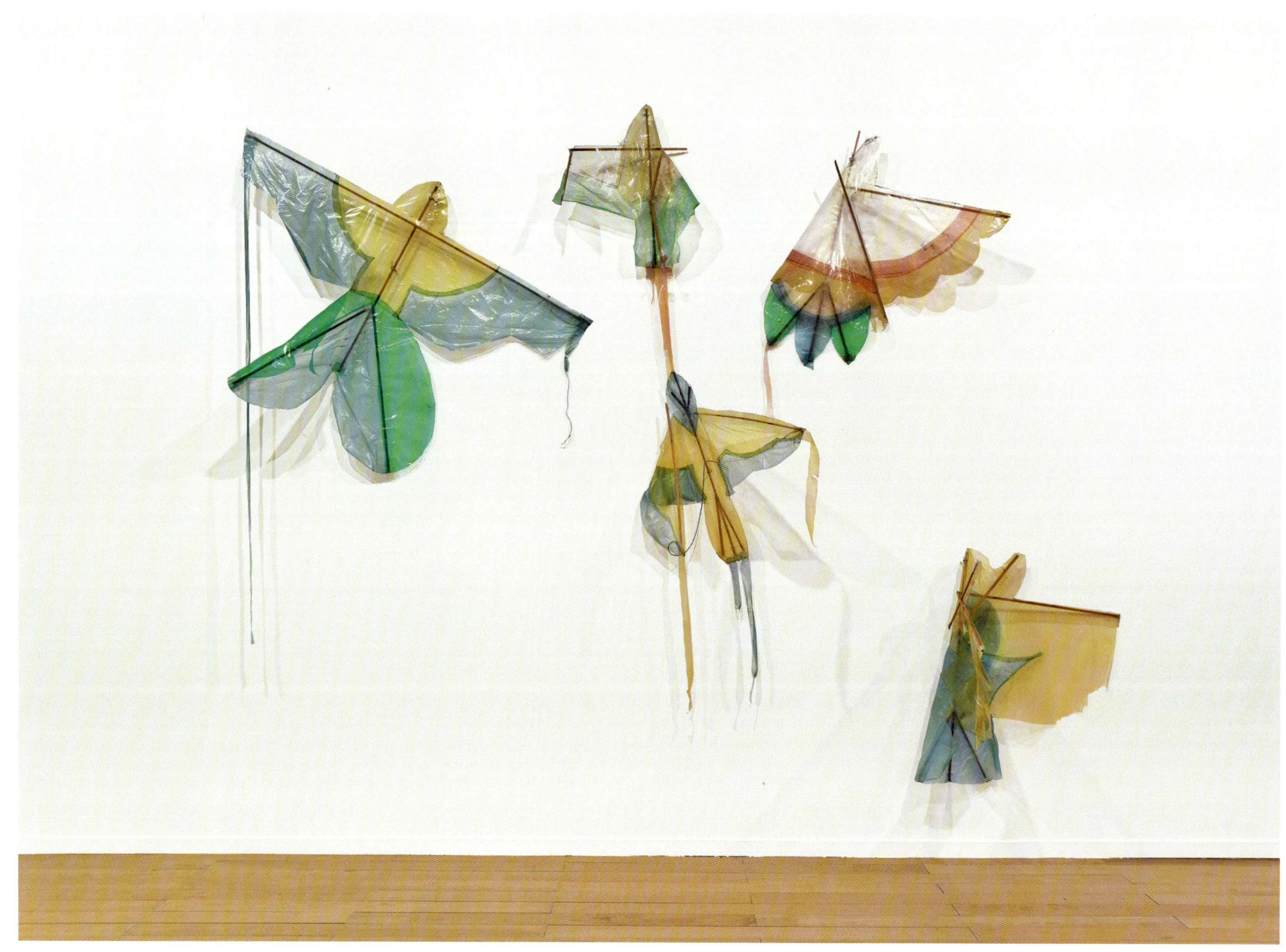

Die Vögel, 2012
Plastic bag kites, wood, tape, staples, ties, dimensions variable
Exhibition views, Laps, Musée d'Art contemporain, Lyon, 2013

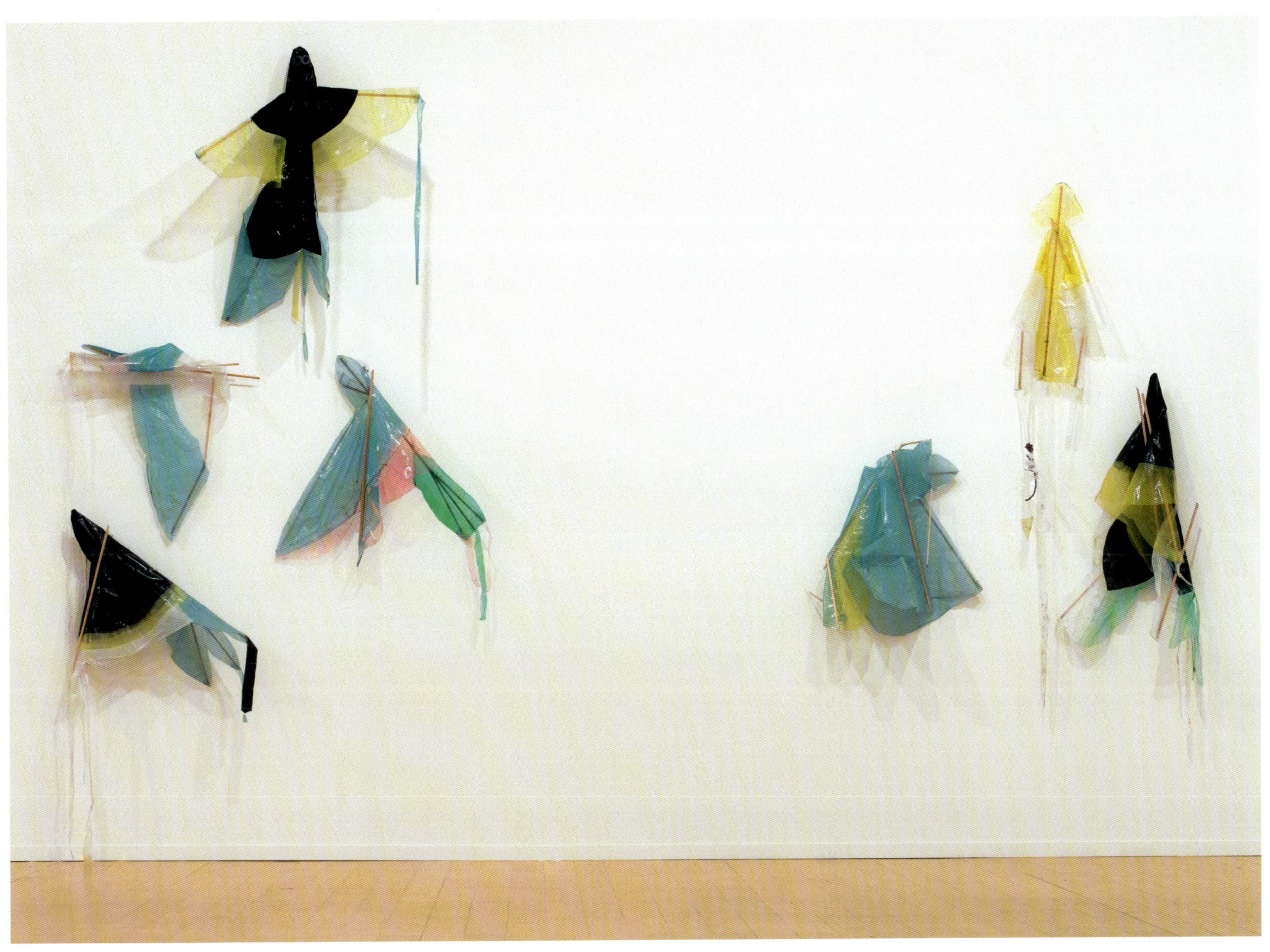

Eivissa (Ibiza)

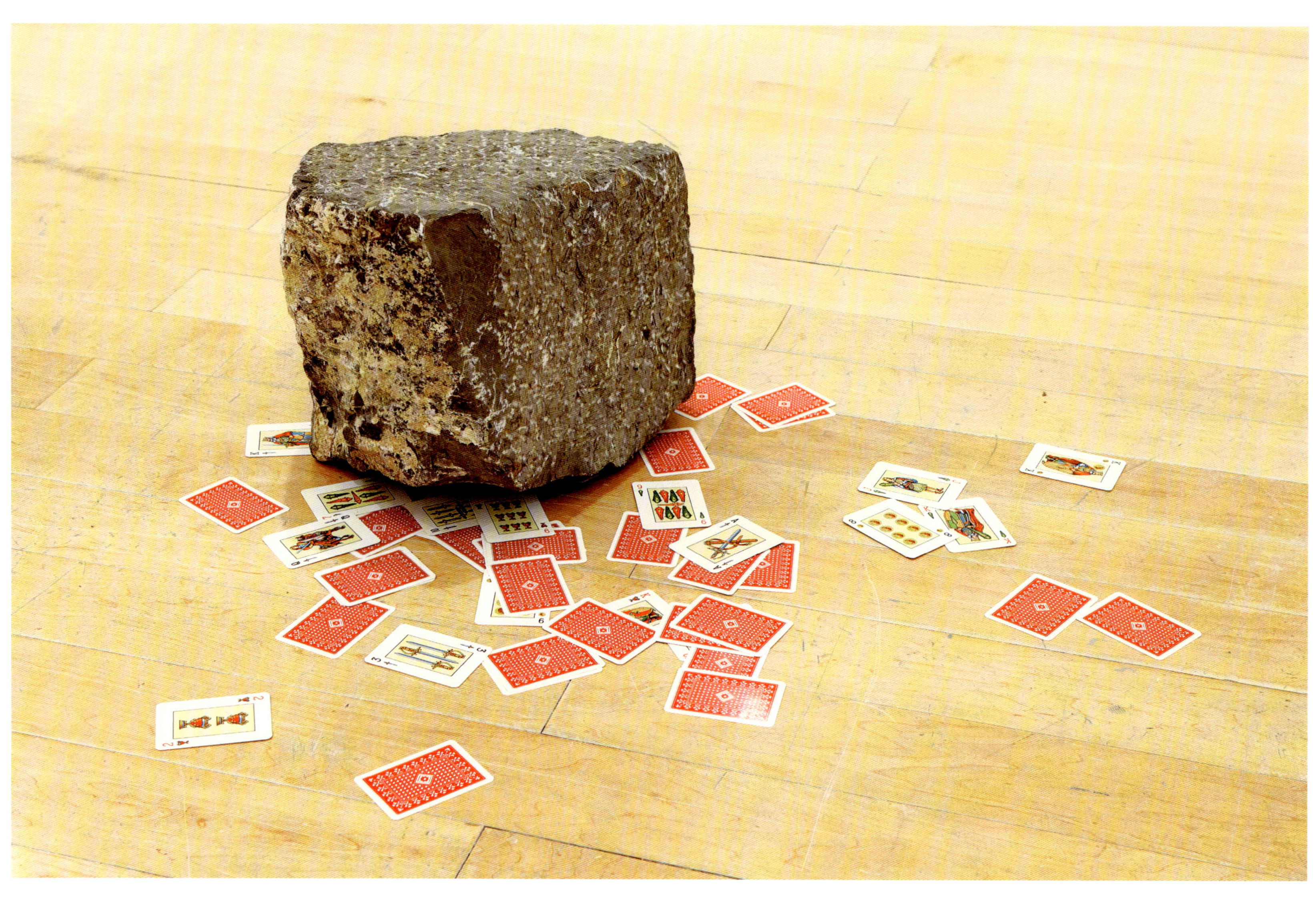

Eivissa (Ibiza), 2010
Playing cards and stones from the platform built in Ibiza to receive the tents of Moroccan soldiers enlisted in the rebel army of General Franco during the Spanish Civil War, dimensions variable
Exhibition views, Laps, Musée d'Art contemporain, Lyon, 2013

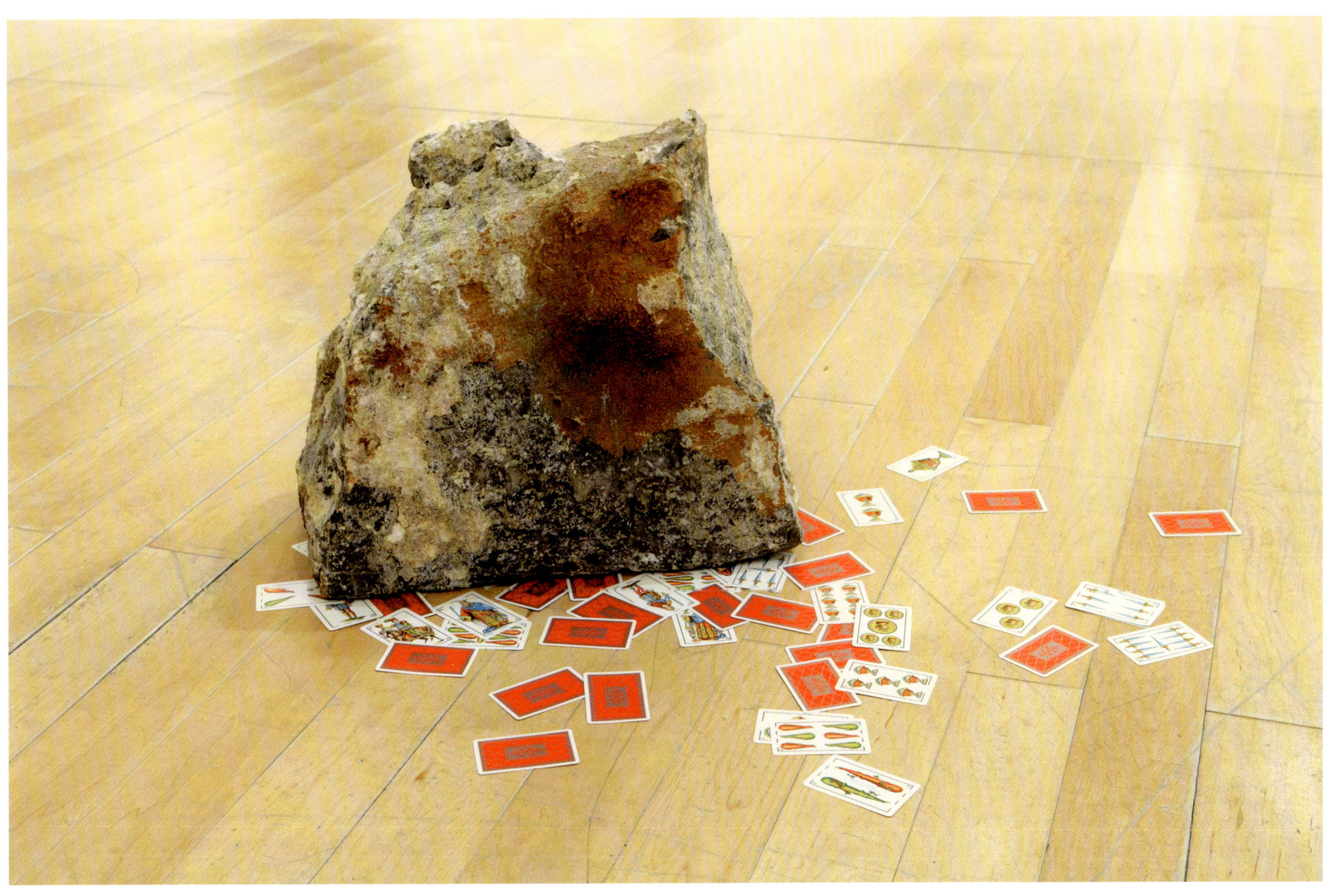

Erratum

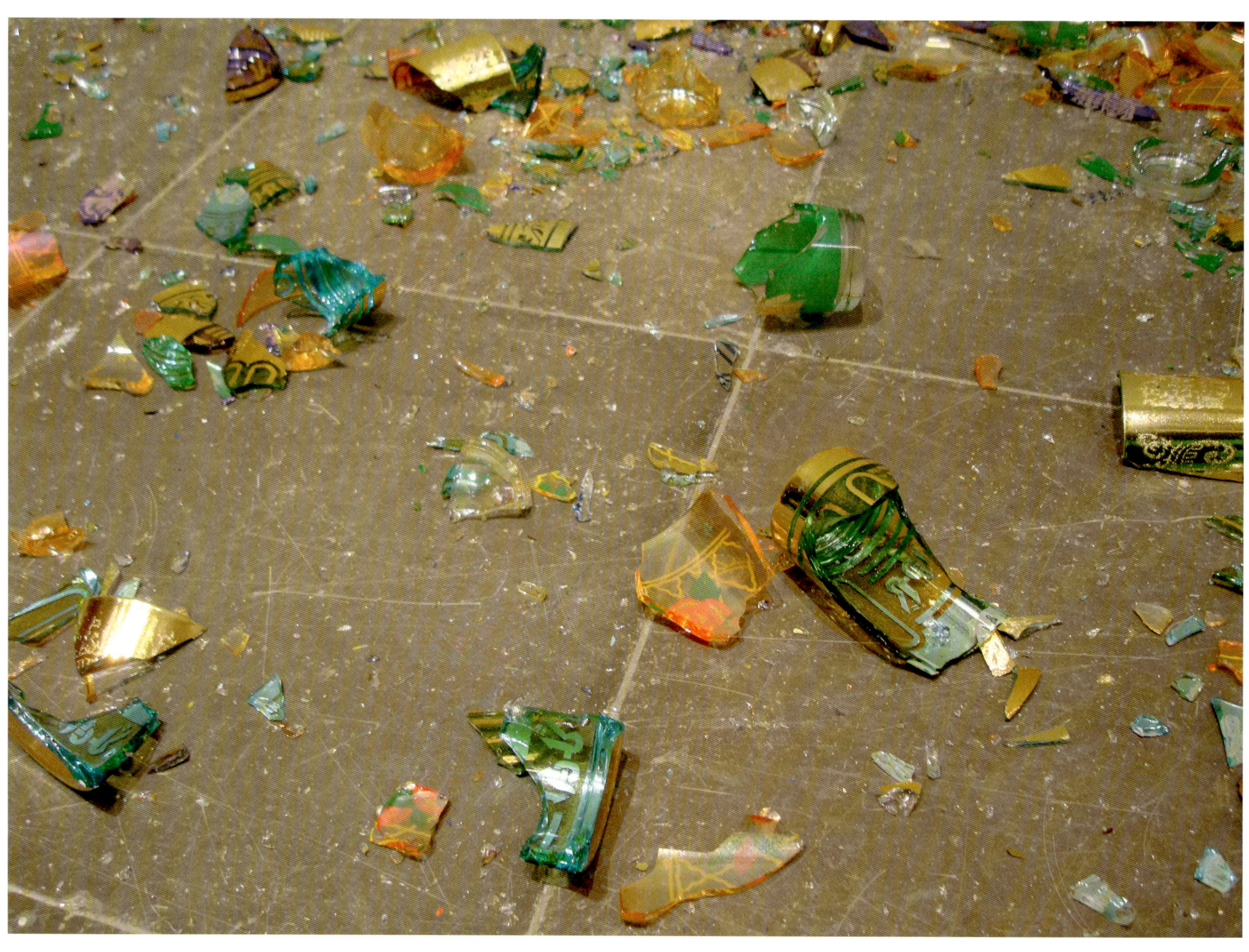

Erratum, 2009
Tea glasses smashed on site, dimensions variable according to the walls
Exhibition views, The Space Between, Konstcentrum, Gävle

Collections Kunstmuseum Liechtenstein, Vaduz; Centre national des arts plastiques, ministère de la Culture et de la Communication

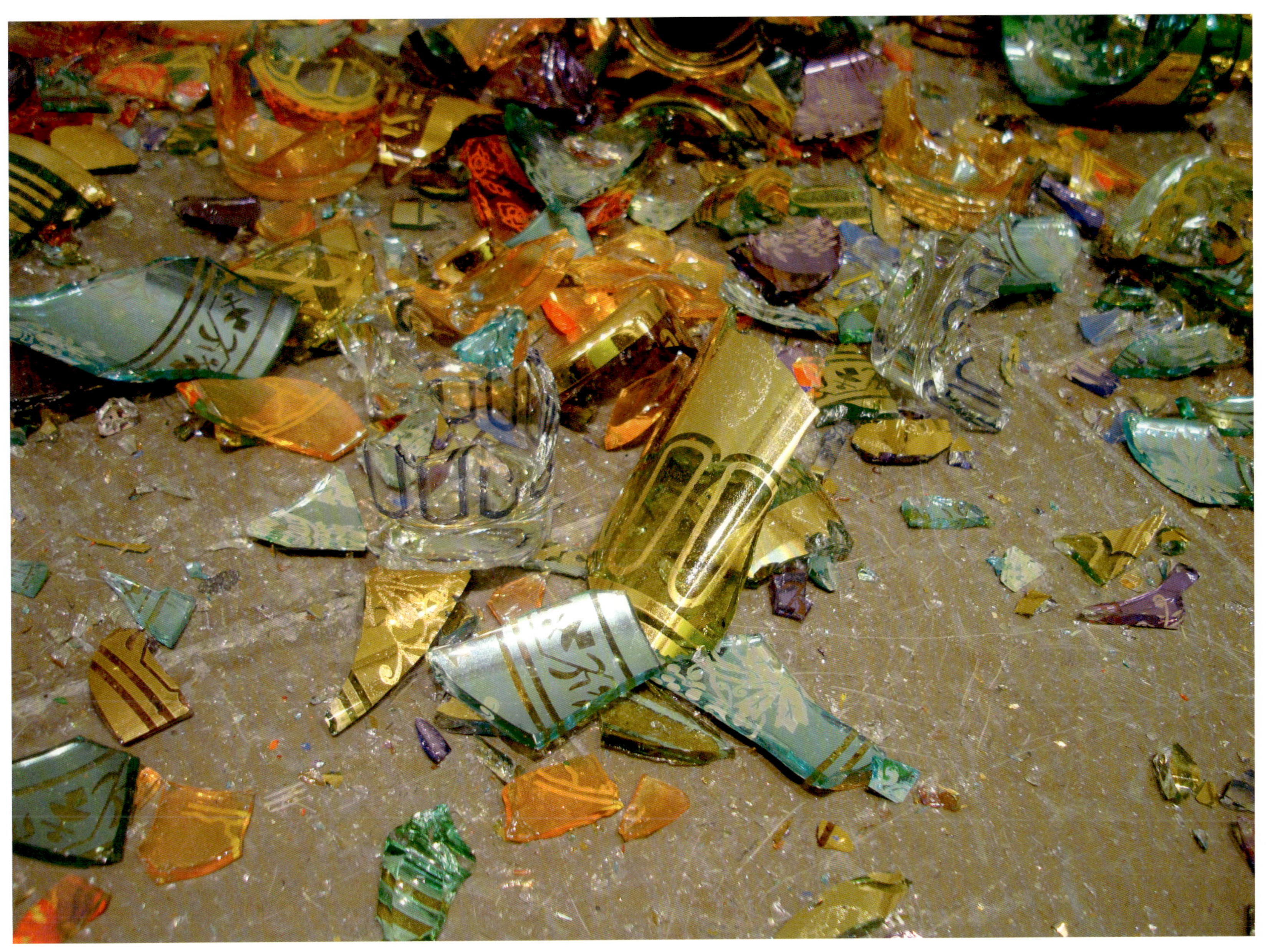

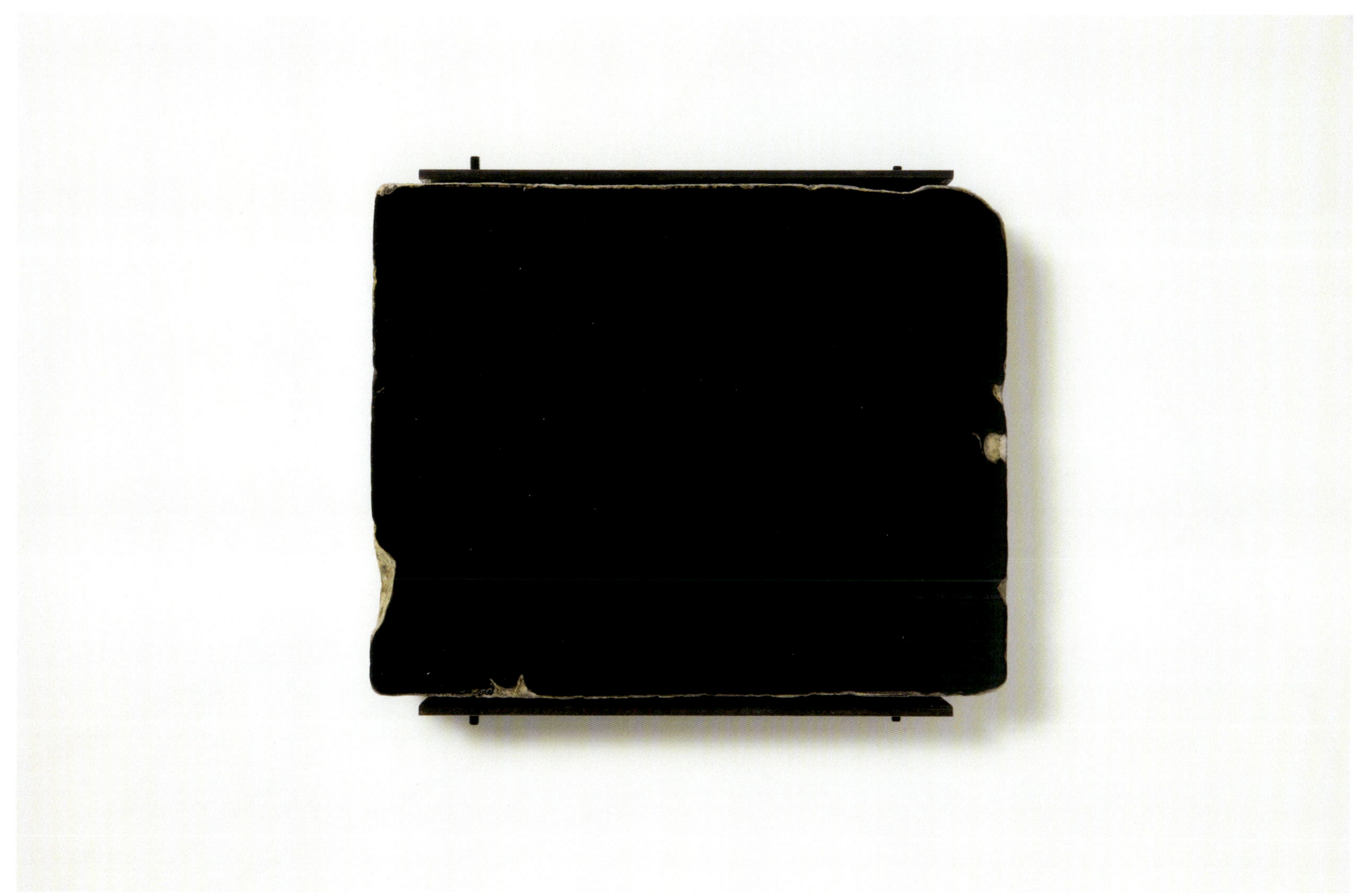

Factory District (W.B.), 2012
Lithographic stone, printing ink,
varnish, steel angles, 24 × 29.5 × 5 cm

Fantasia

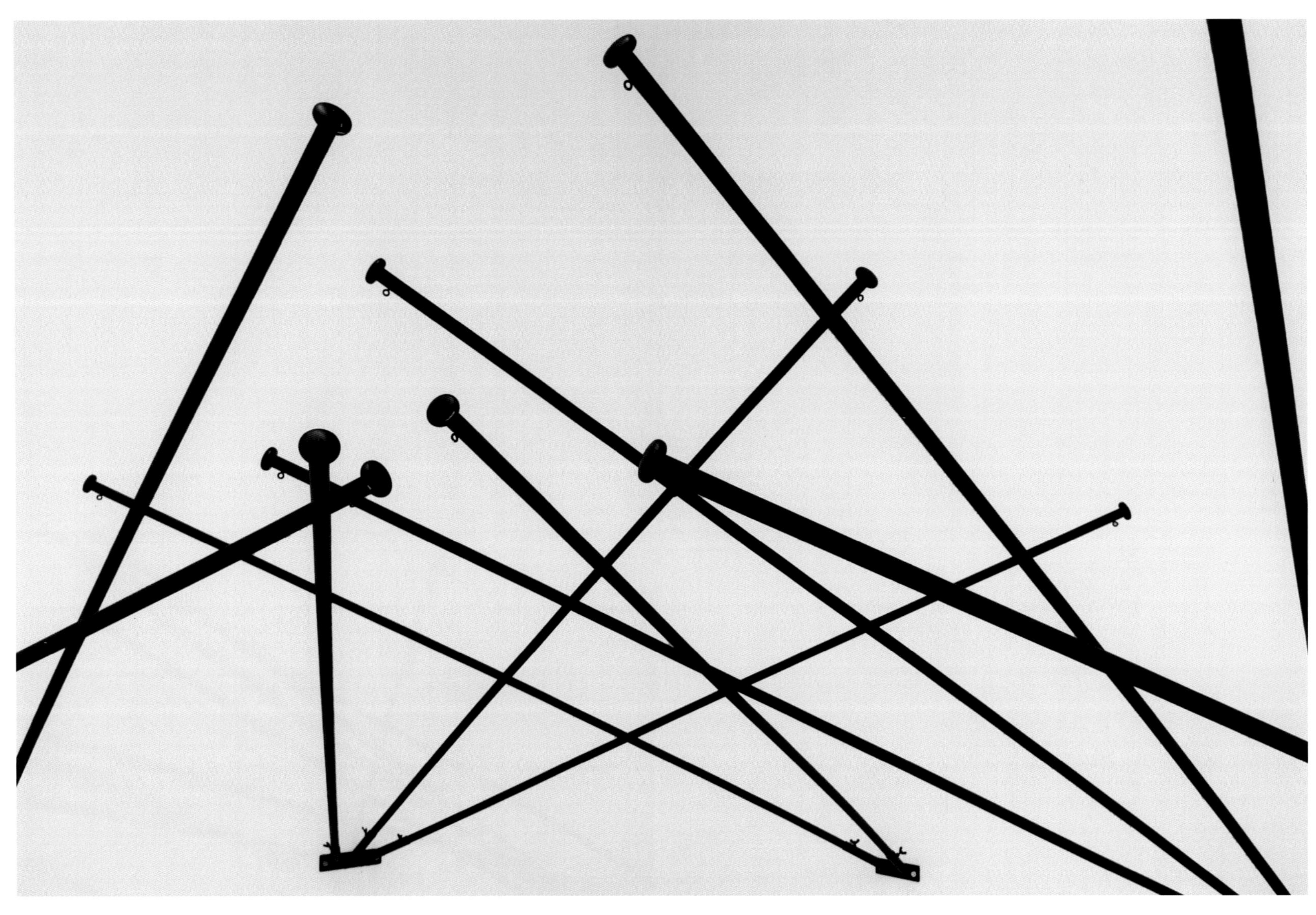

Fantasia (Empty Flag, Black)
4 Walls in a Room, 2008 (detail)
Fiberglass flagpoles, steel bases,
dimensions variable, length: 3 m

Collection Kunsthaus Zürich, Zurich

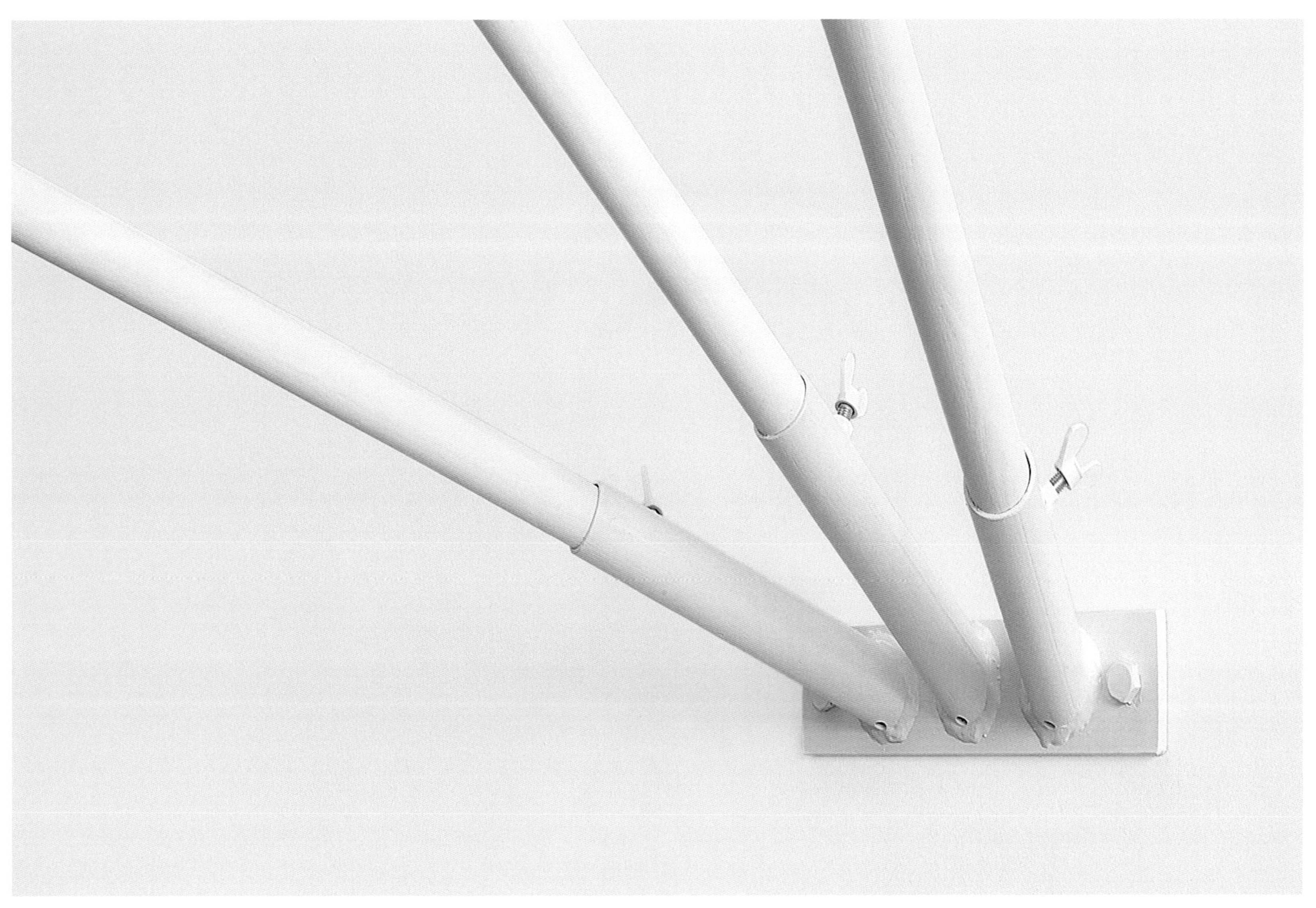

Fantasia (Empty Flag, White)
4 Walls in a Room, 2008 (detail)
Fiberglass flagpoles, steel bases,
dimensions variable, length: 3 m

Fantôme

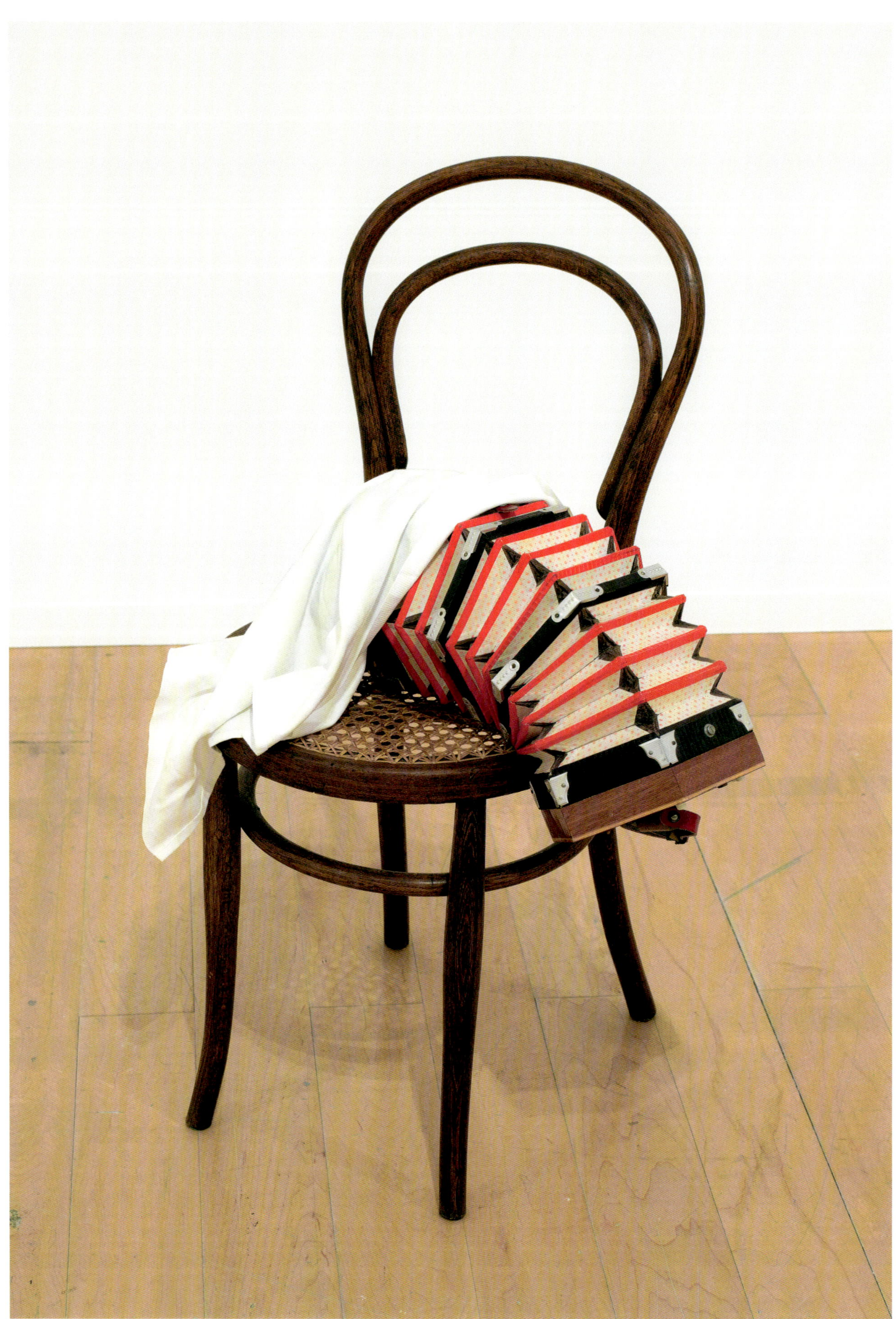

Fantôme, 2011
Thonet chair, Italian bandonion, restaurant napkin, 80 × 43 × 43 cm
Exhibition view, Laps, Musée d'Art contemporain, Lyon, 2013

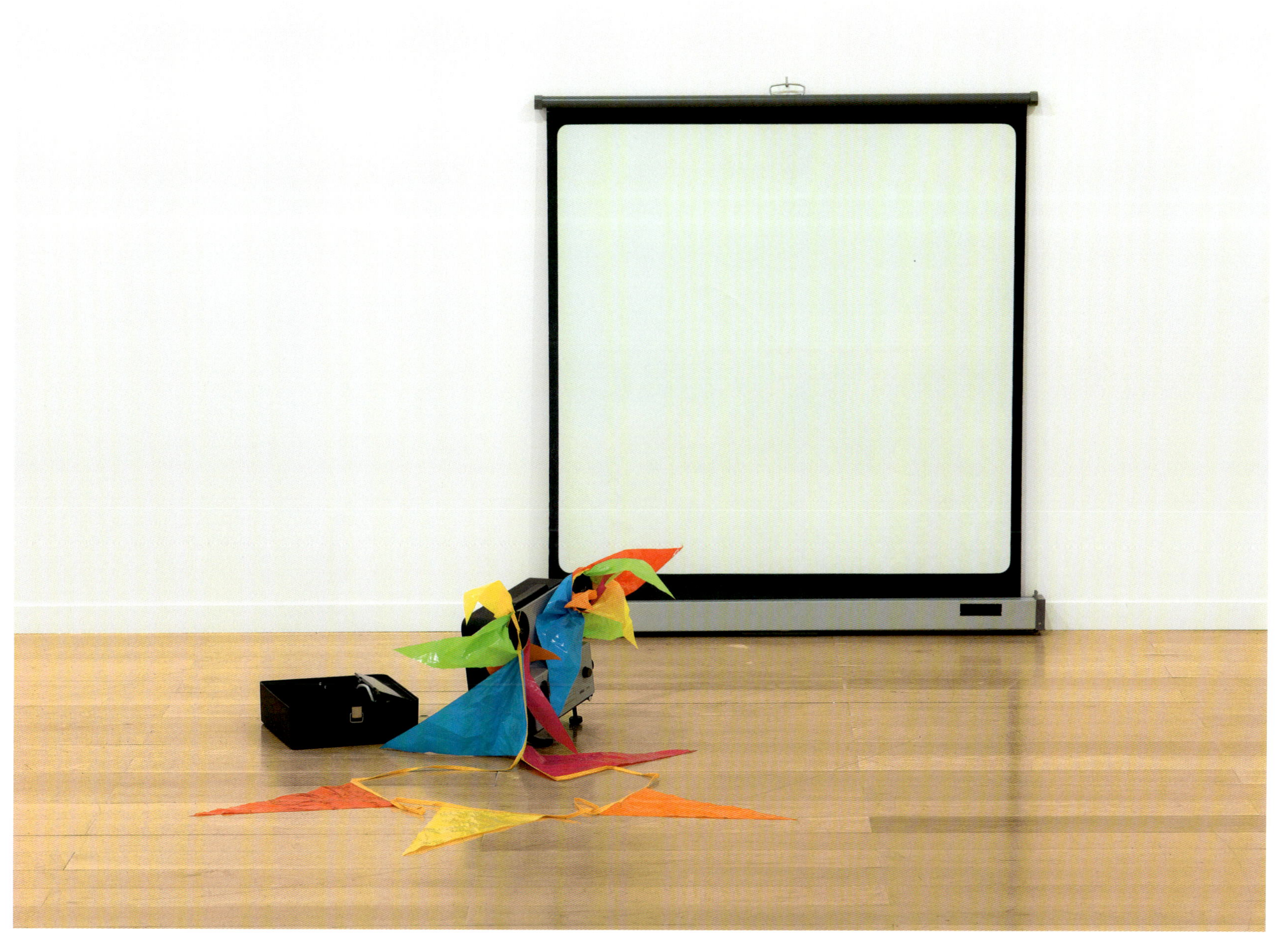

Fantôme, 2013
Portable Super-8 player, plastic club flags, portable screen, dimensions variable
Exhibition view, Laps, Musée d'Art contemporain, Lyon, 2013

Fantôme

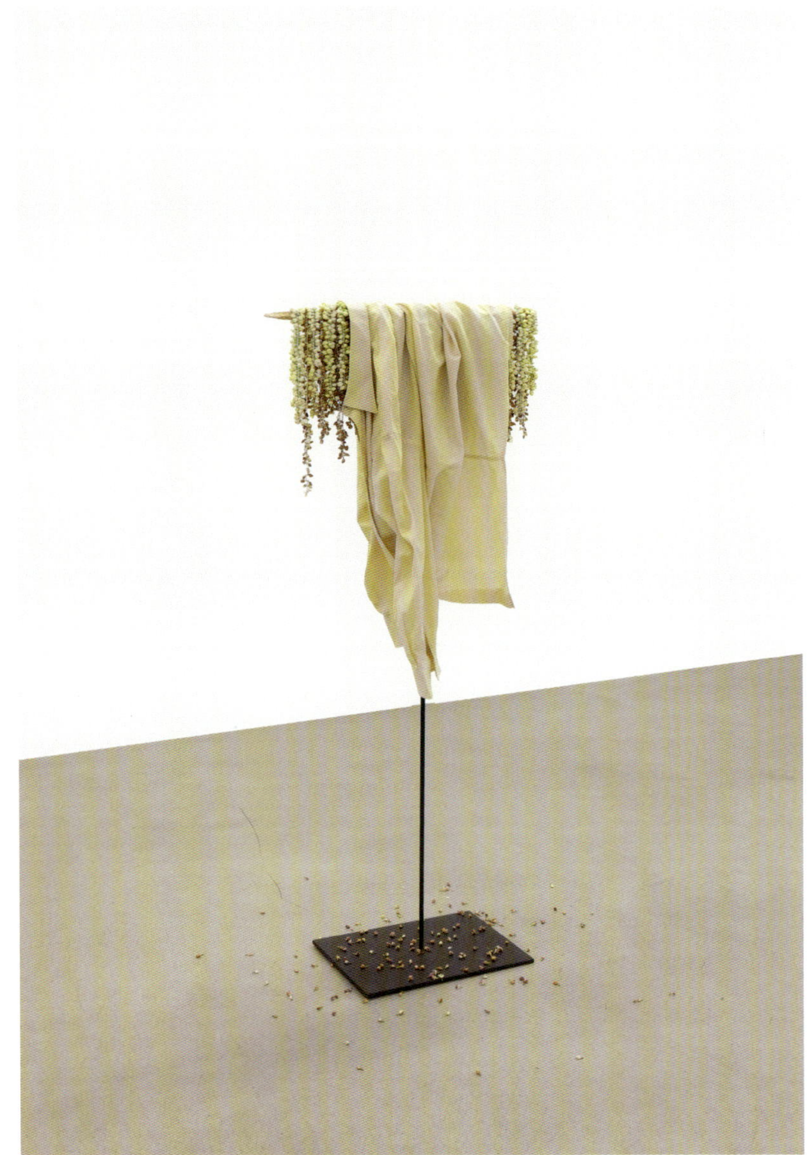

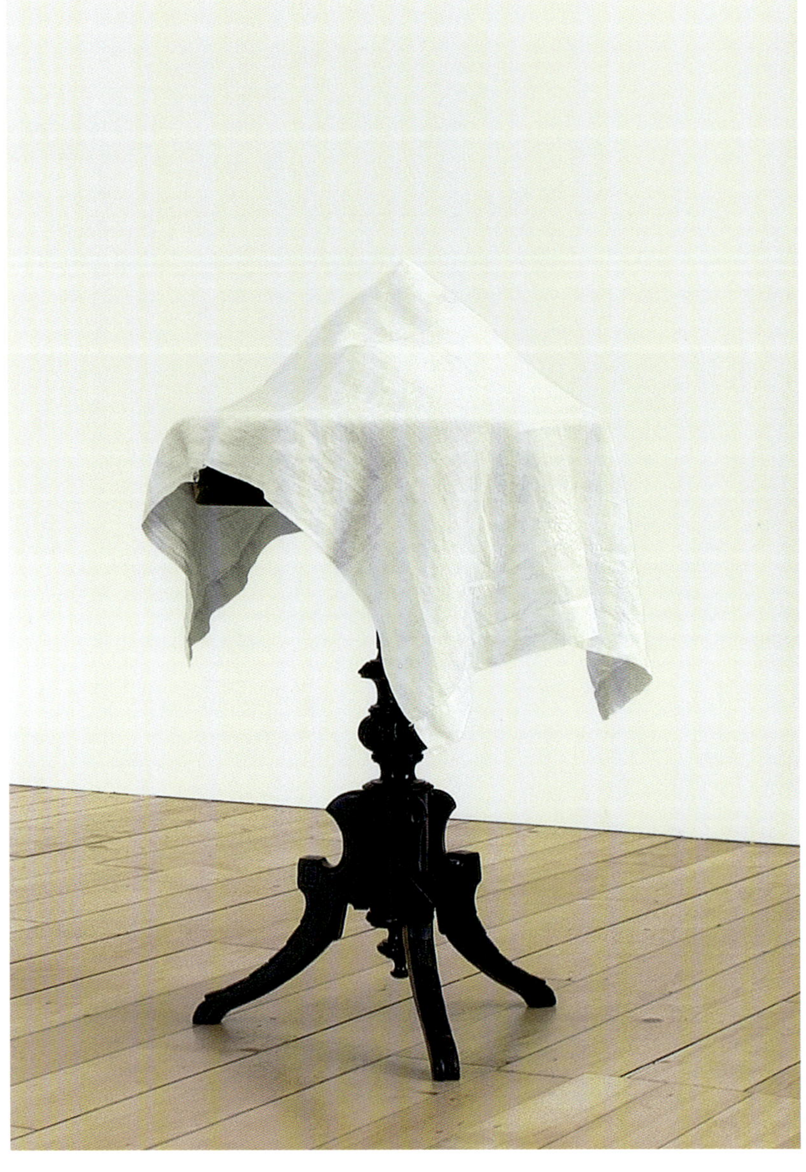

Fantôme (Jasmin), 2011
Steel, wood, shirt, more or less fresh jasmine garlands, 141 × 61.5 × 30 cm
Exhibition view, Tkaf, kamel mennour, Paris, 2011

Collection François Pinault Foundation

Fantôme, 2010
Pedestal table, handwoven linen, teapot, 2 gold tea glasses, 76 × 52 × 52 cm

Collection Fondation Ricola

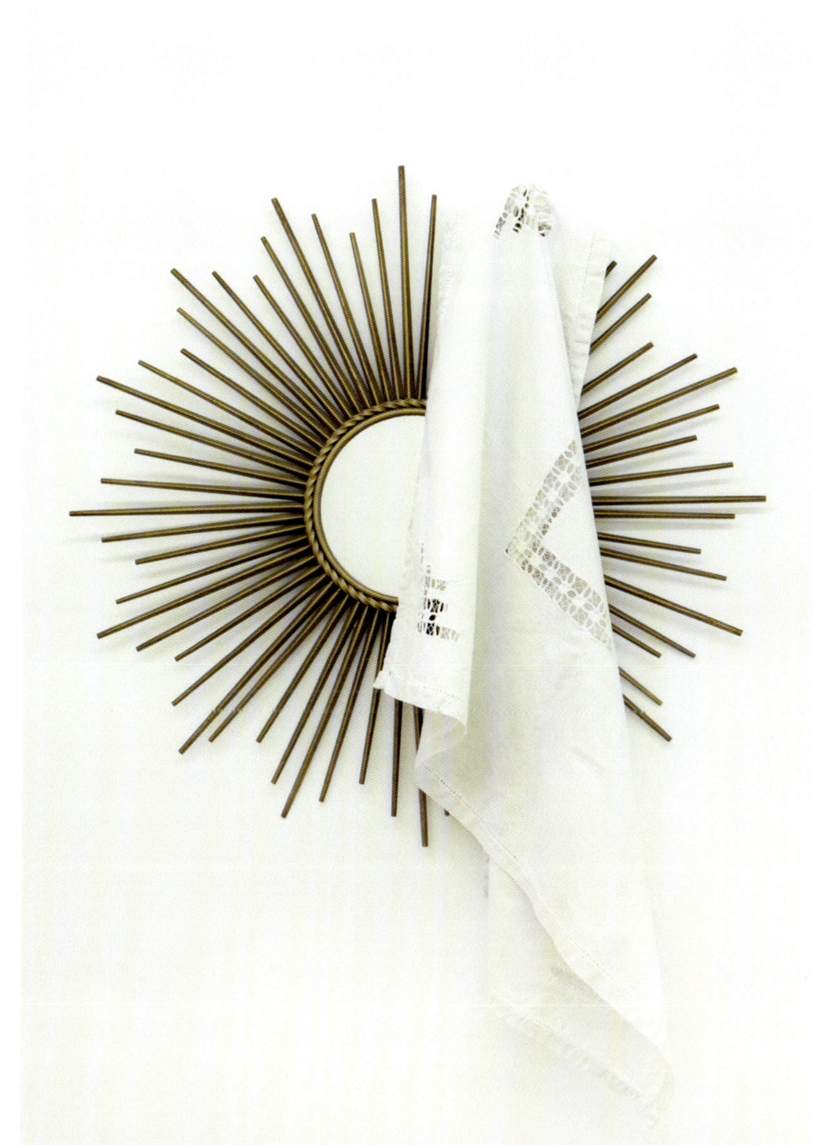

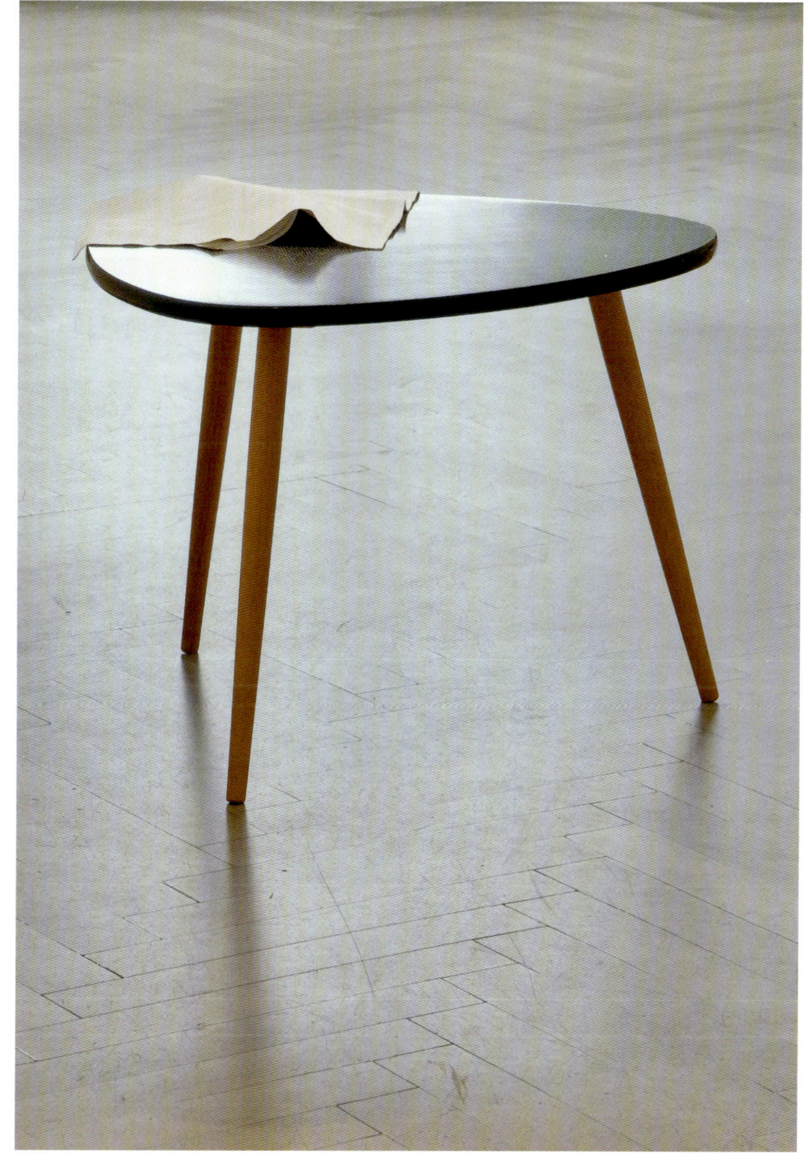

Fantôme, 2011
Chaty Vallauris mirror, antique linen,
c. 110 × 115 cm

Fantôme (Paul Celan), 2011
Table, book, white napkin, 80 × 43 × 43 cm
Exhibition view, From Threshold to Threshold, Mies van der Rohe Haus der Esters, Kunstmuseen, Krefeld, 2011

Frame

Frame, 2008
Polyester carpet borders,
103 × 145 cm
Exhibition view, Le rappel des oiseaux, GAMeC, Bergamo, 2010

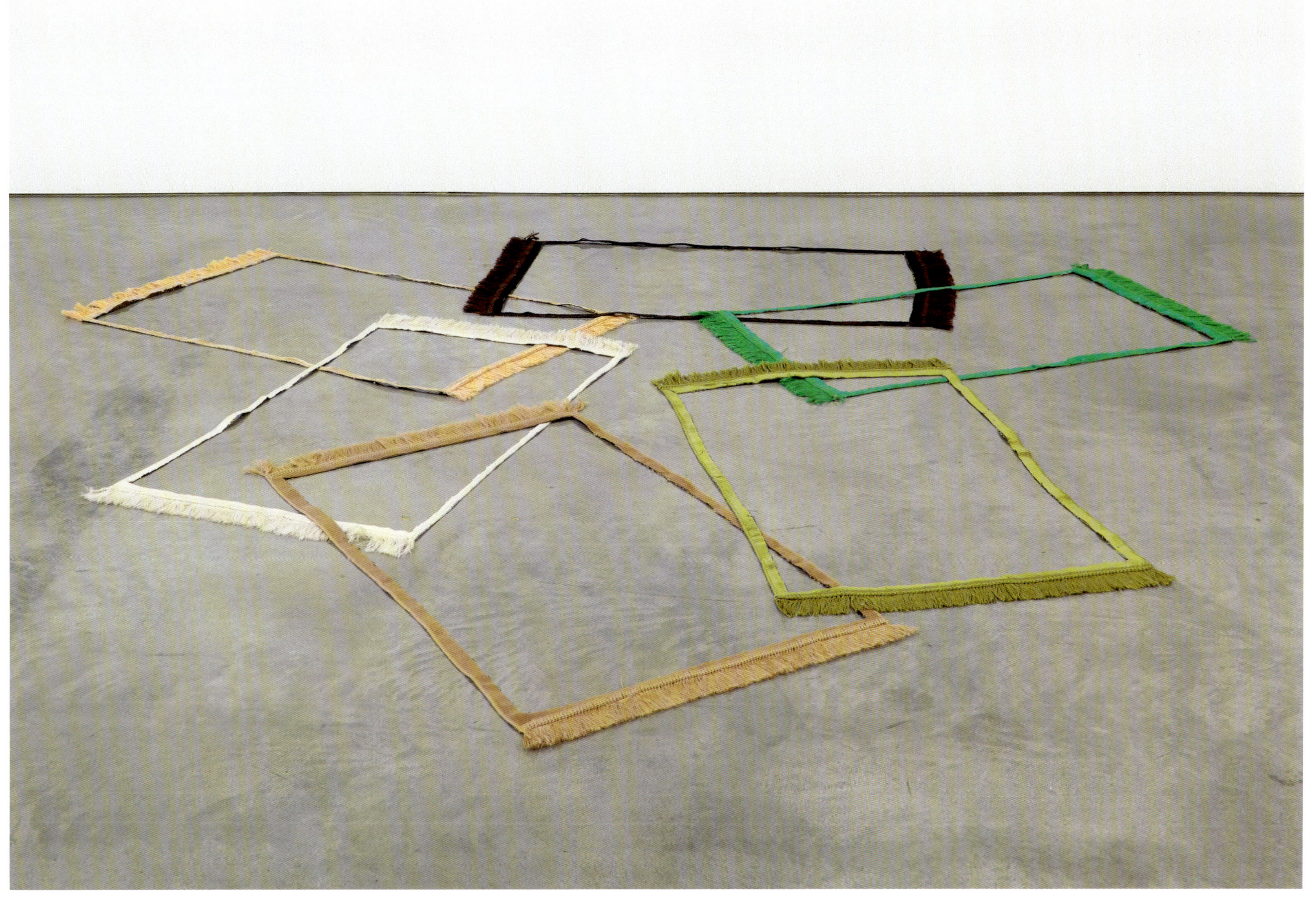

Frames (Olive, miel, beige, vert, brun, paille), 2012
6 polyester carpet borders, dimensions variable
Exhibition view, The Spirit Level, Gladstone
Gallery, New York, 2012

Collection Kunstmuseum Liechtenstein, Vaduz

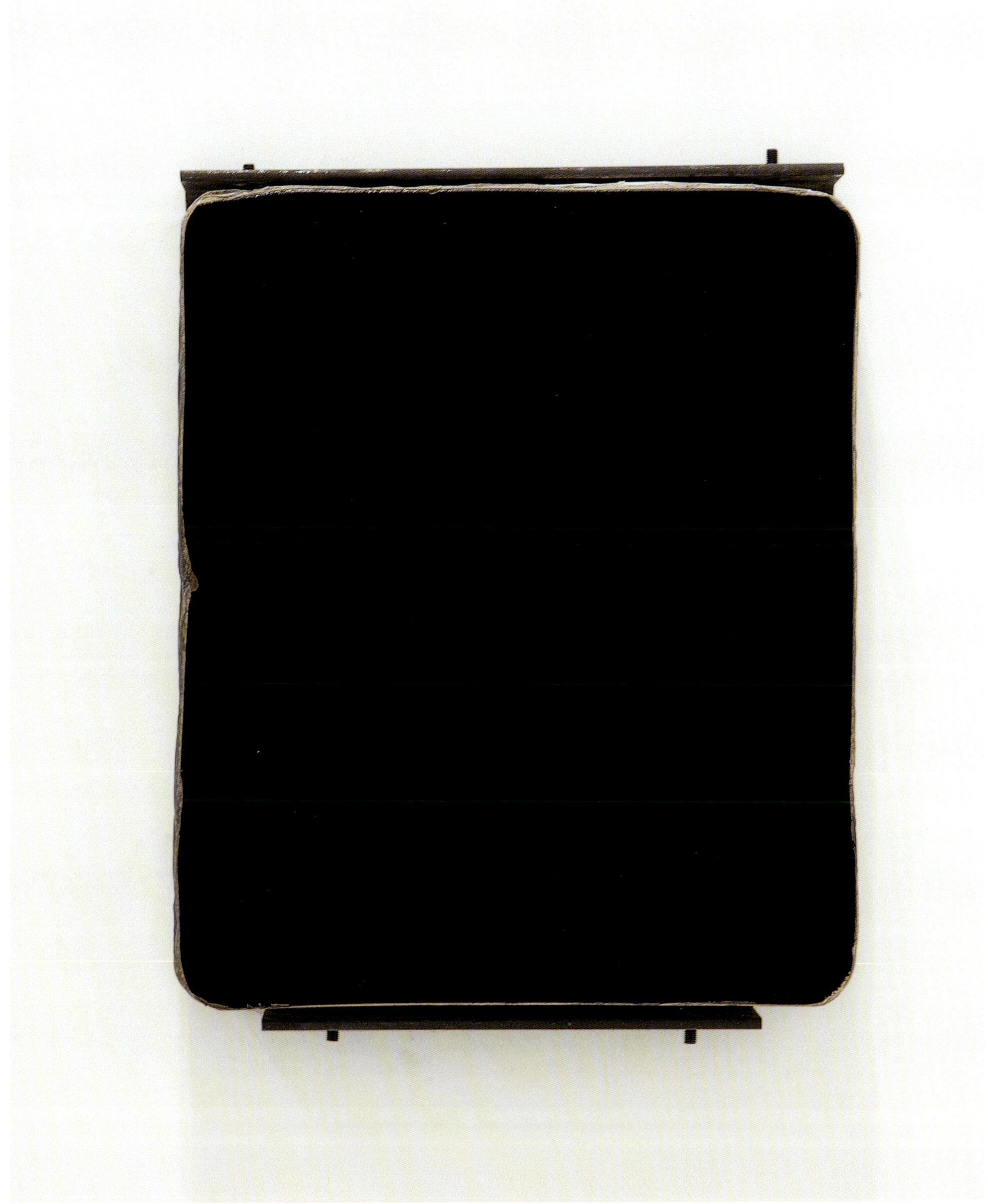

Fringed Scarf (M.G.), 2012
Lithographic stone, printing ink,
varnish, steel angles, 30 × 24.5 × 5 cm

Gaya (E102)

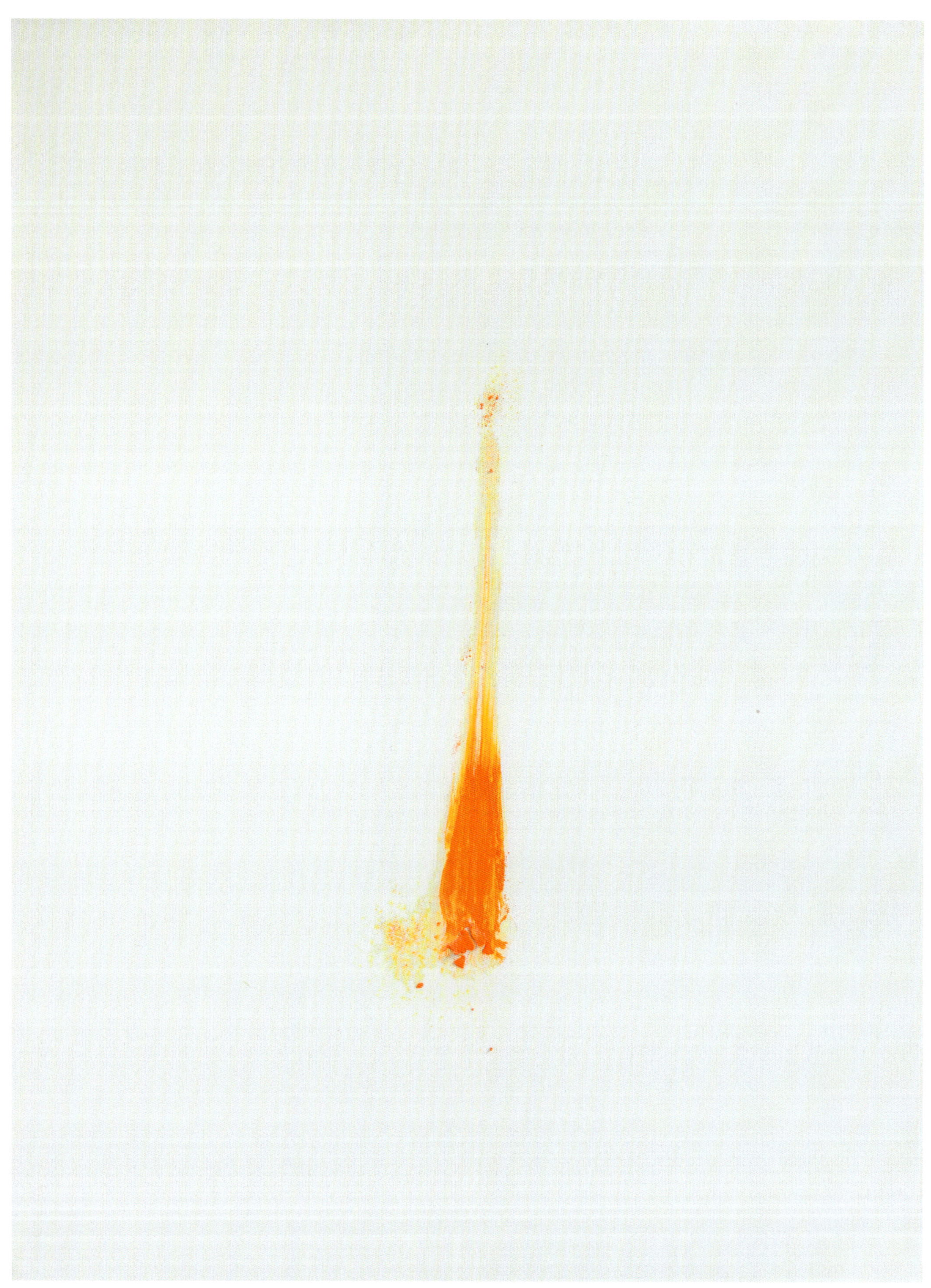

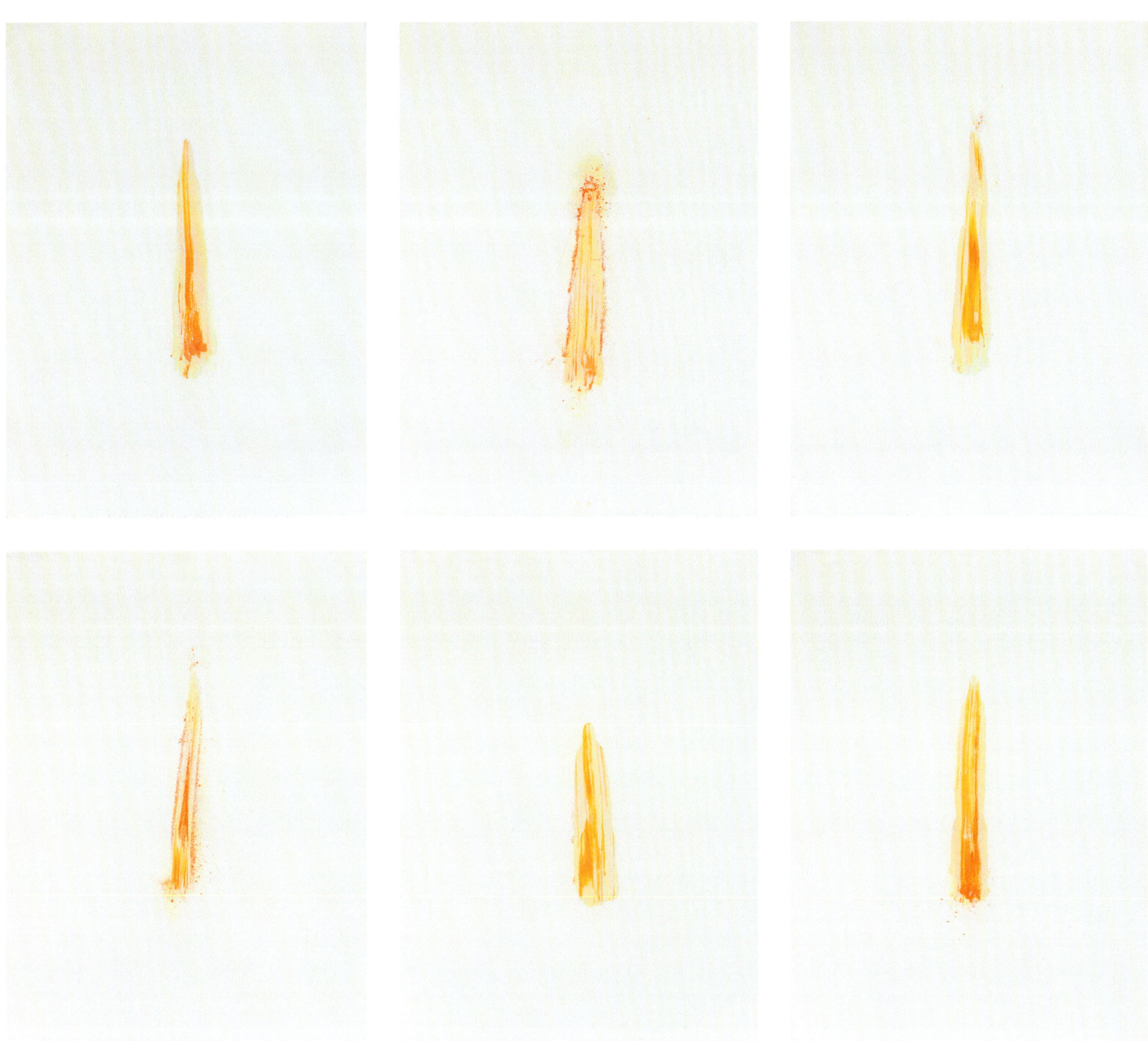

<u>Gaya (E102)</u>, 2004
E102 synthetic food dye and saliva
on canvas, 46 × 33 cm each

Globus

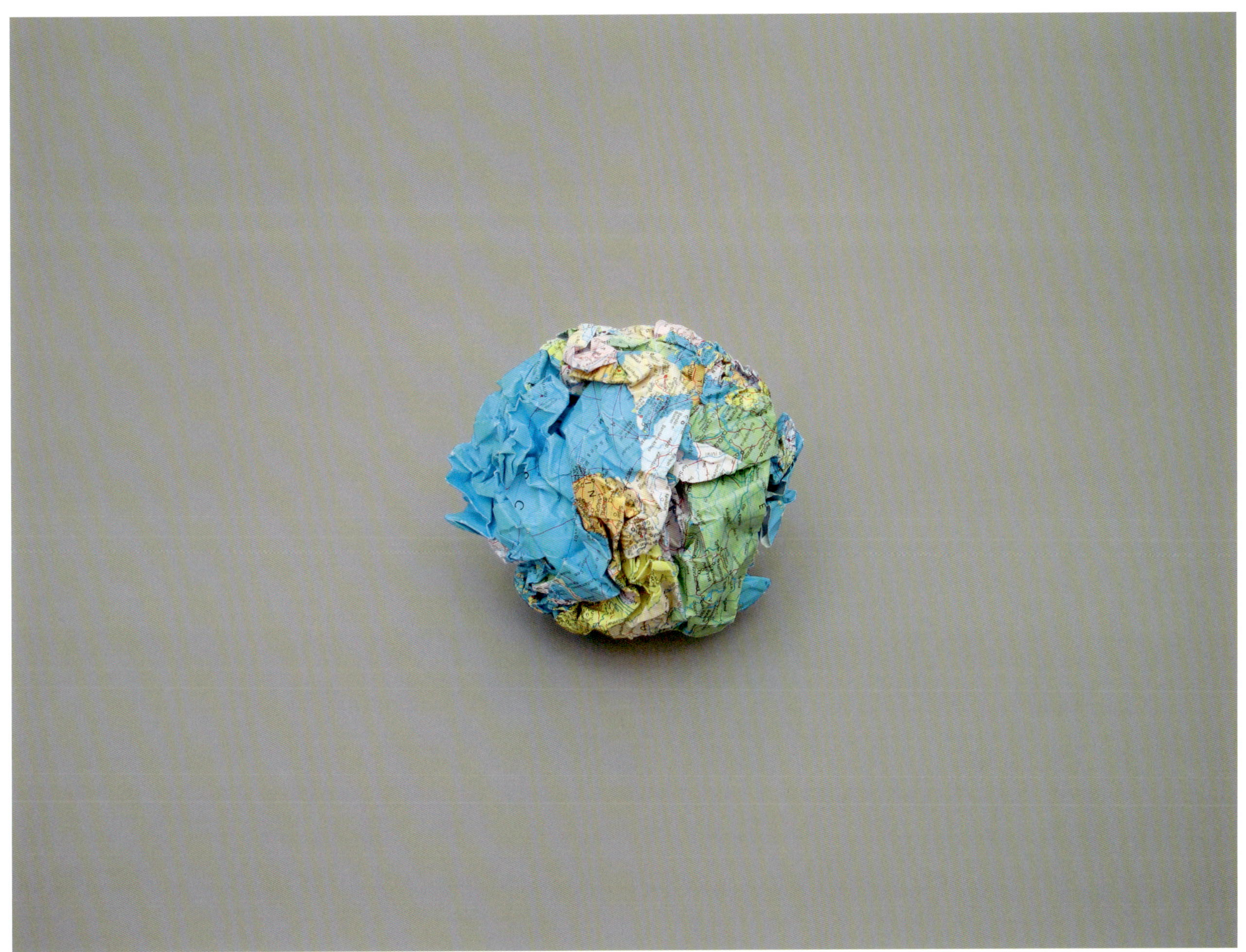

Globus a, 2007
Creased and varnished fabric globe, ø 22 cm

HLM

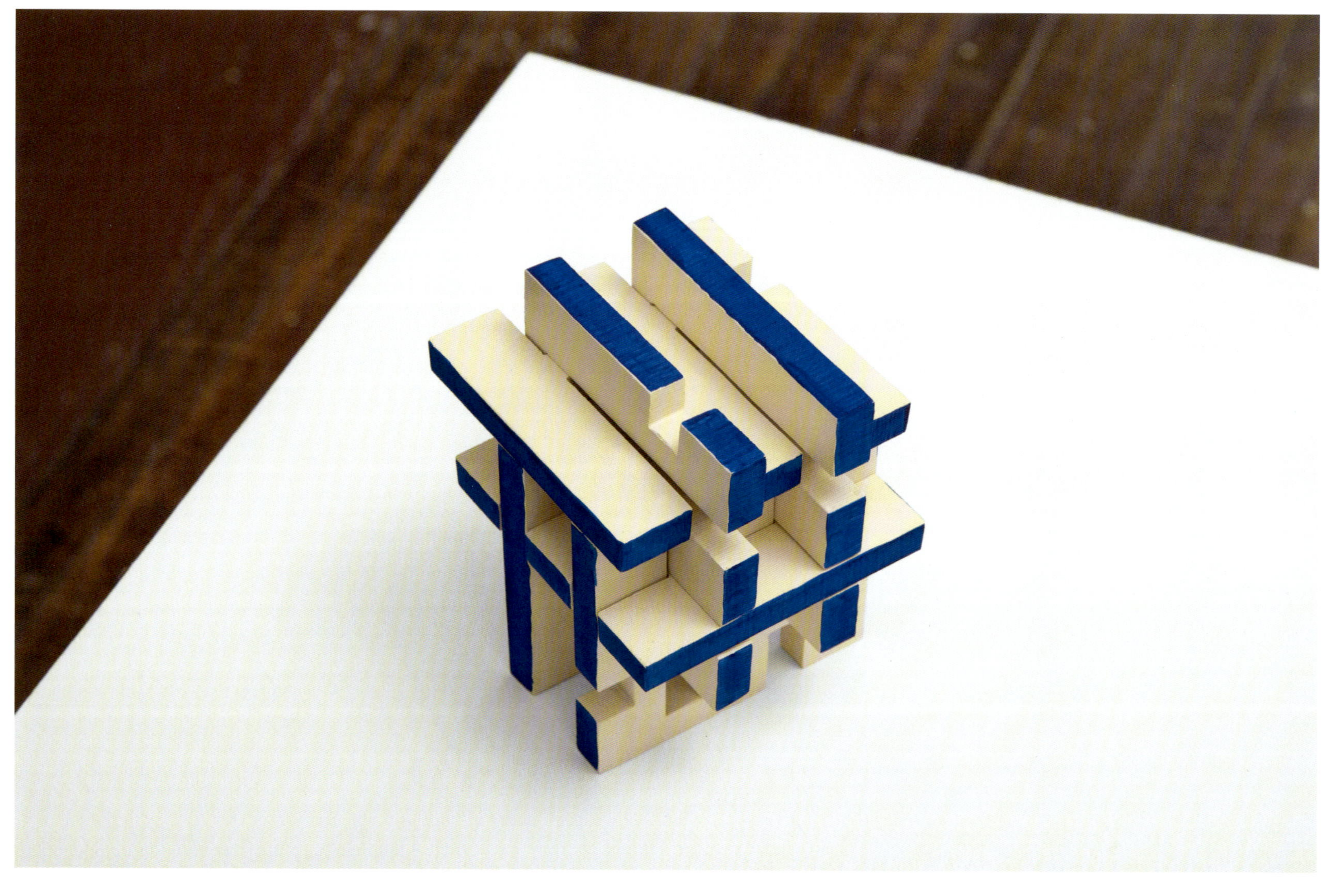

HLM (L'Artimon, La Corène, La Misaine, La Vigie, Le Beaupré, Le Grand Pavois), 2009 (details)
6 painted wooden puzzles on pedestals, pedestal height: 86 cm, each puzzle c. 15 × 15 cm
Left: L'Artimon; right: La Vigie

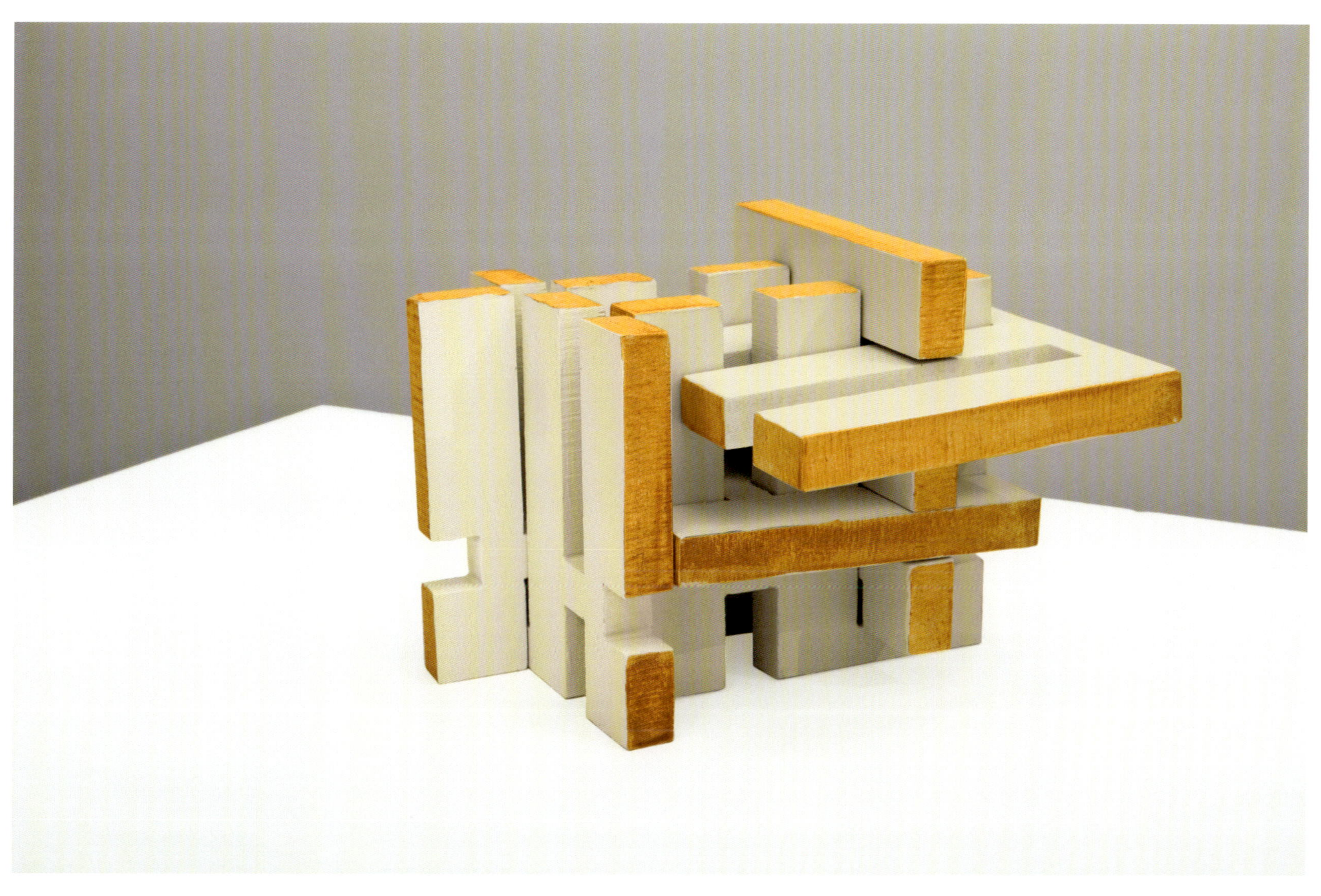

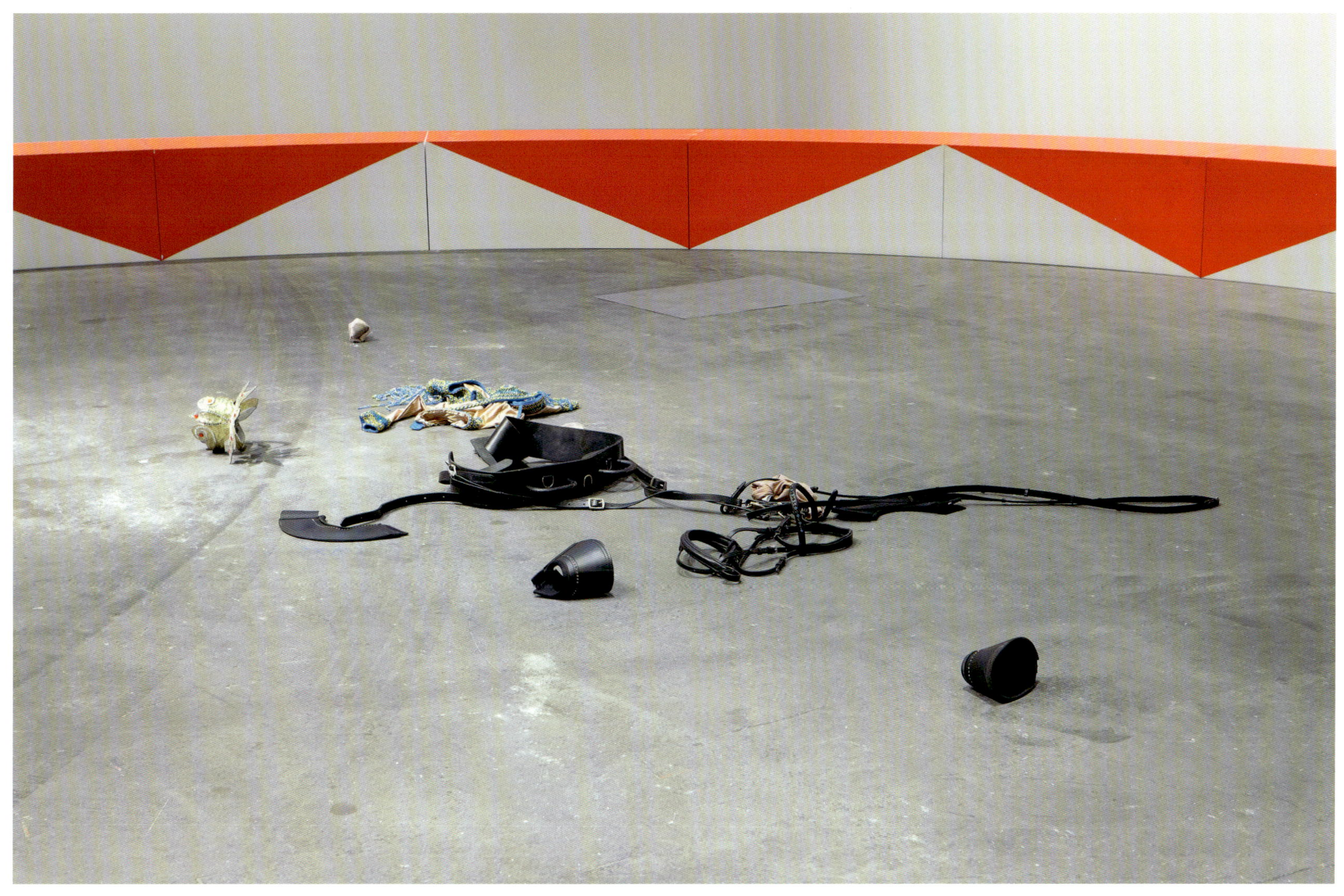

Horse and Figure, 2012 (detail)
Circus ring, hardboard, paint, costumes, pumps, helmets, horse reins, harness, 50 × 1000 × 1000 cm
Installation view, Art Unlimited, Art Basel, 2013

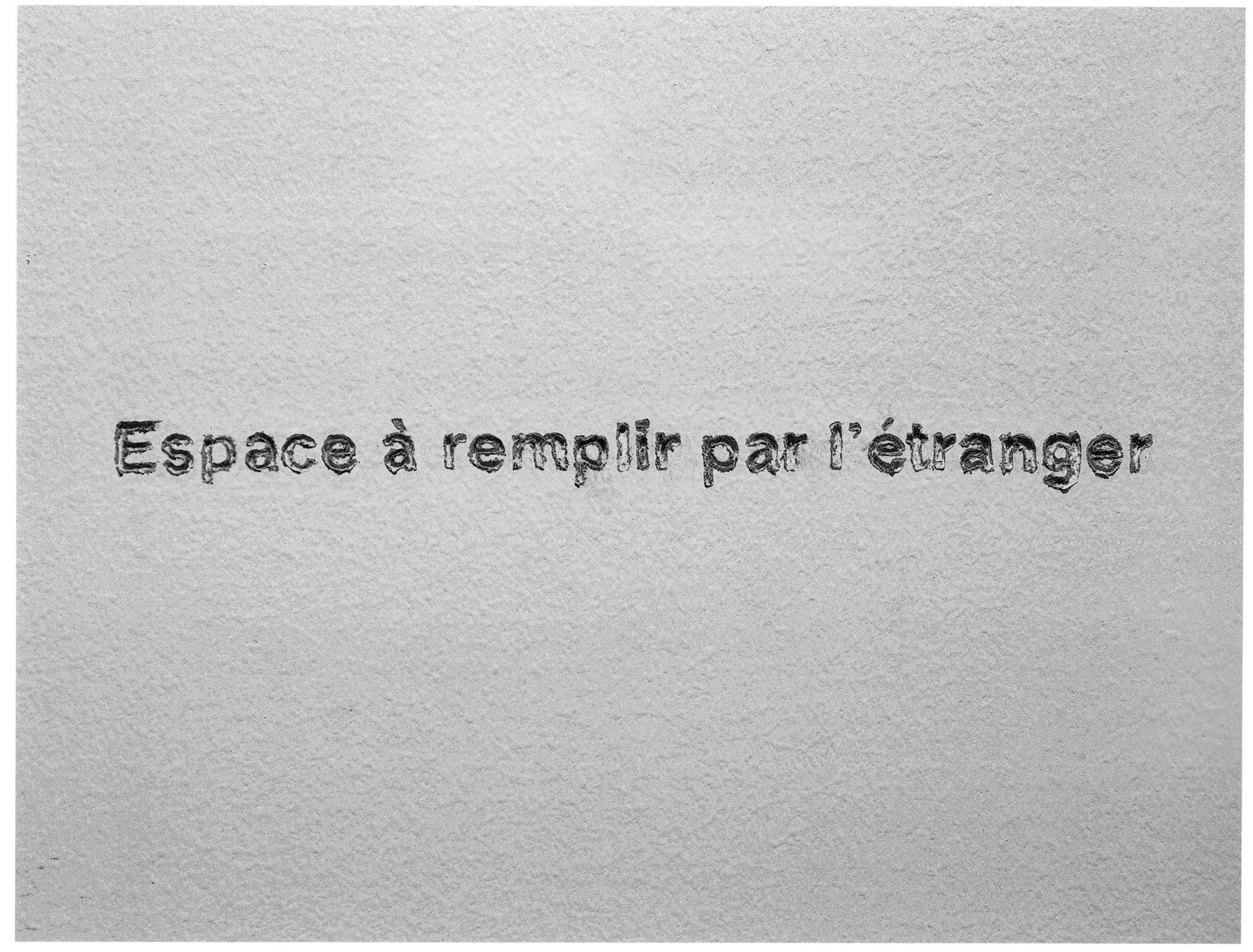

Hospitalité, 2006
Engraving on wall, length: 29 cm

Collections Institut d'Art contemporain, Villeurbanne/Rhône-Alpes; Musée national de l'histoire et des cultures de l'immigration/CNHI, Paris

Is this the Meaning of Life (L.K.)

Is this the Meaning of Life (L.K.), 2012
Lithographic stone, printing ink, varnish, steel angles, 38 × 49 × 6.5 cm

Kasseler Parkbänke

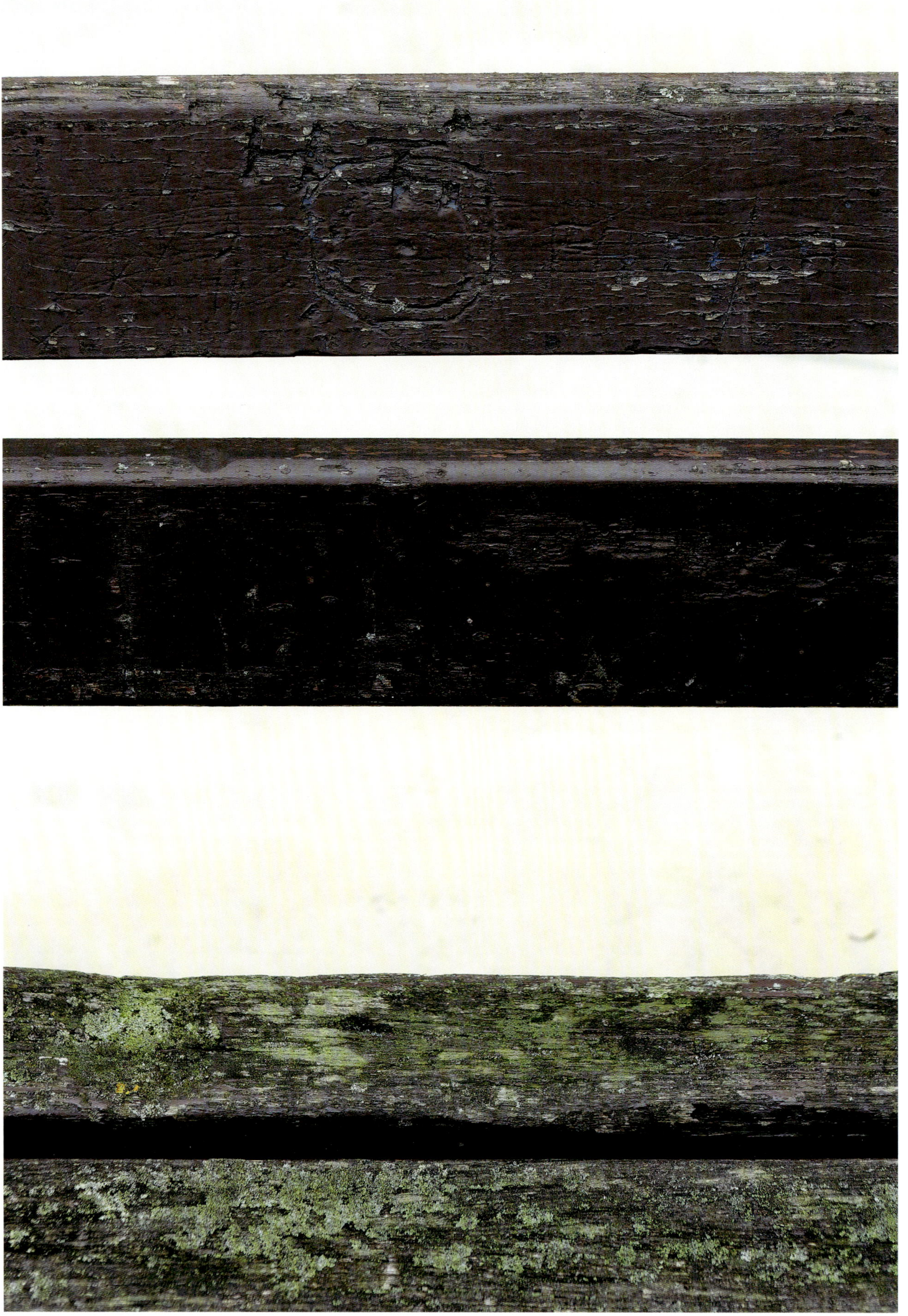

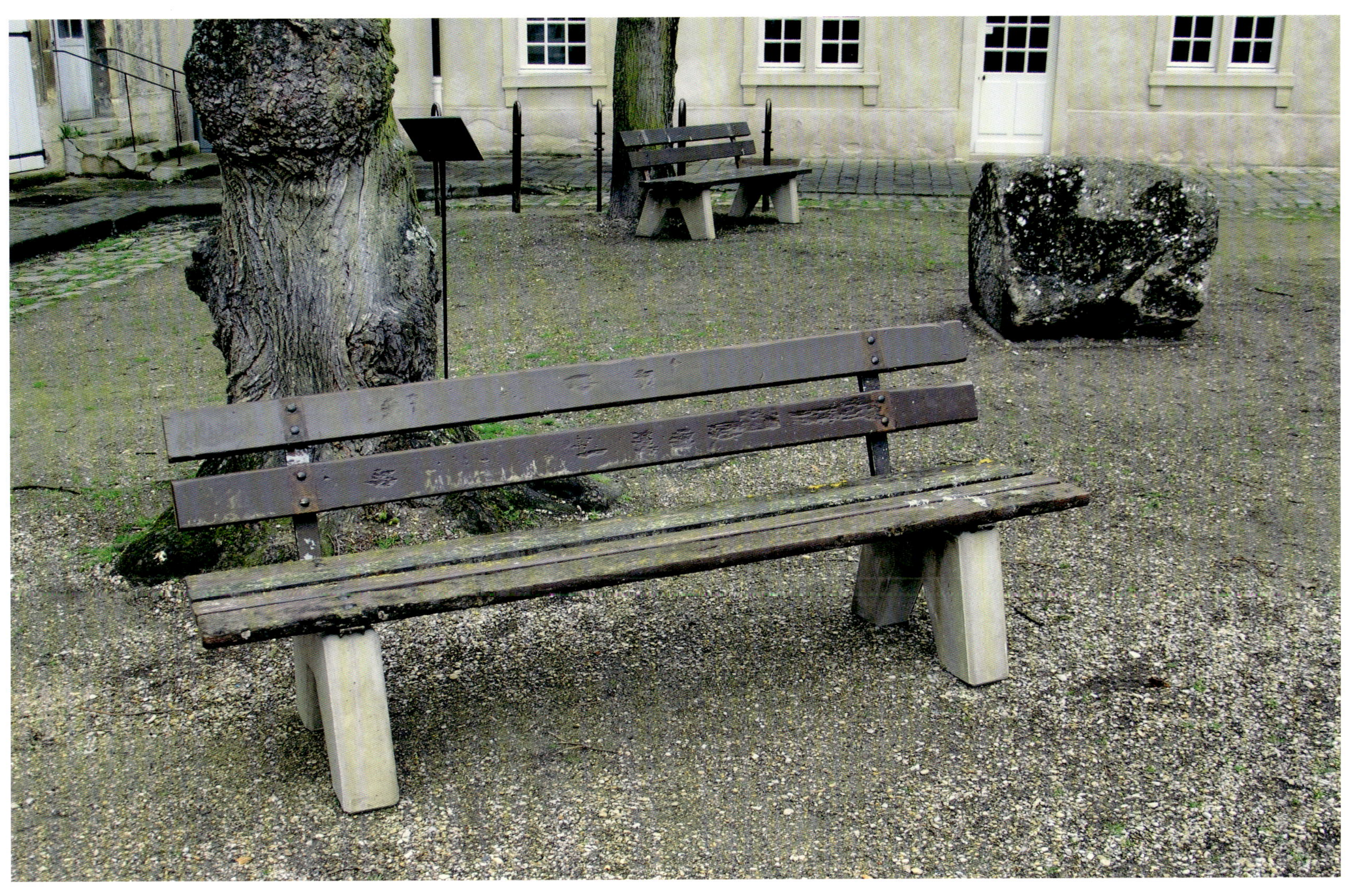

Kasseler Parkbänke, 2009 (details)
Kassel public benches,
76 × 200 × 60 cm each
Exhibition view, Le rappel des oiseaux,
FRAC Champagne-Ardenne, Reims, 2010

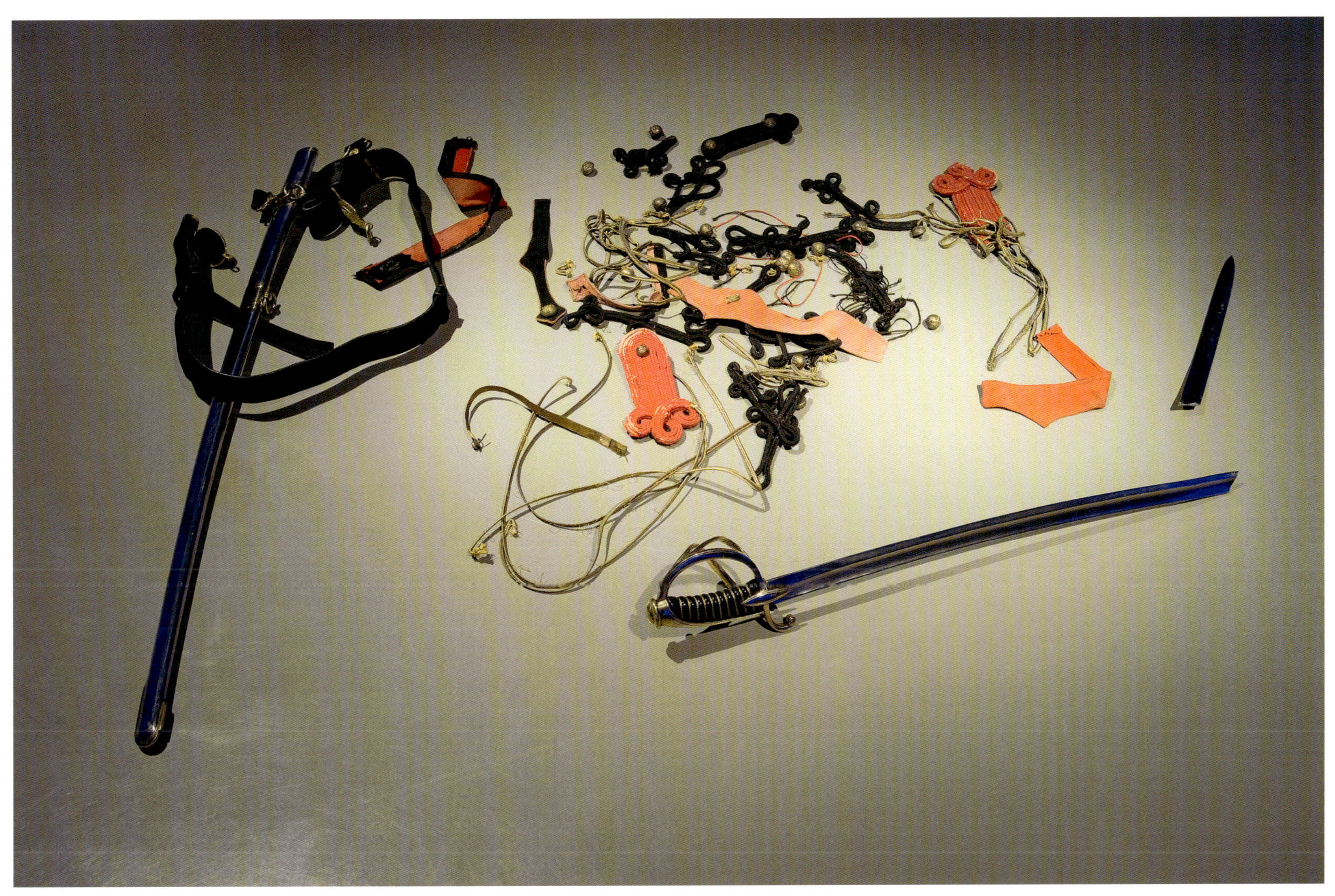

La dégradation, 2009
Buttons, stripes, epaulettes, leather belt, saber, case from a 19th-century French army officer's uniform, dimensions variable

Les fruits de mon ami

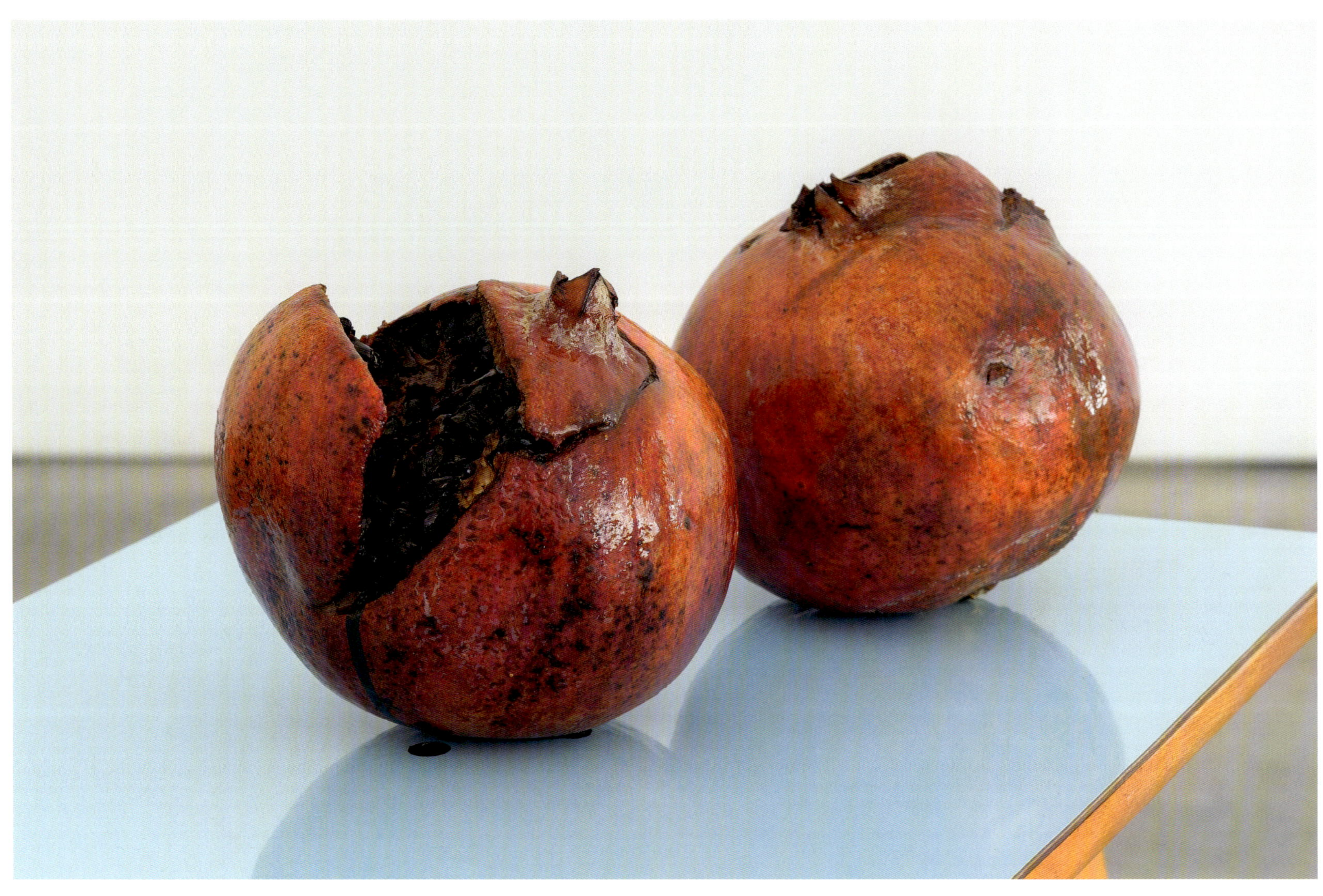

Les fruits de mon ami, 2013
Cast pomegranates on a blue Formica and wood table, India ink; pomegranates 13 × 13 cm each, table: 54 × 33 × 60 cm

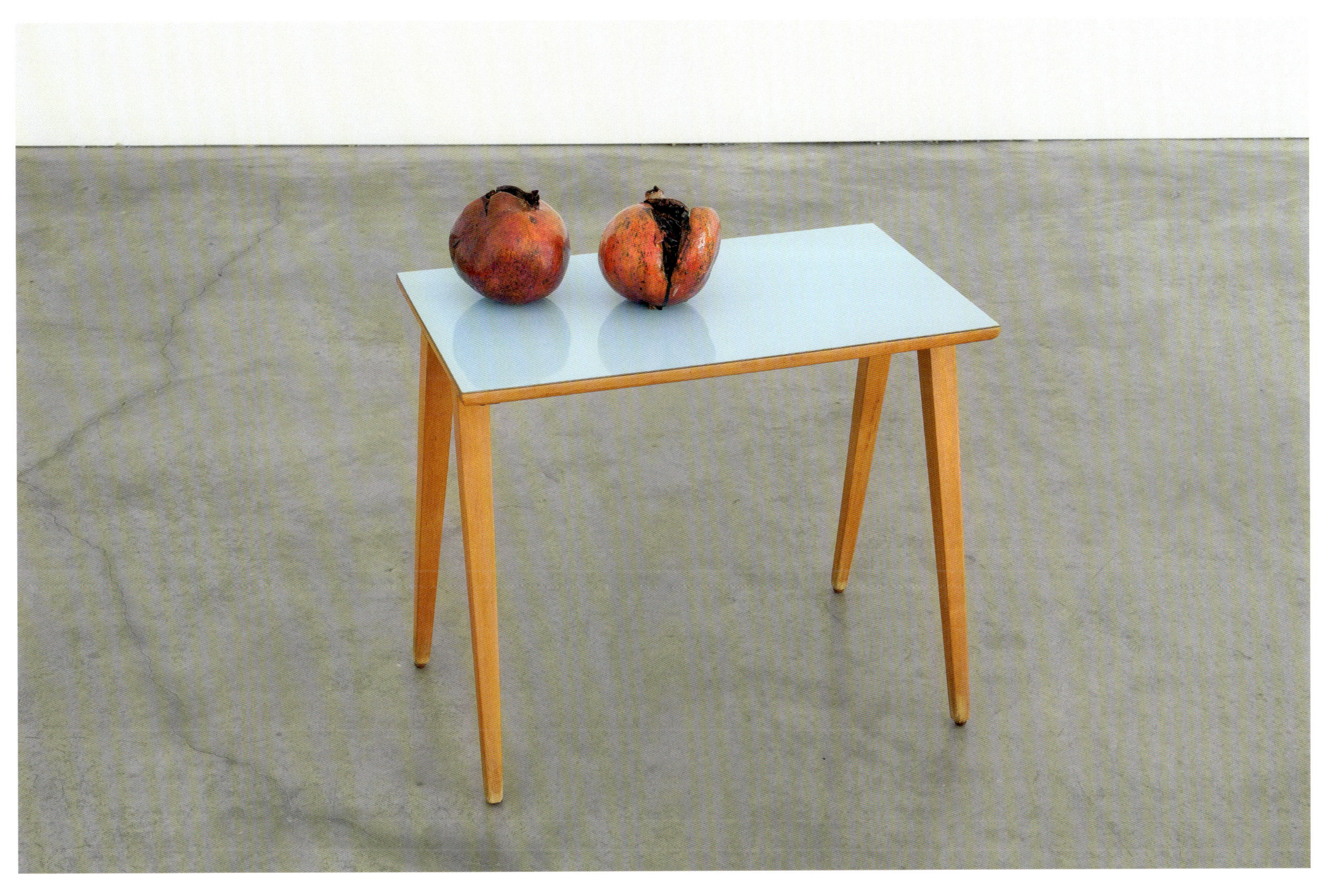

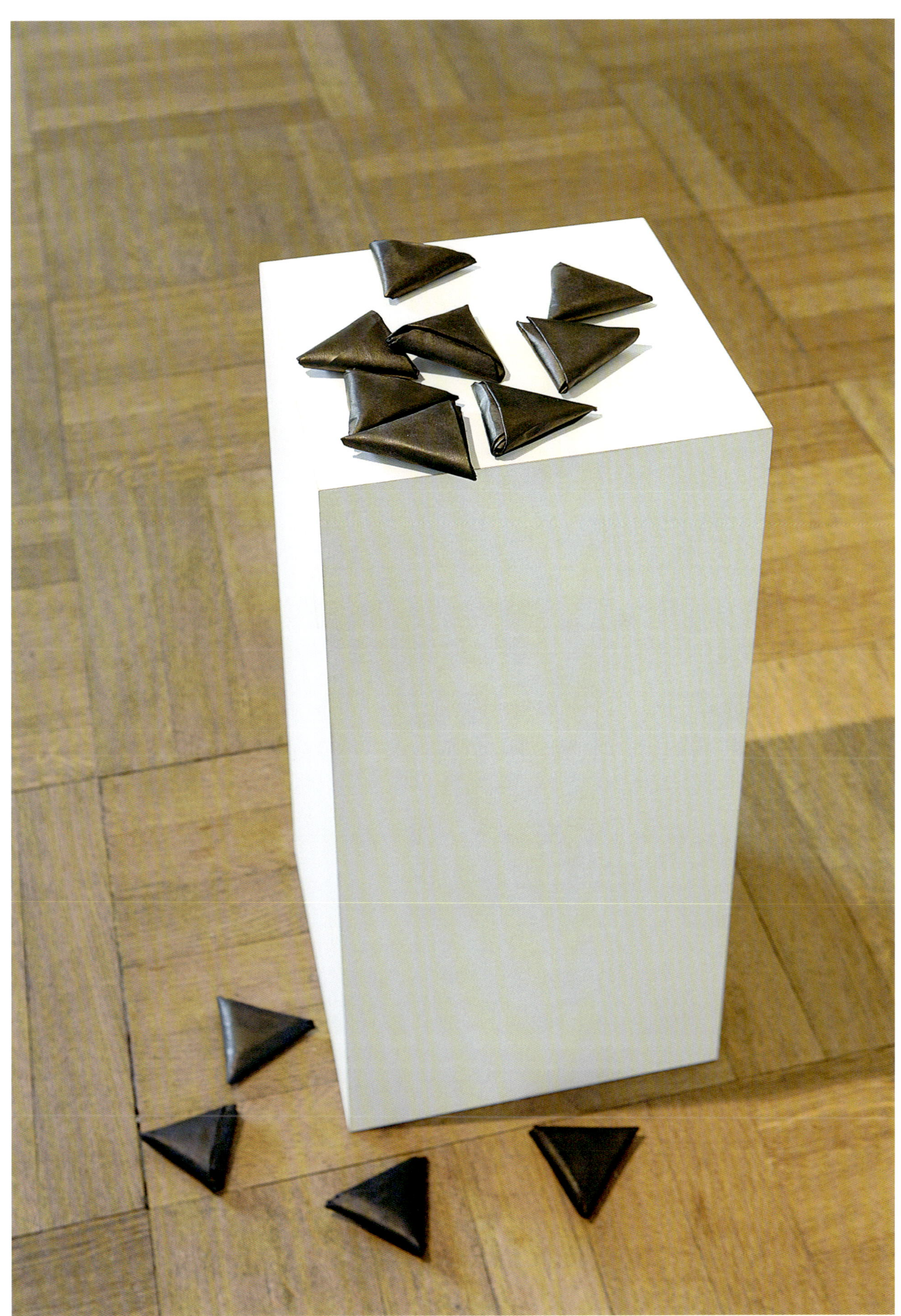

Les petites lettres, 2009
12 pieces of paper dyed with black Chinese ink on pedestal; pedestal height: 70 × 43 × 43 cm
Exhibition view, Partitas, Bielefelder Kunstverein, Bielefeld, 2009

Le thé de Saïd

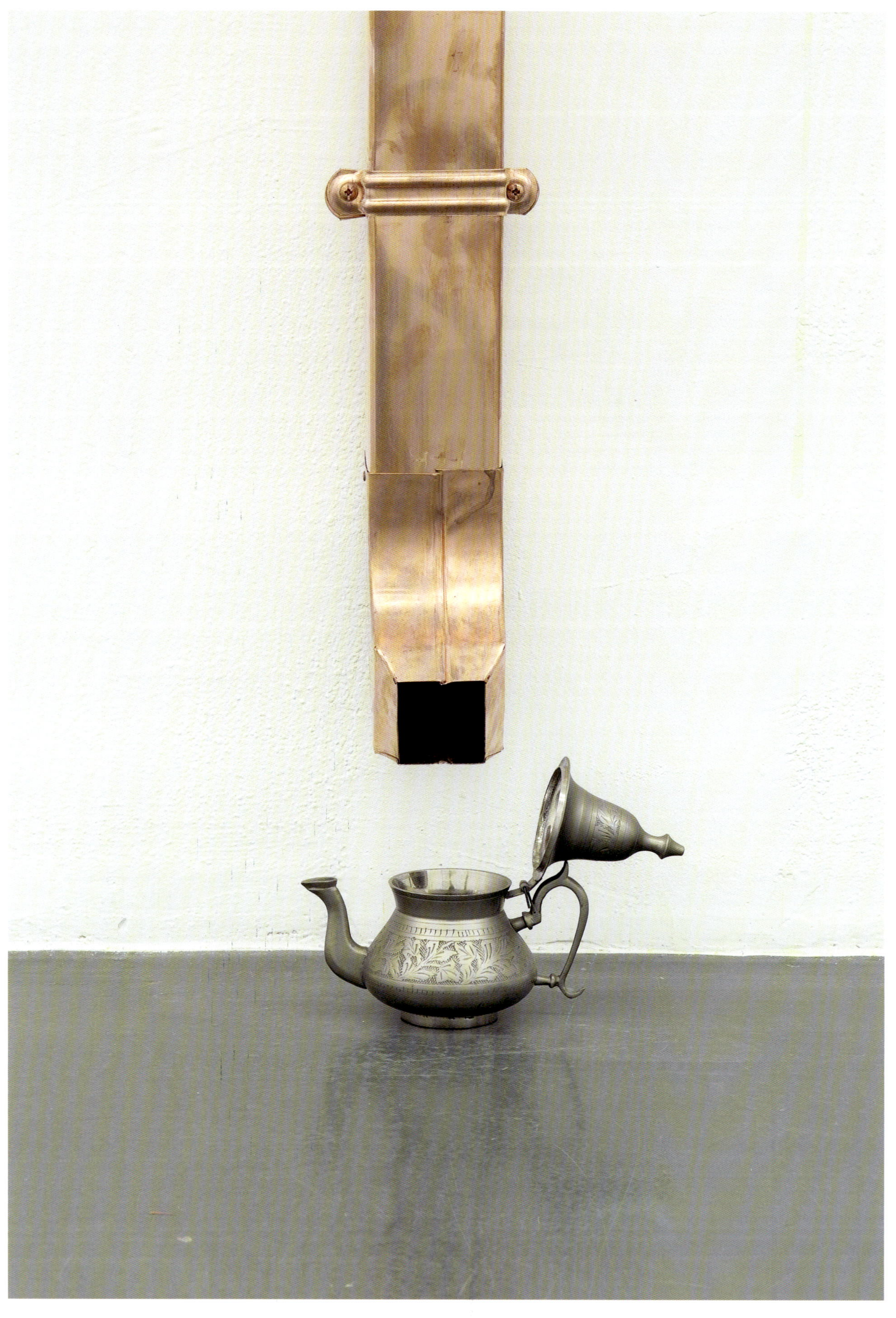

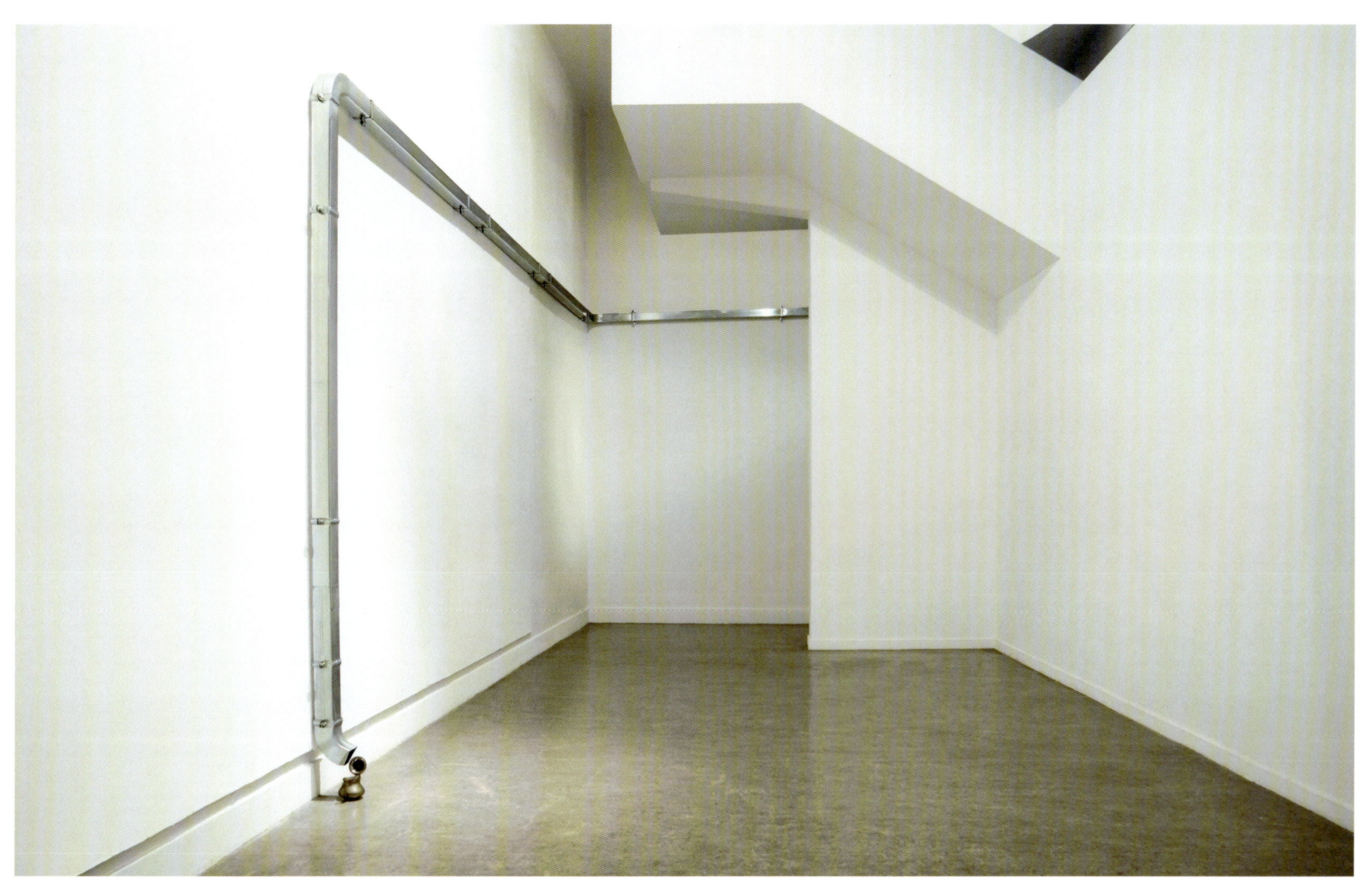

Le thé de Saïd, 2010
One-person teapot and gutter running from the exterior to the interior of the exhibition space, dimensions variable
Exhibition views, Le rappel des oiseaux, GAMeC, Bergamo, 2010 (left); FRAC Champagne-Ardenne, Reims, 2010 (above)

Loan Shop (M.J.)

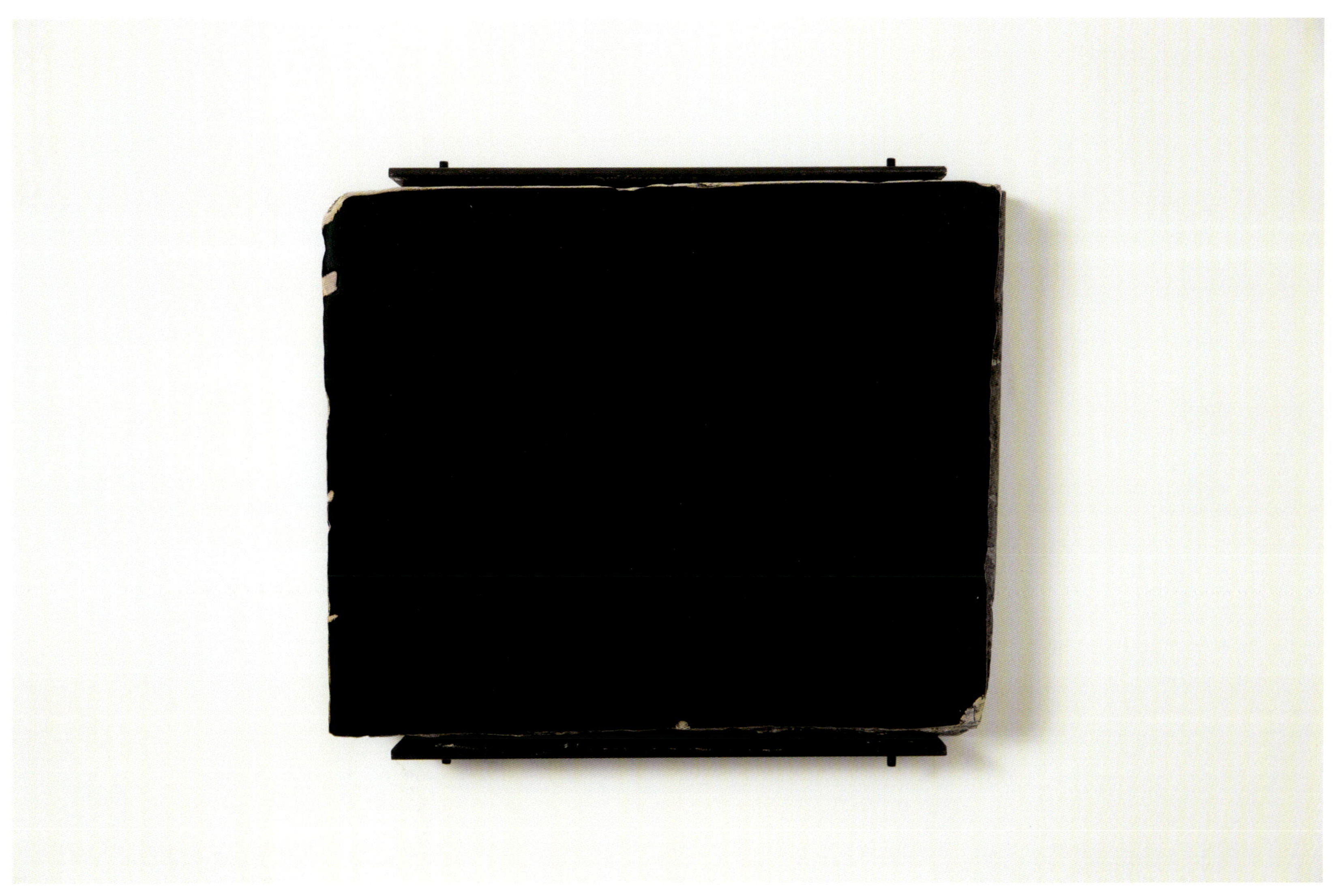

Loan Shop (M.J.), 2012
Lithographic stone, printing ink, varnish,
steel angles, 26 × 31.5 × 6 cm

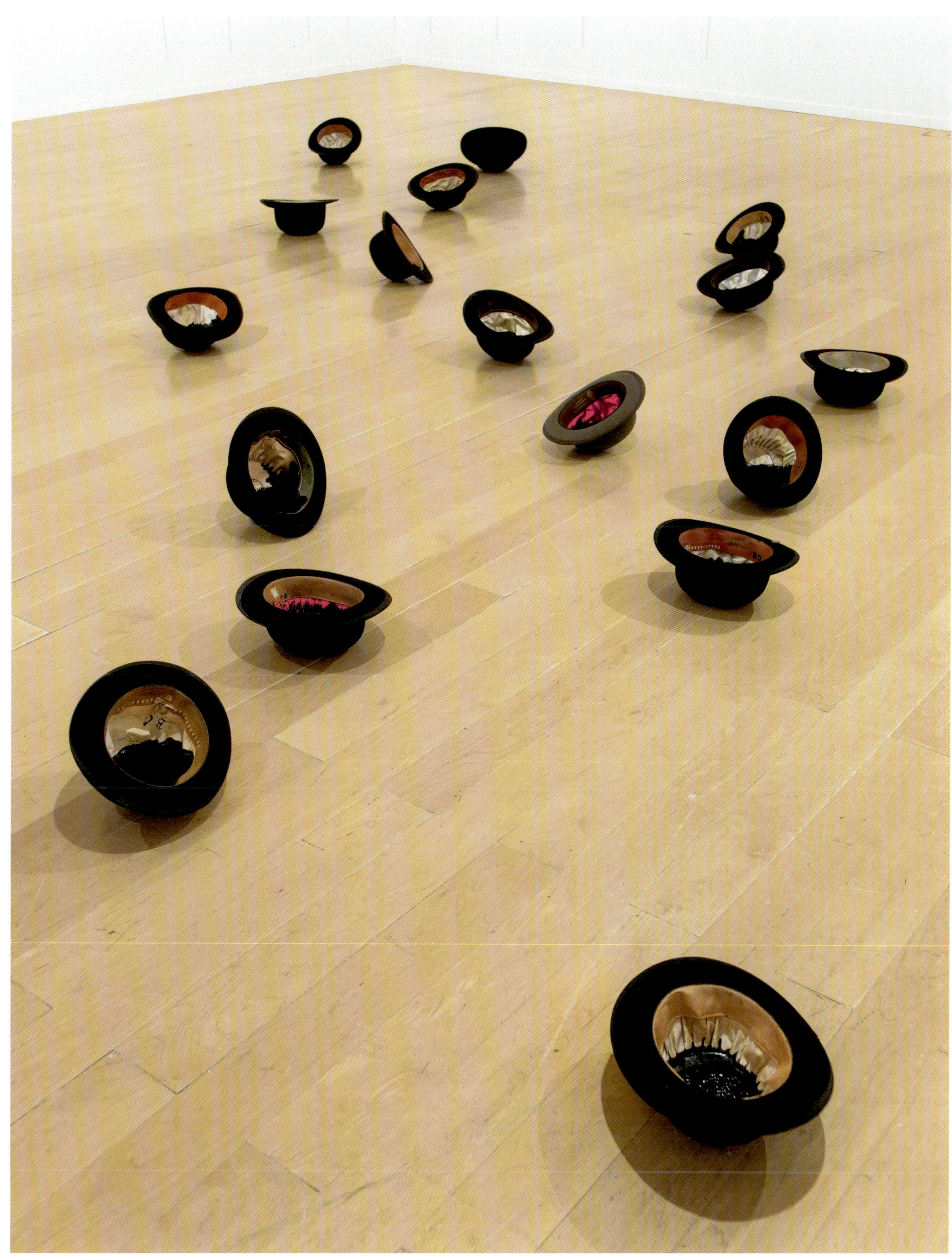

Mer d’encre, 2012
24 Belgian hats, polyester resin,
India ink, dimensions variable
Exhibition view, Laps, Musée
d’Art contemporain, Lyon, 2013

Micro vide

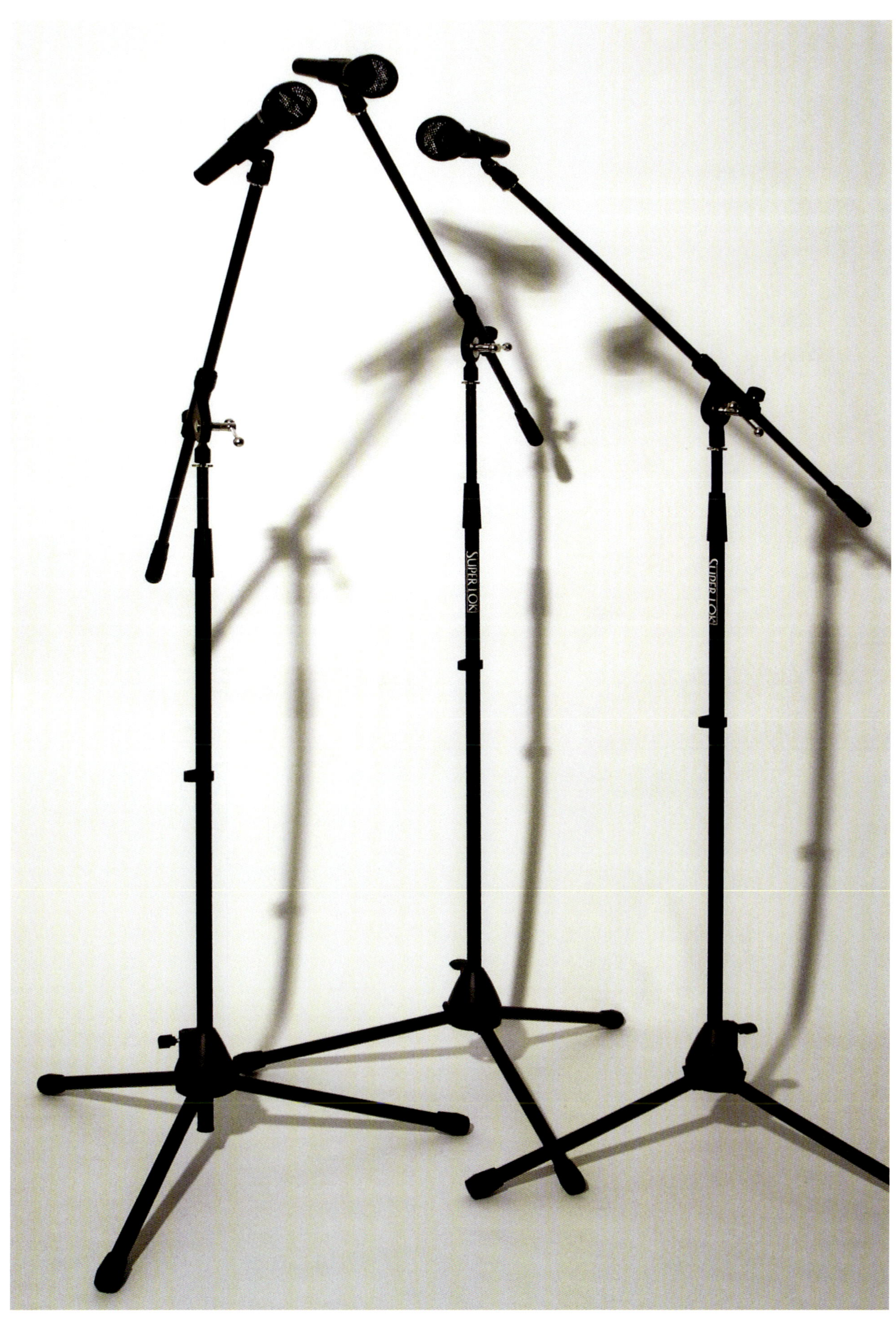

Micro vide, 2006
3 tripods and hollow microphones,
tripod height: 150 cm

Morgenlied

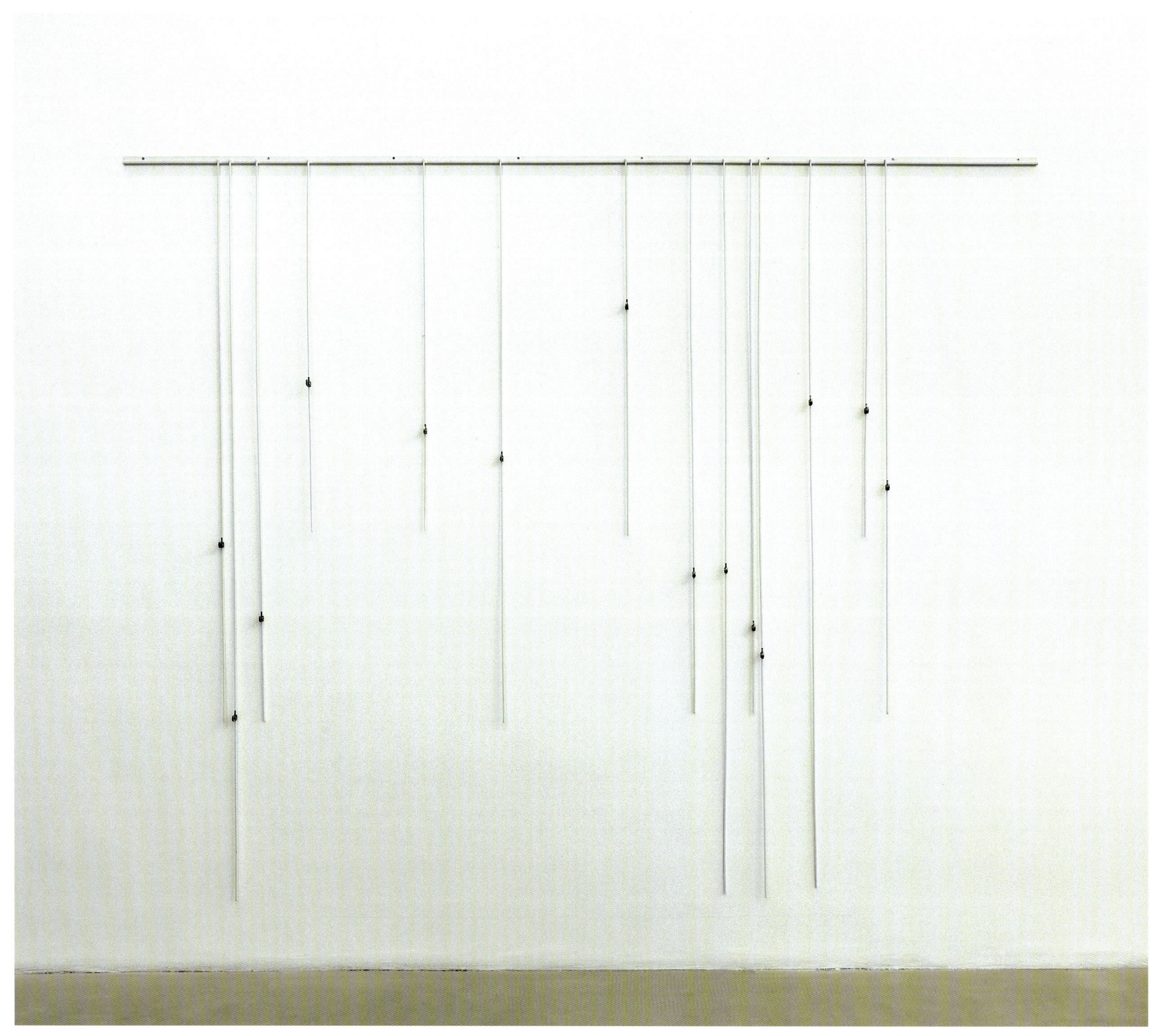

Morgenlied (la do si ré), 2012
Picture hanging systems, 200 × 250 cm

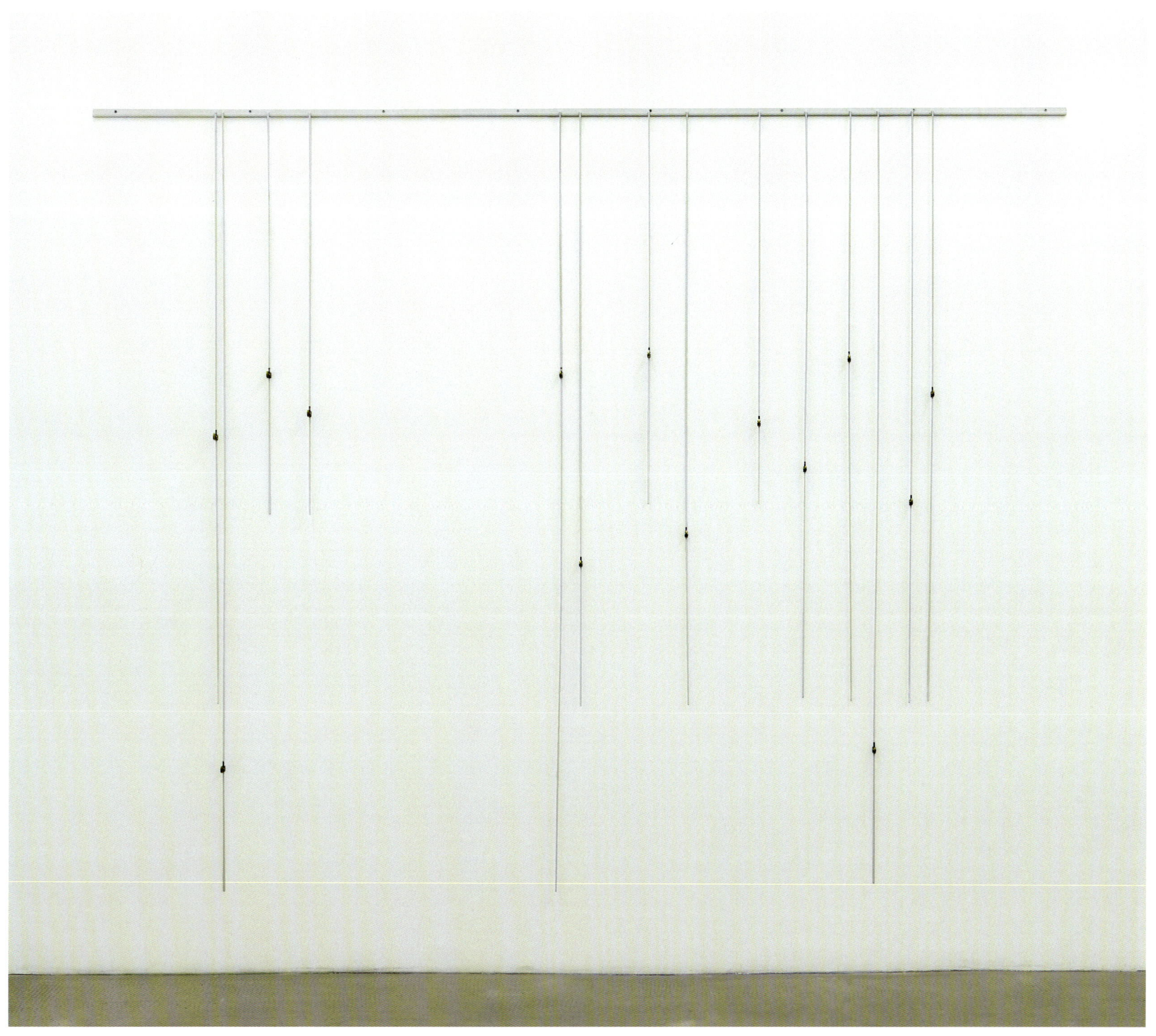

Morgenlied (III), 2012
Picture hanging systems, 205 x 200 cm

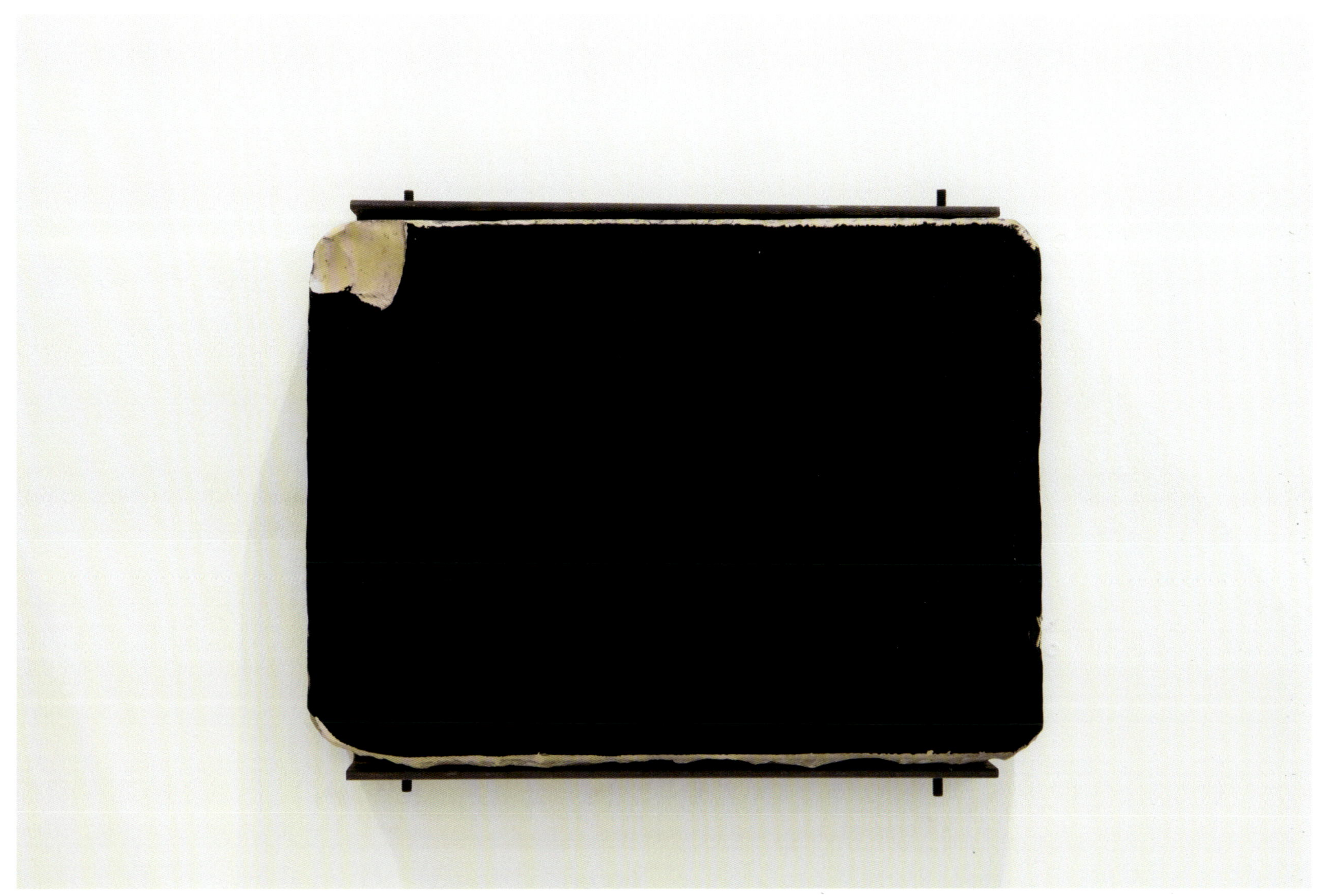

One Summer Night (S.K.), 2012
Lithographic stone, printing ink, varnish,
steel angles, 24 × 32.4 × 4.5 cm

Plainte

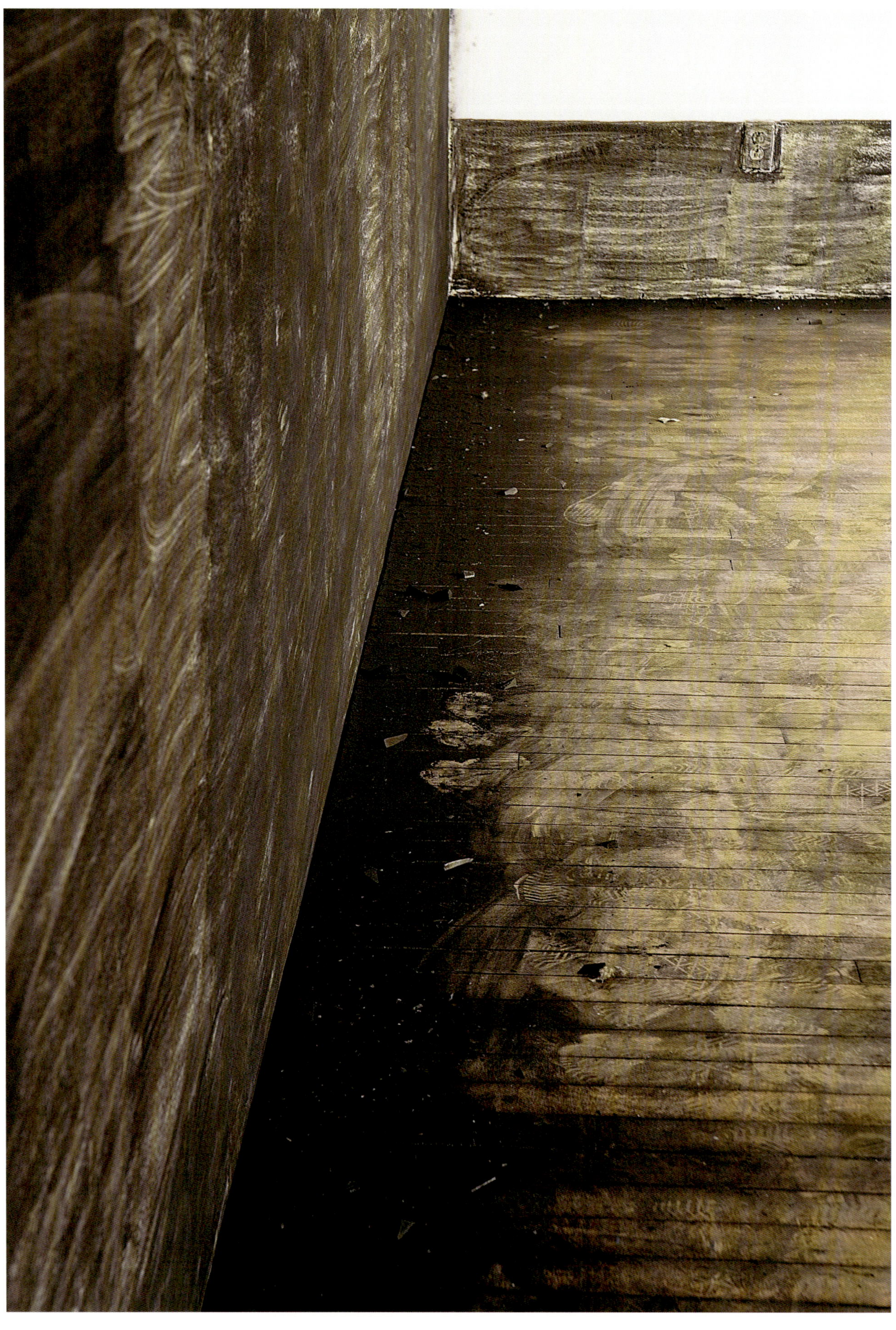

Plainte, 2009 (details)
Charcoal on walls, various heights: 27 cm, 43 cm, 70 cm, 86 cm, 113 cm, 140 cm, 183 cm, 226 cm
Exhibition views, Movement and Complication, Swiss Institute, New York, 2009 (far left); Partitas, Bielefelder Kunstverein, Bielefeld, 2009 (left)

Principe d’économie

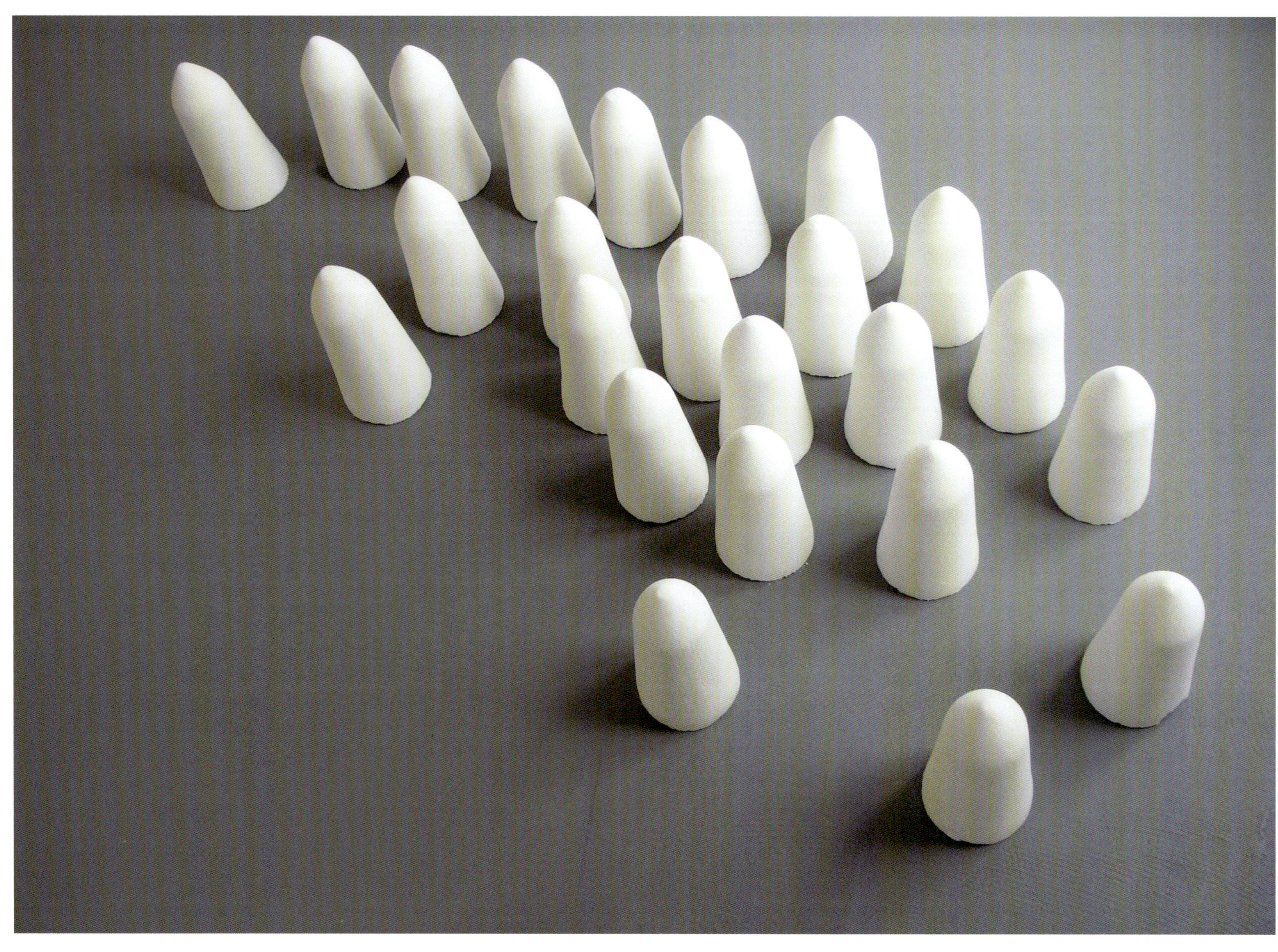

Principe d’économie I, 2005–2009
24 Moroccan sugarloaves, 2 kilos each,
sugarloaf height: 30 cm,
overall dimensions variable

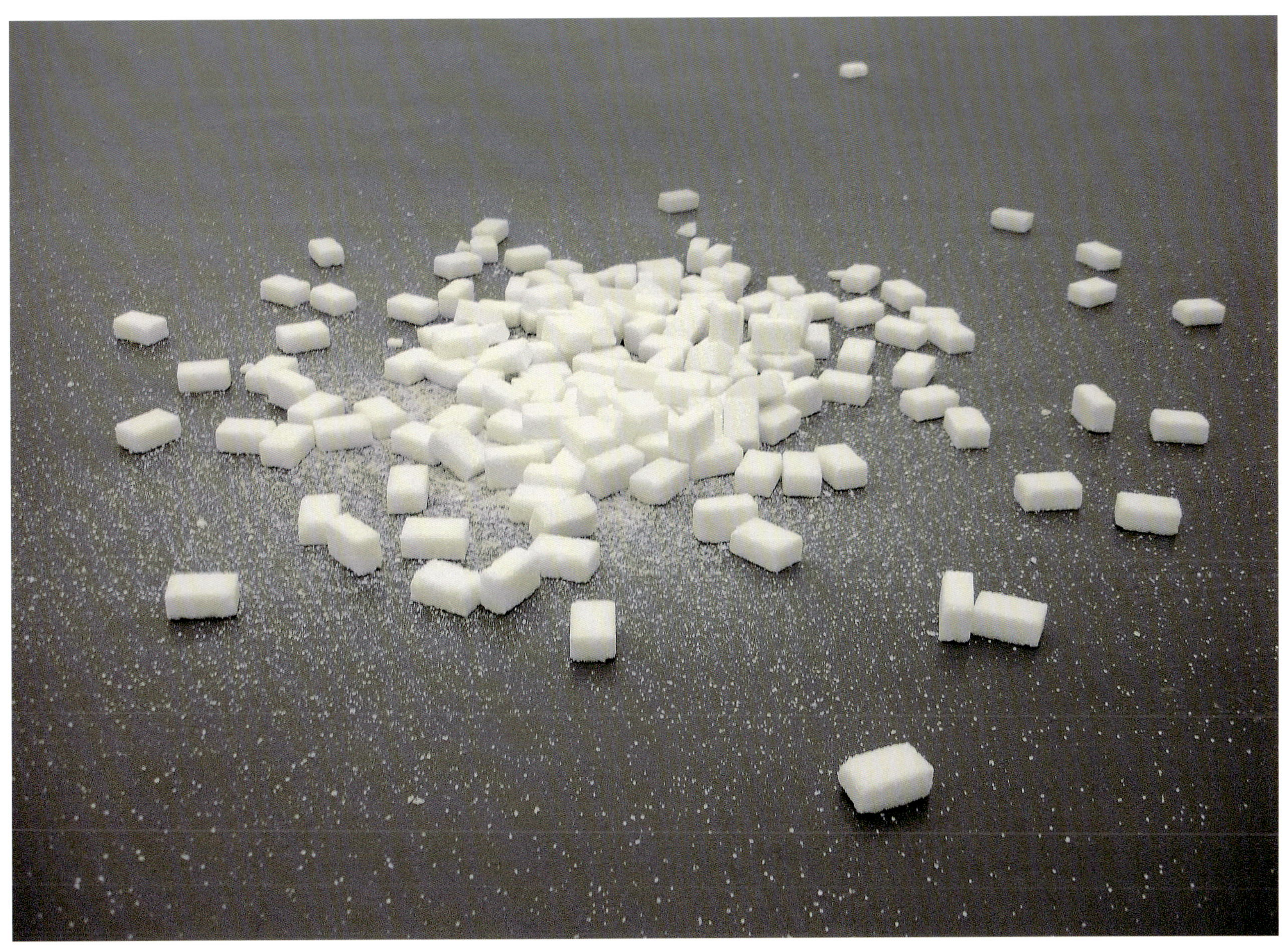

Principe d'économie II, 2007–2009
One kilo of French sugar cubes,
dimensions variable

Résolutions

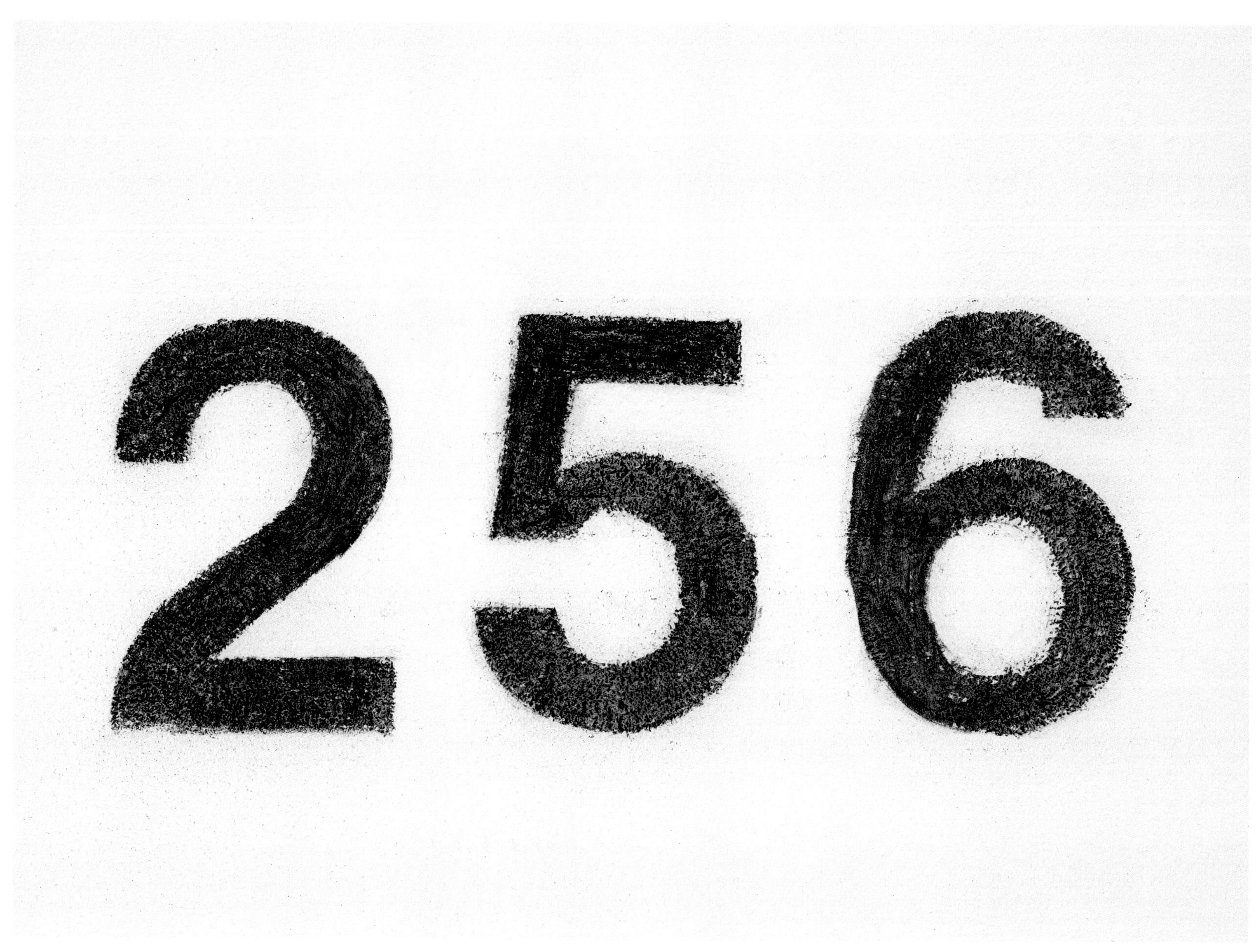

Résolutions, 2009–in progress (details)
Charcoal on wall, dimensions variable
Exhibition views, Jean Genet: Prisoners of Love, Act Two, Nottingham Contemporary, Nottingham, 2011

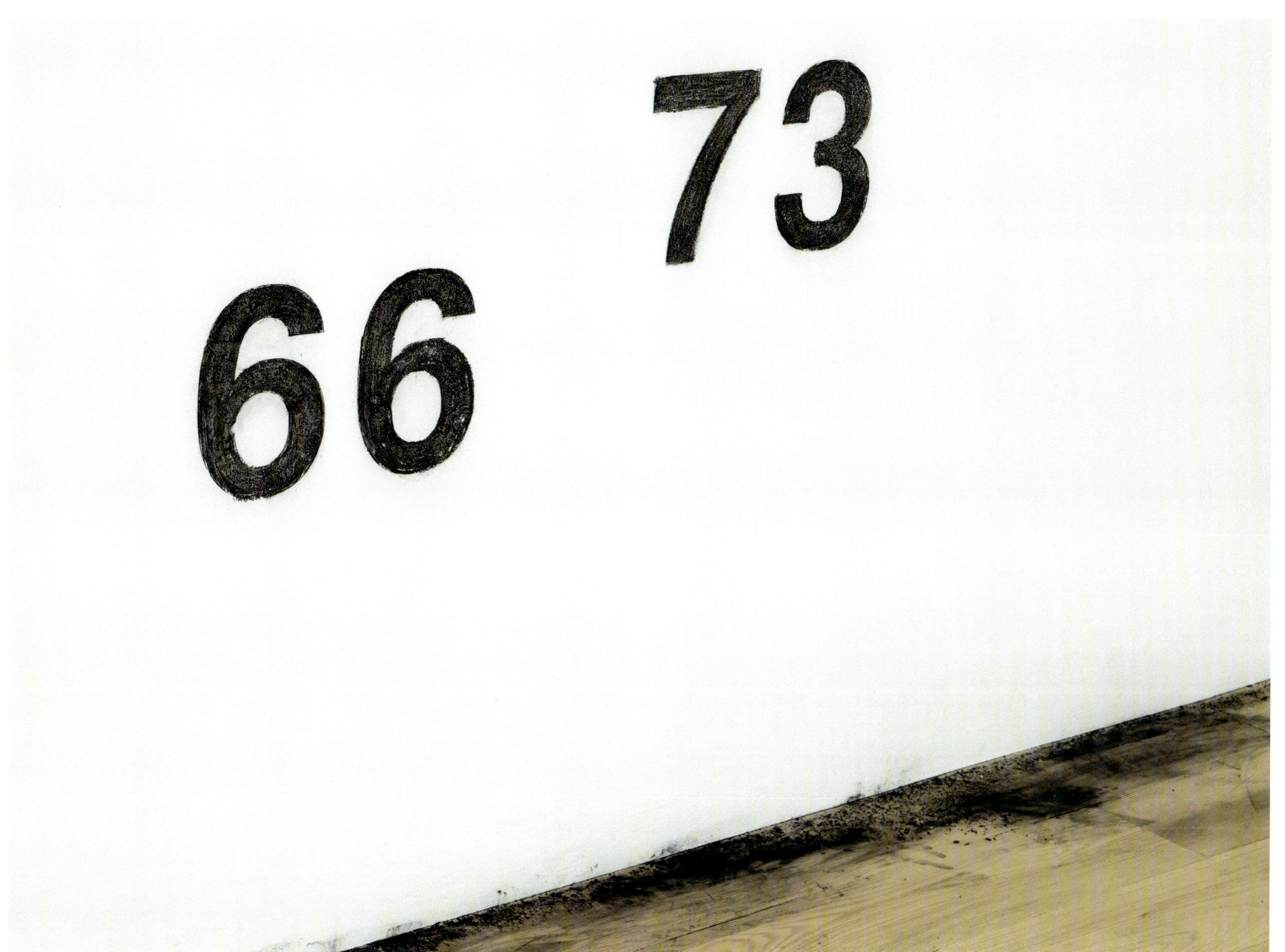
73
66

Sans titre, 11 mars 2005

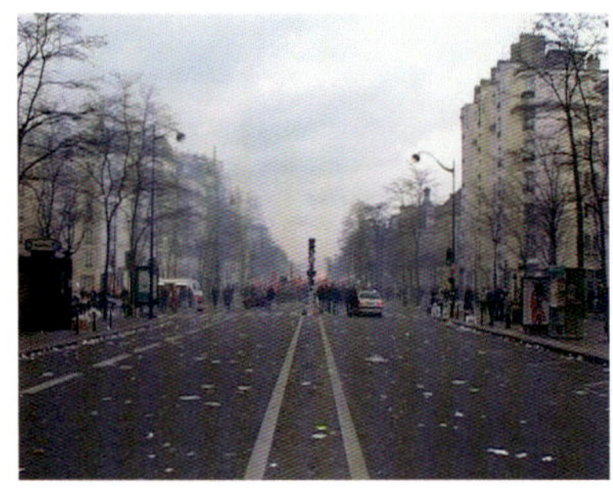
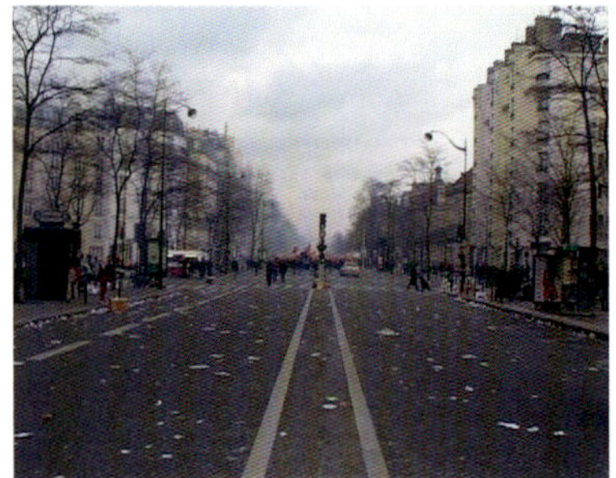
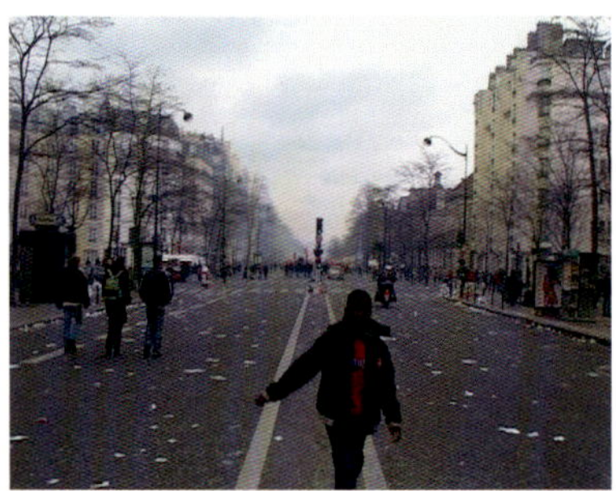
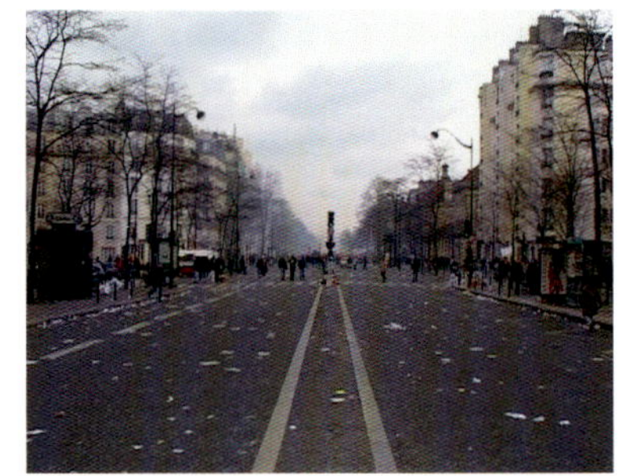
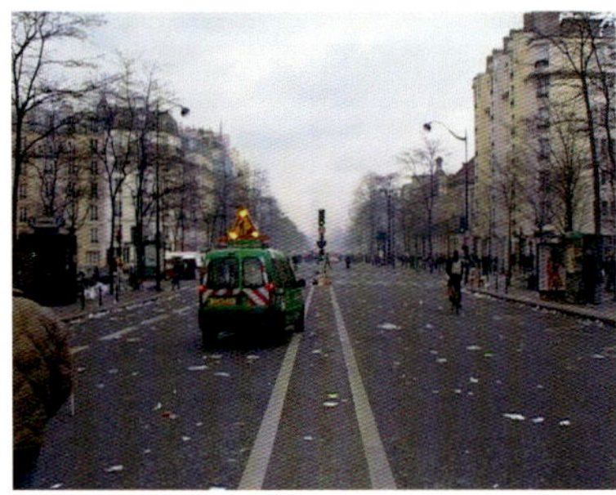
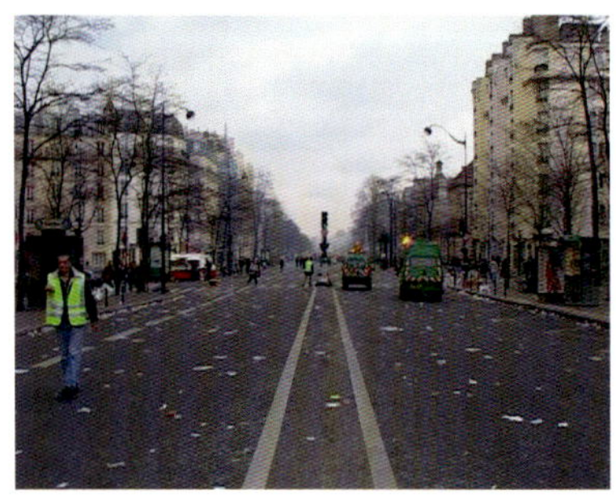
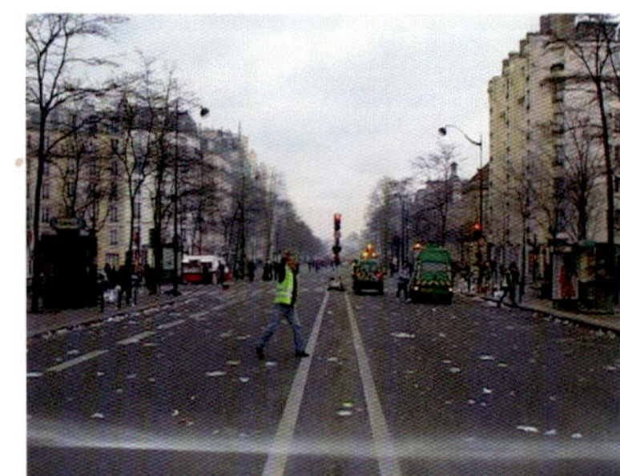
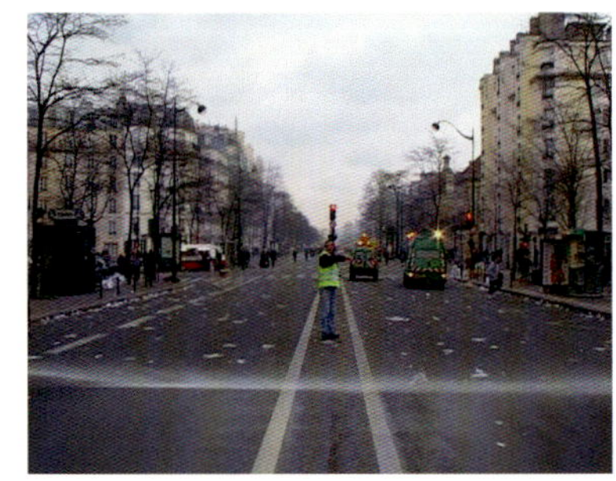
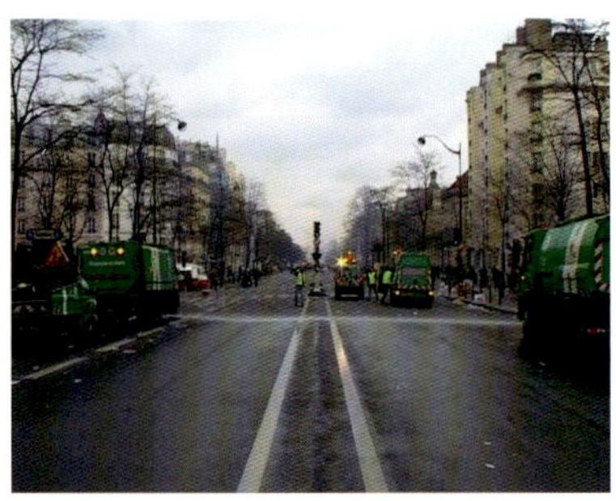
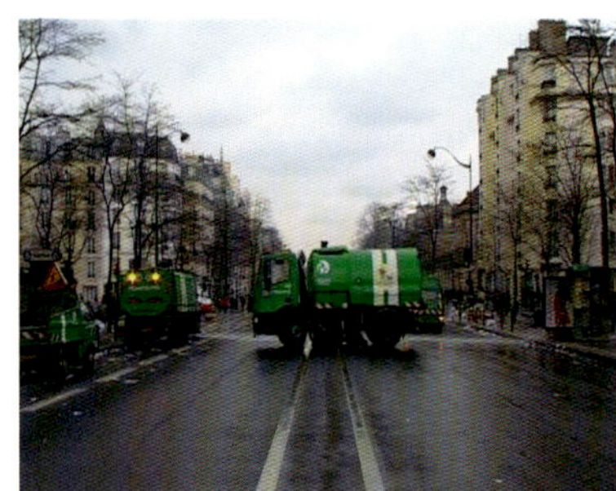
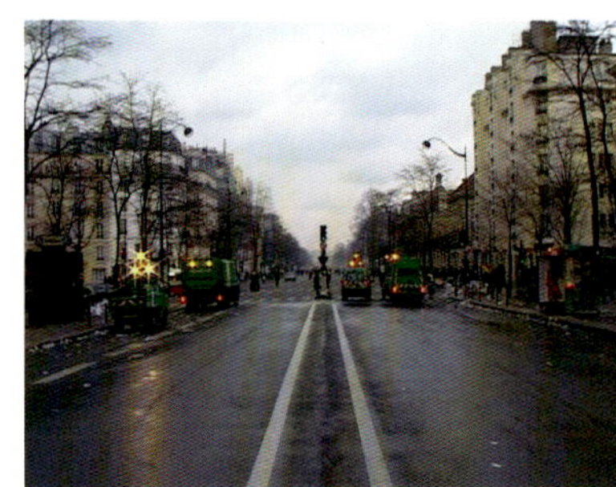
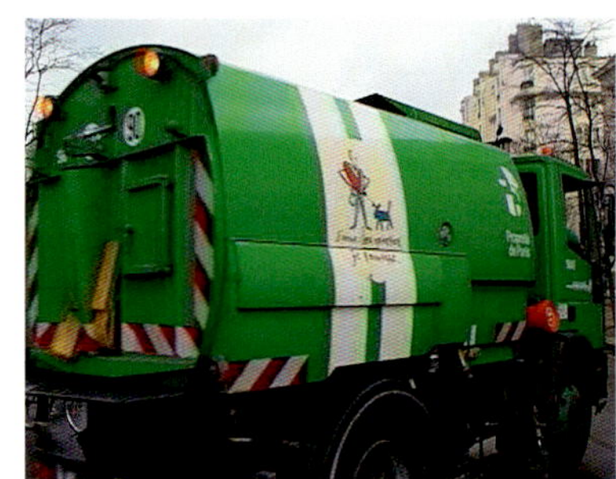

Sans titre, 11 mars 2005, 2005
Video, color, sound, 23′ loop

Collection FRAC Champagne-Ardenne, Reims

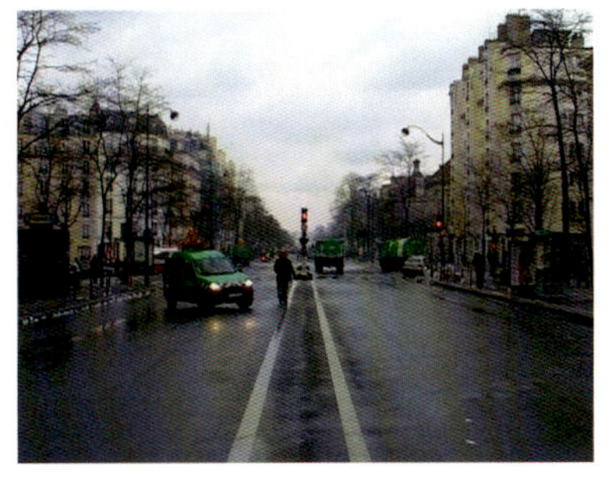
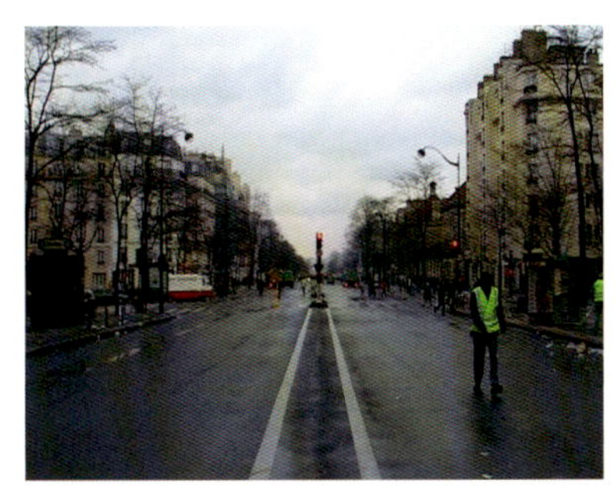
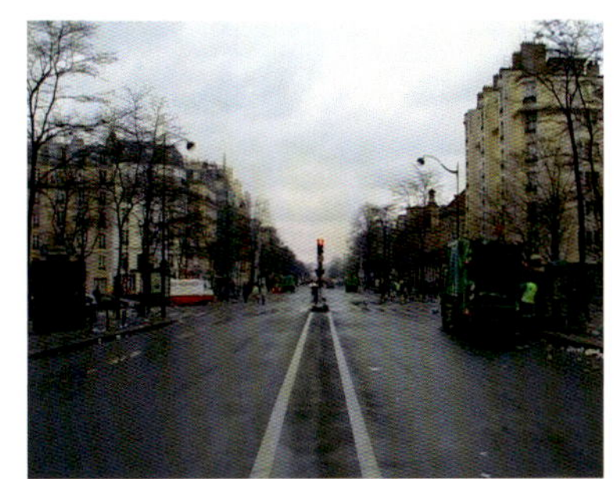
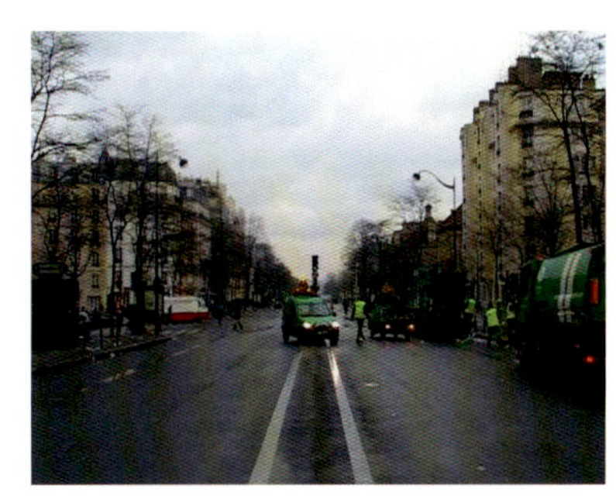
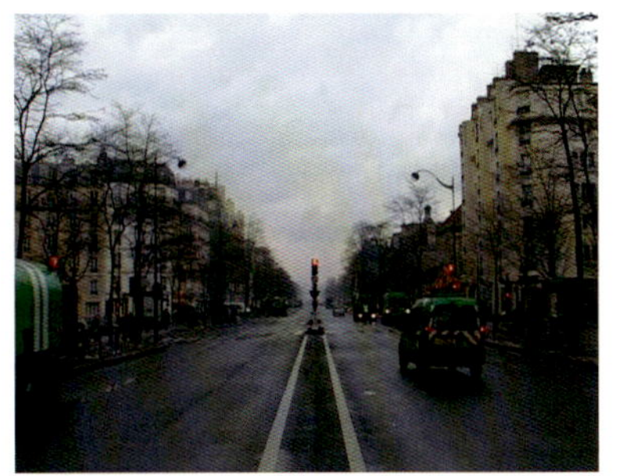
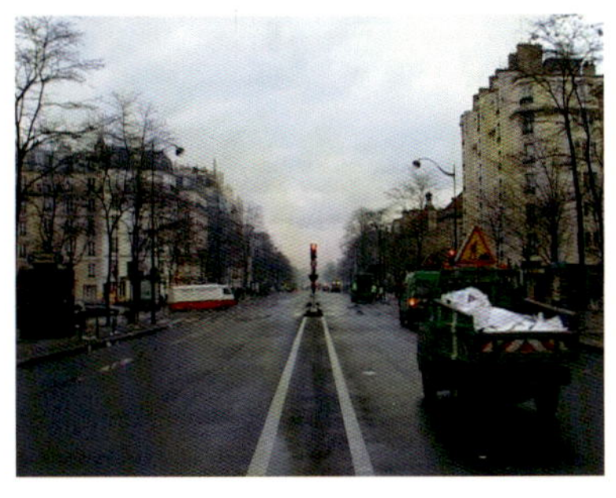
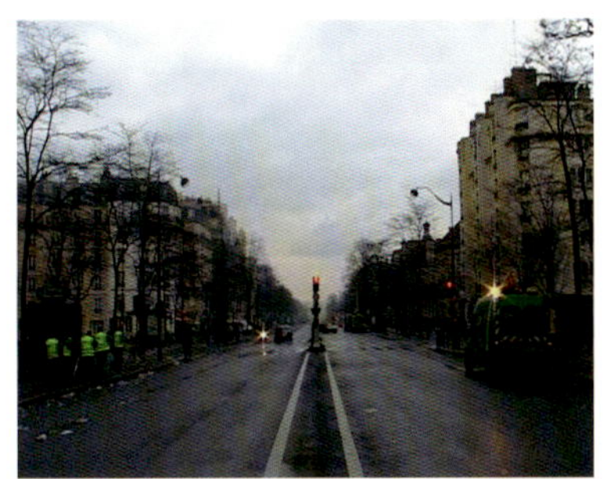
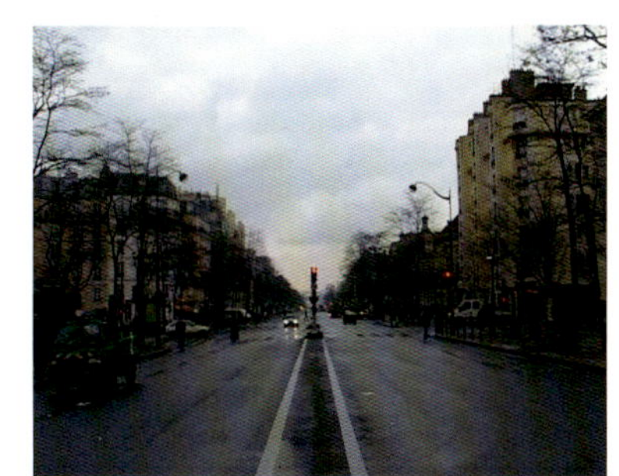
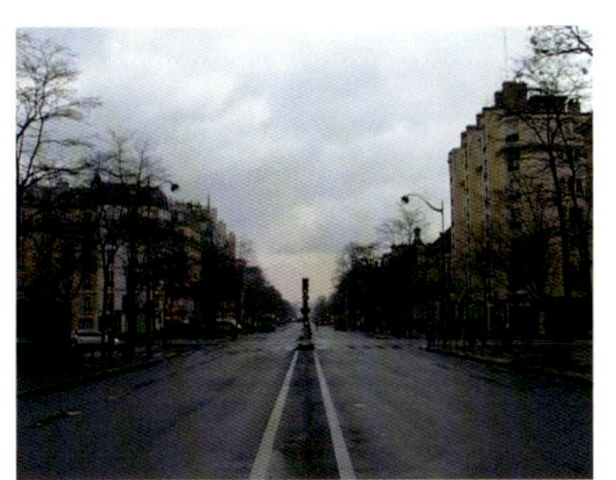
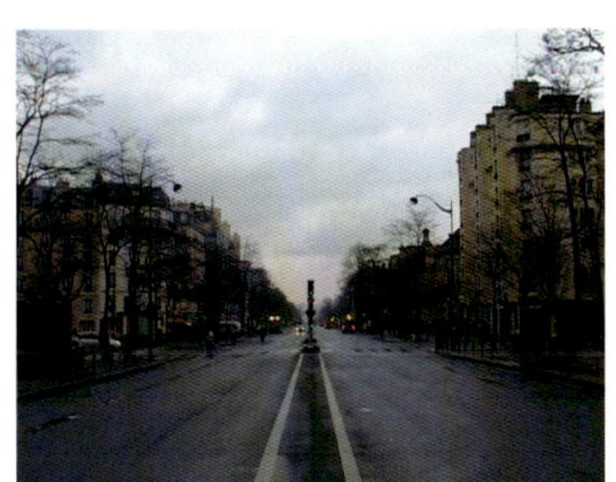
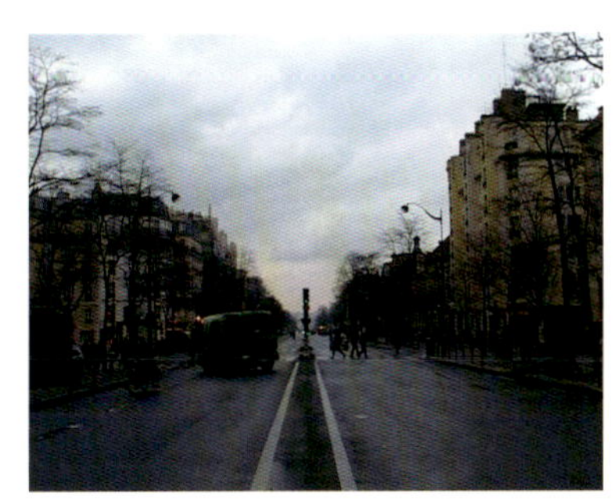
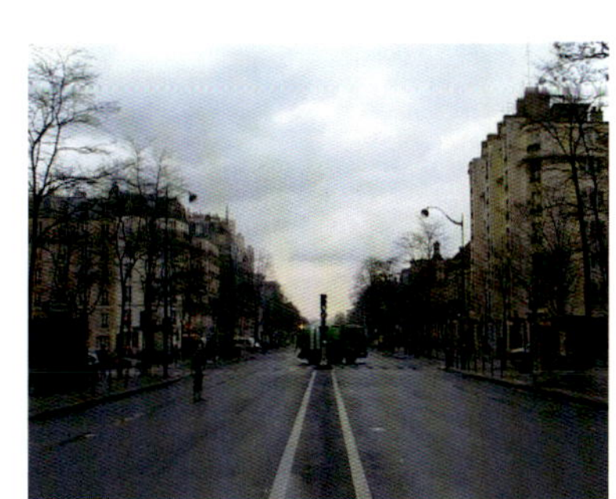

Sans titre XIX

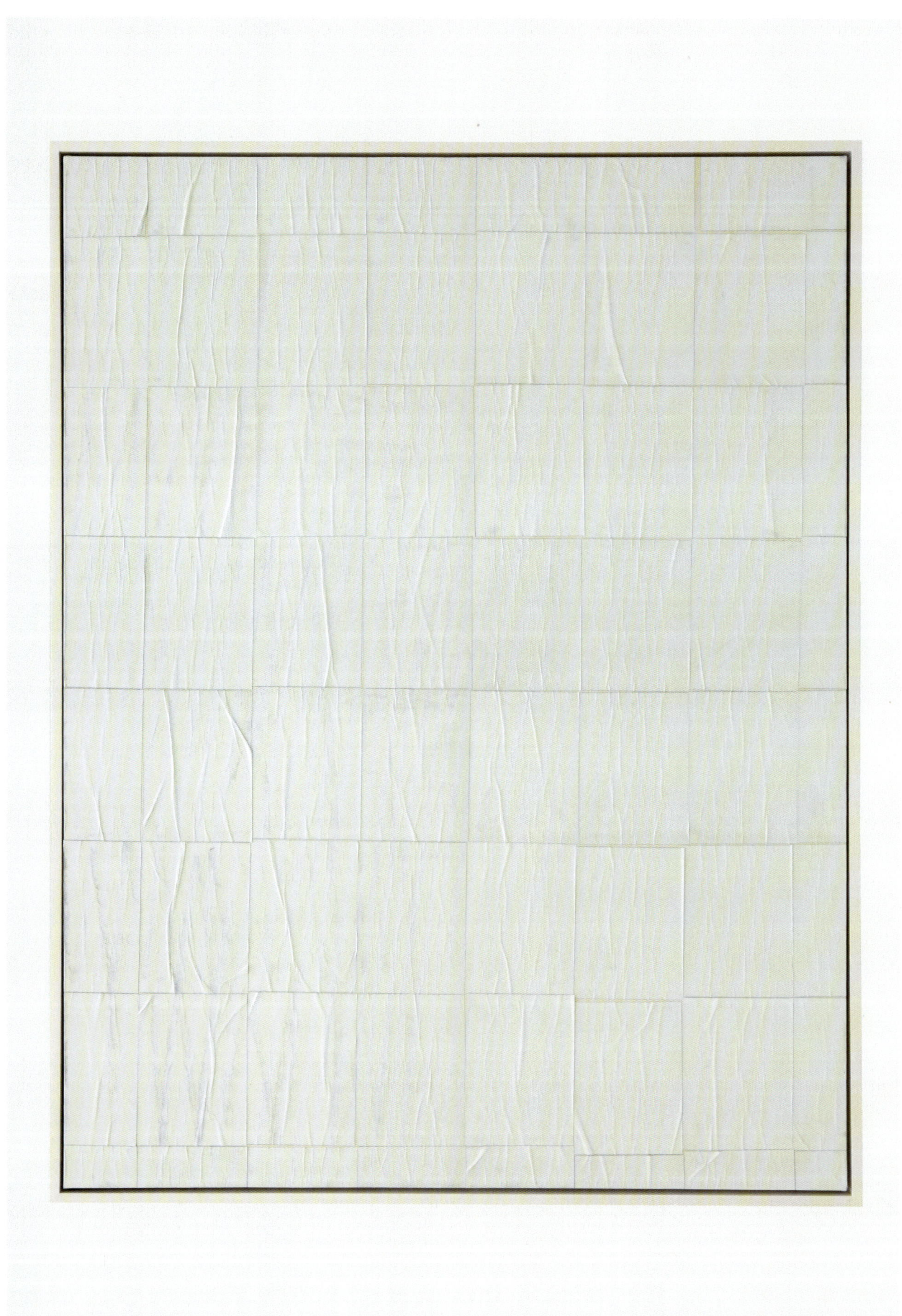

Sans titre XIX, 2010
White carbon paper on canvas,
wood frame, 206 × 156 cm

Sans titre XXVI, 2010
Black carbon paper on canvas,
wood frame, 206 × 156 cm

Sans titre (Gunpowder)

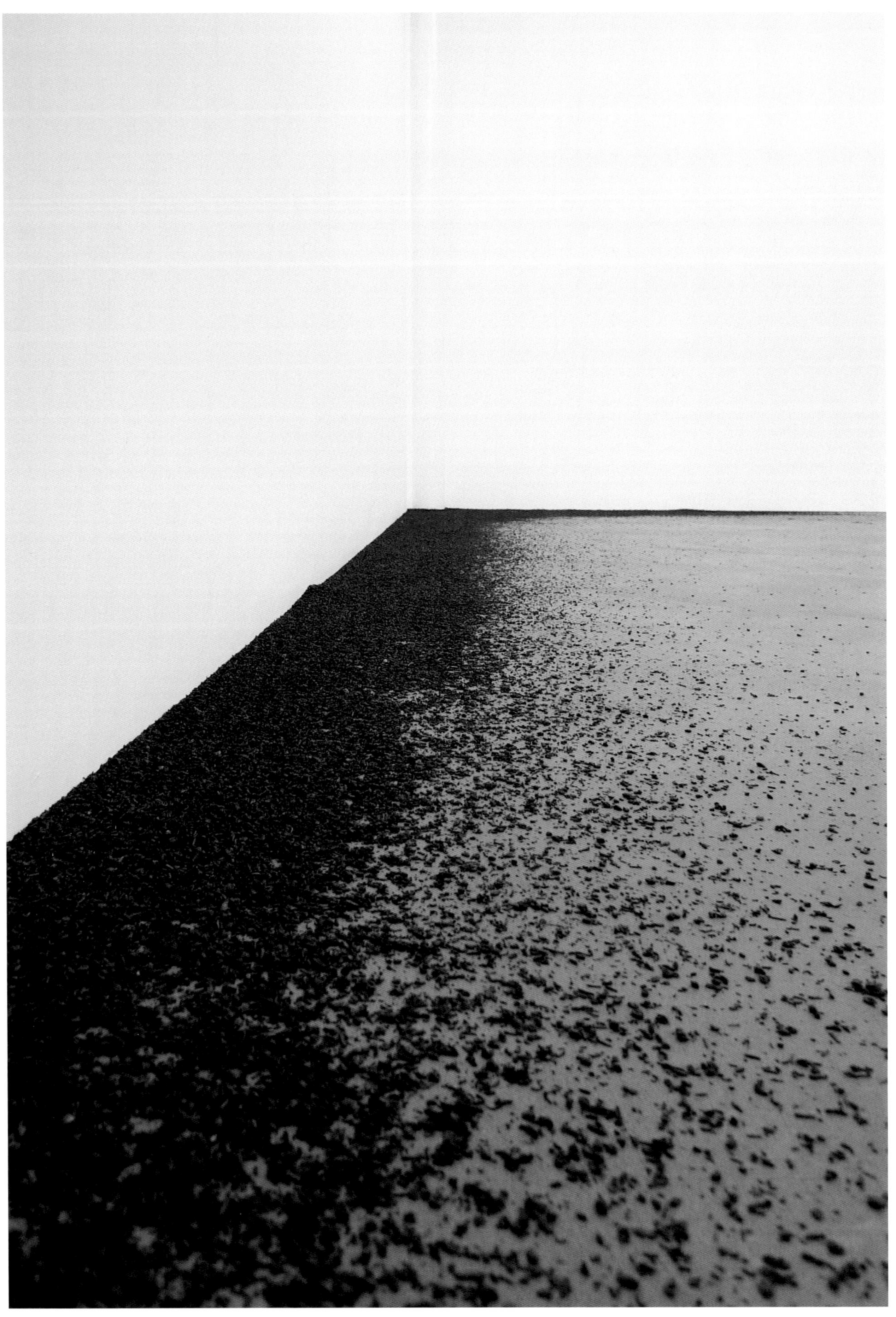

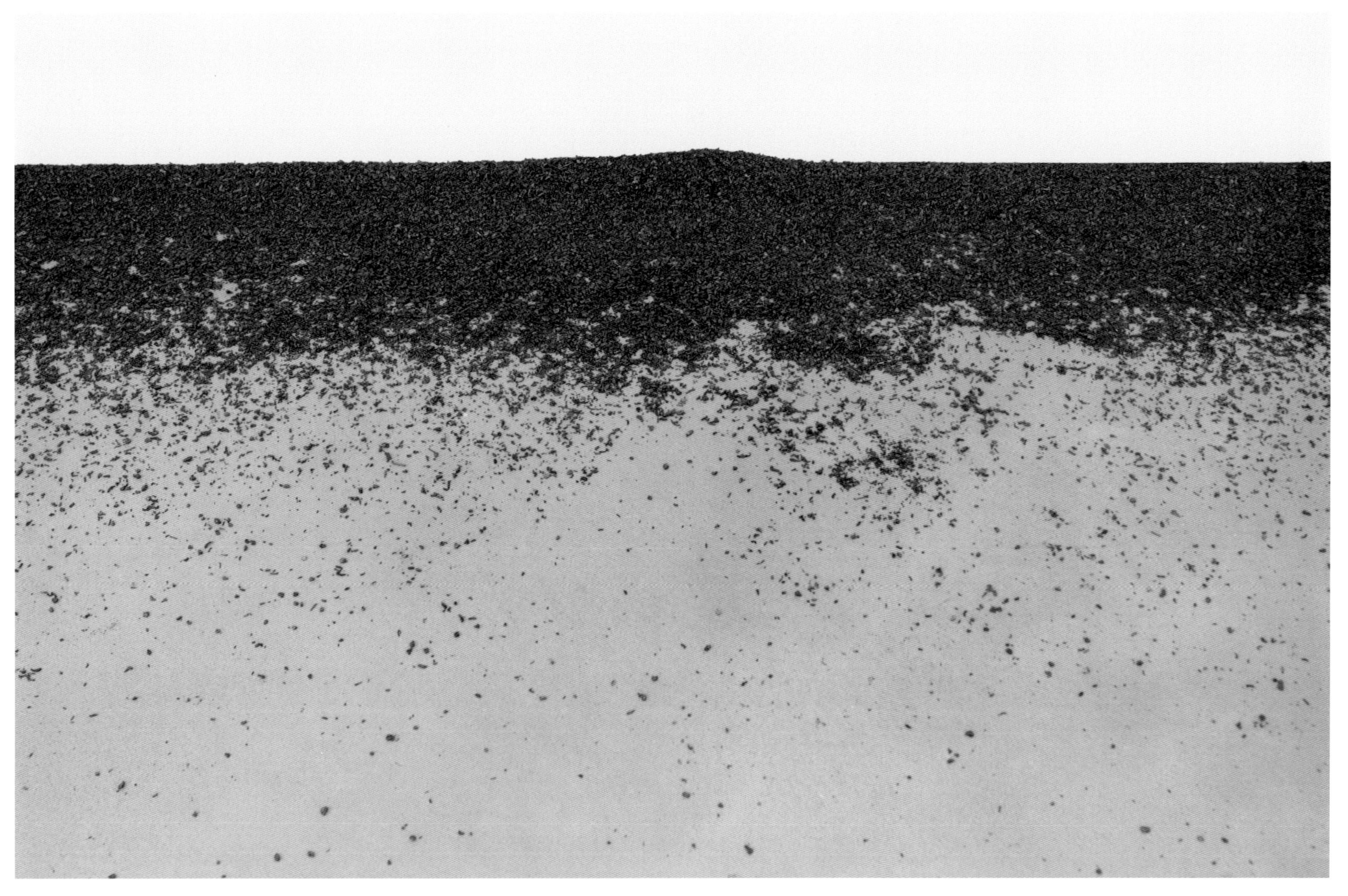

Sans titre (Gunpowder), 2008
Gunpowder green tea, dimensions variable
Exhibition view, Still life, Frame still,
Fri Art, Fribourg, 2010

Sans titre (Joueur de tambour)

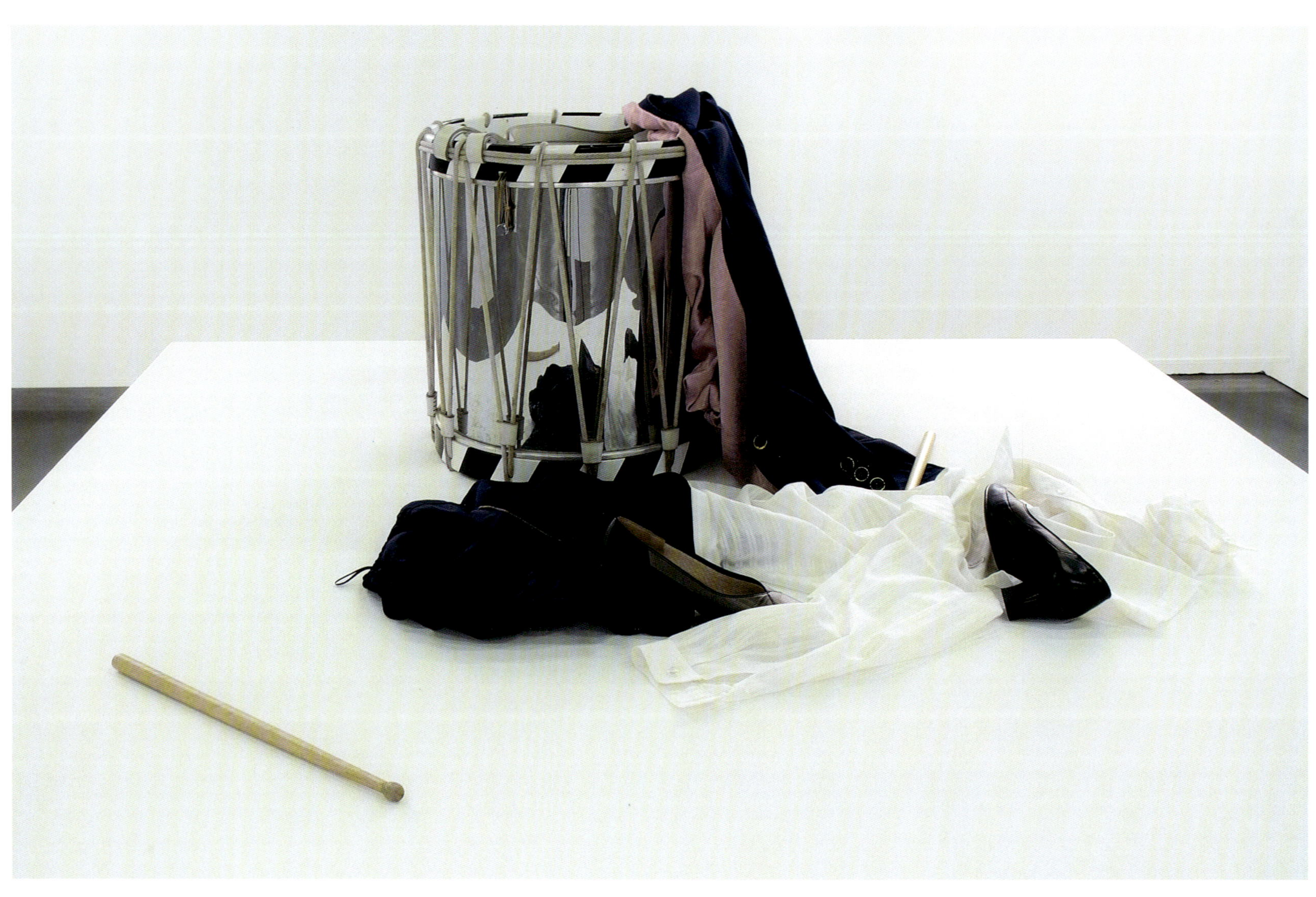

Sans titre (Joueur de tambour a), 2010
Skirt suit, shoes, Basel drum on pedestal,
183 × 183 × 55 cm; drum height: 105 cm
Exhibition view, Still life, Frame still,
Fri Art, Fribourg, 2010

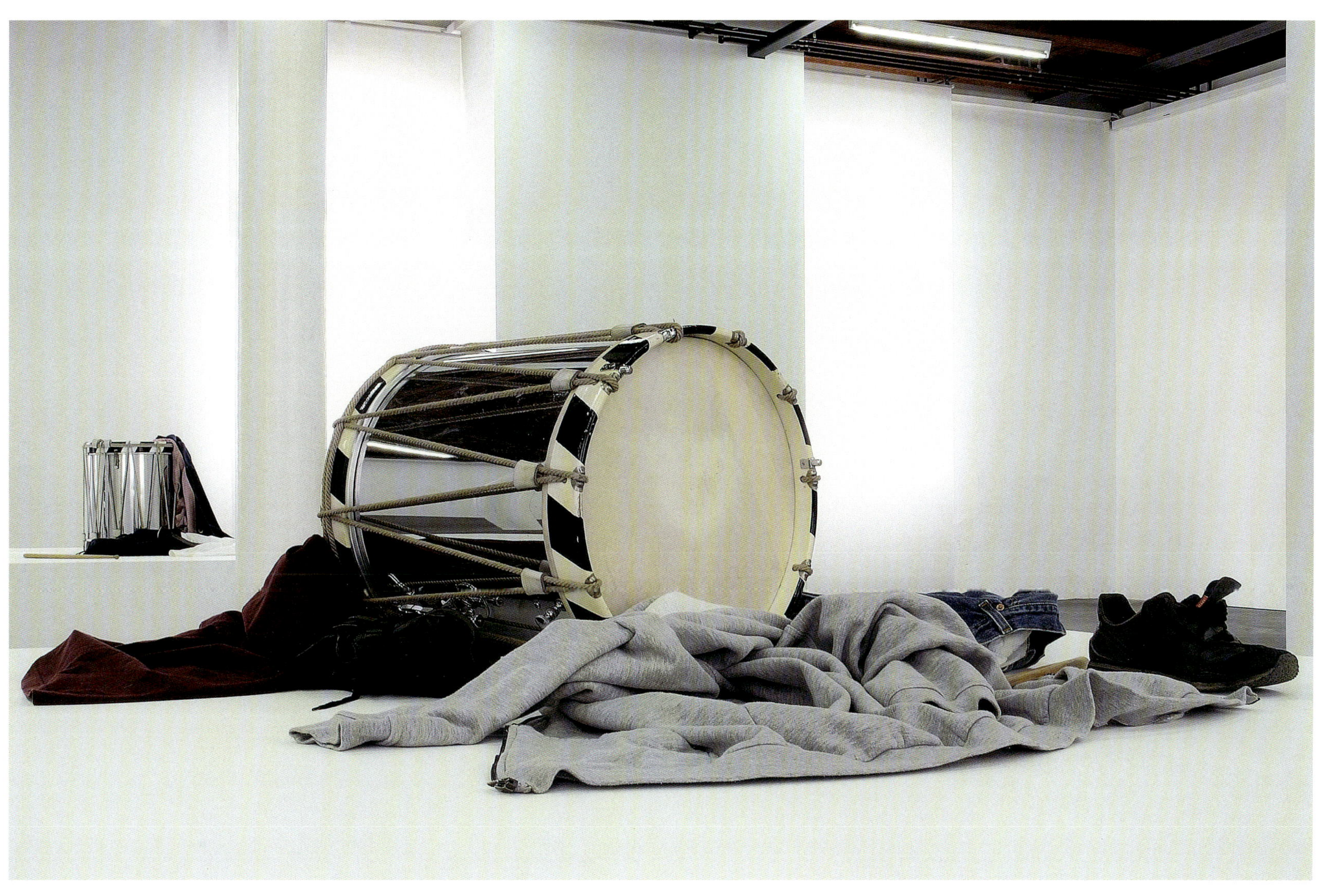

Sans titre (Joueur de tambour b), 2010
Sweatshirt with hood, T-shirt, jeans,
sneakers, Basel drum on pedestal,
183 × 183 × 55 cm; drum height: 105 cm
Exhibition view, Still life, Frame still,
Fri Art, Fribourg, 2010

Sans titre (Les étrangers)

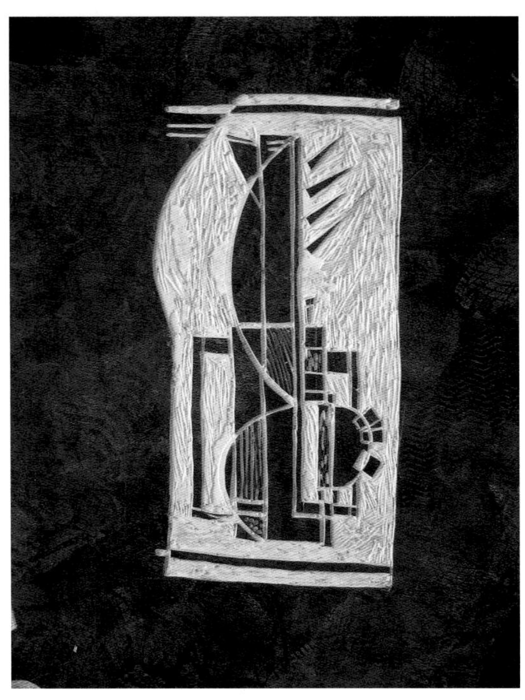

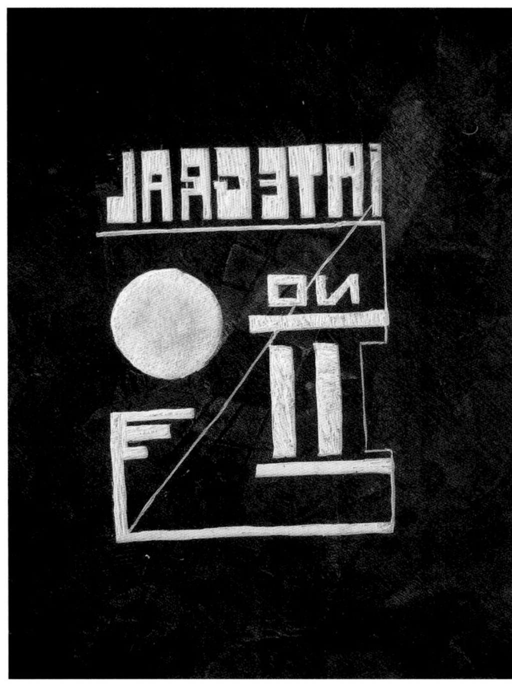

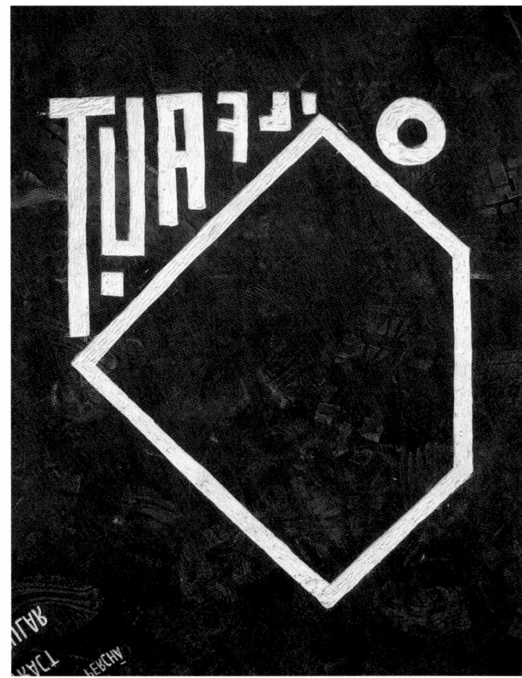

Sans titre (Les étrangers), 2006 (details)
Engravings on linoleum, dimensions variable,
c. 50 sq. m.
Exhibition view, Strategies of Learning,
Periferic Biennale, Palais de la Culture, Iasi, 2006

Collection FRAC des Pays de la Loire, Carquefou

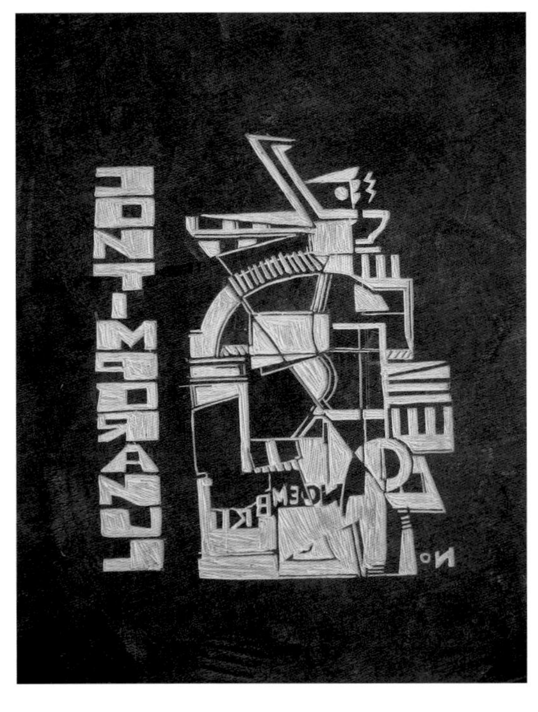

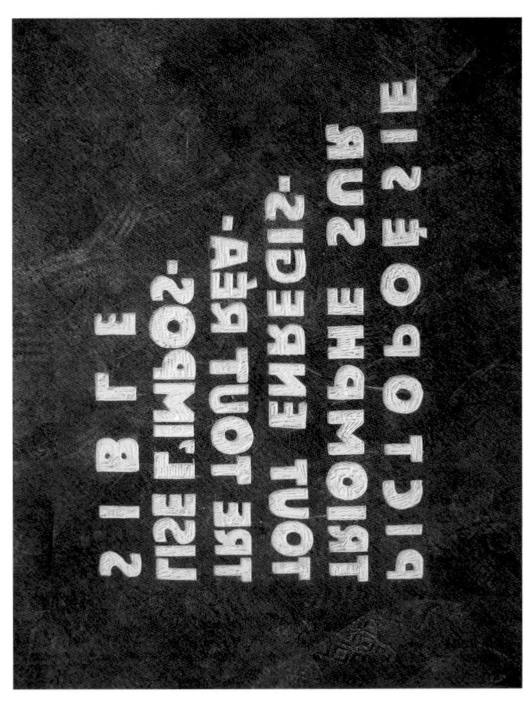

Sans titre (Pole Dancer)

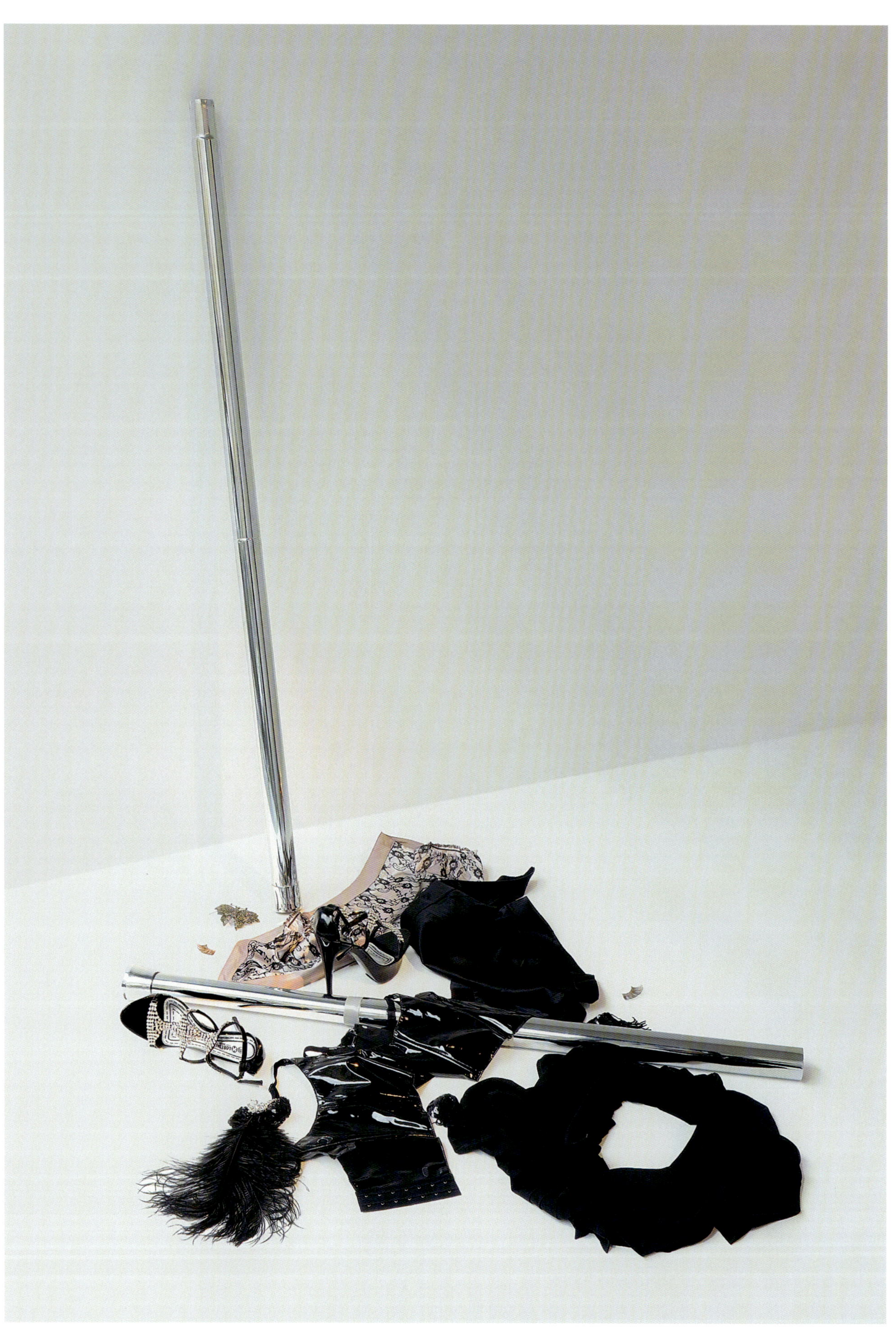

Sans titre (Pole Dancer b), 2011
Collapsible pole, shoes, skirt, corset, bolero, stocking, garter, brooch, feather headband, nipple tassels, fake eyelashes, dimensions variable
Exhibition view, The Door, Sorry we're closed, Brussels, 2011

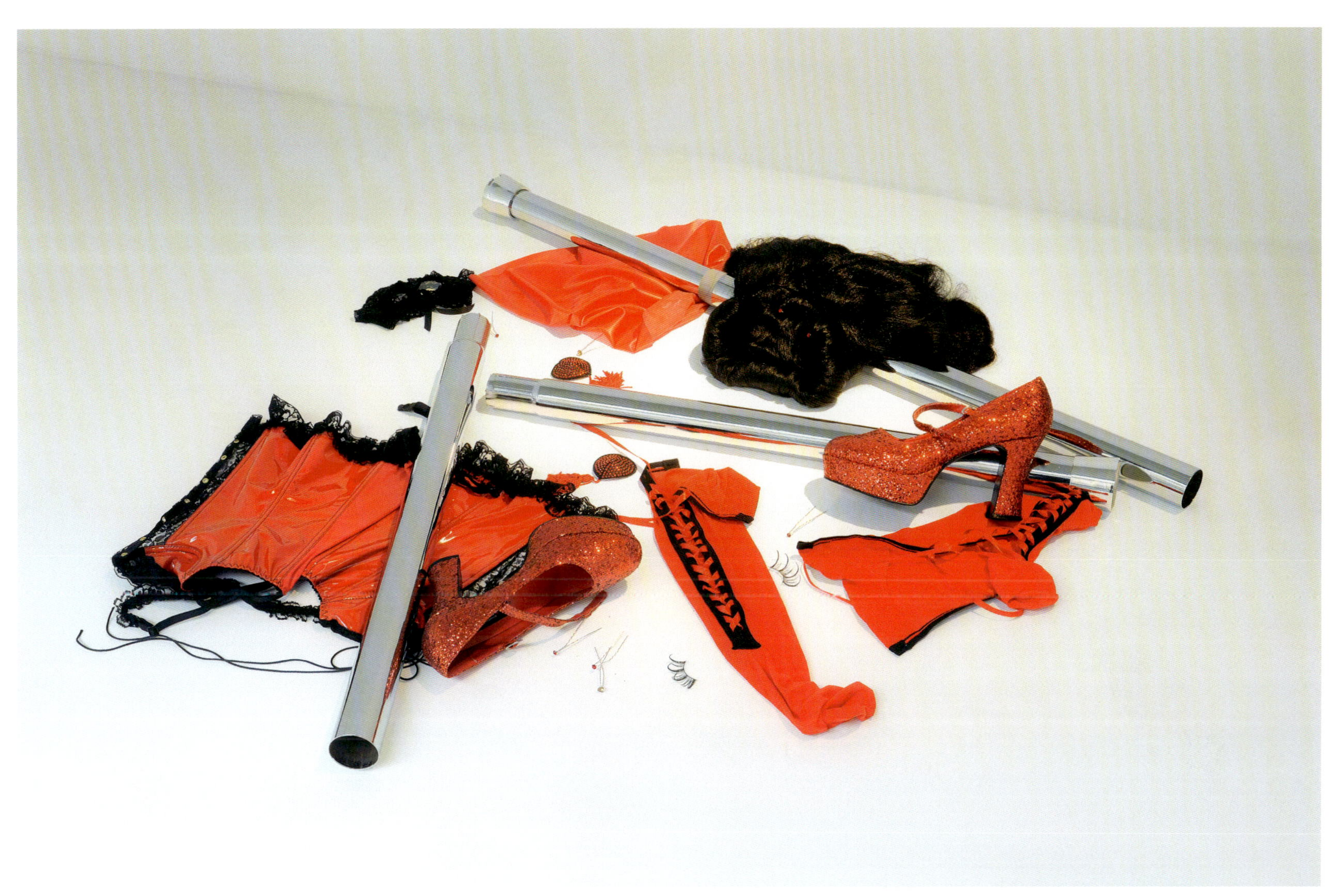

Sans titre (Pole Dancer c), 2011
Collapsible pole, shoes, skirt, corset, stocking, garter, glitter, hair clip, nipple tassels, fake eyelashes, wig, dimensions variable
Exhibition view, The Door, Sorry we're closed, Brussels, 2011

Seuils

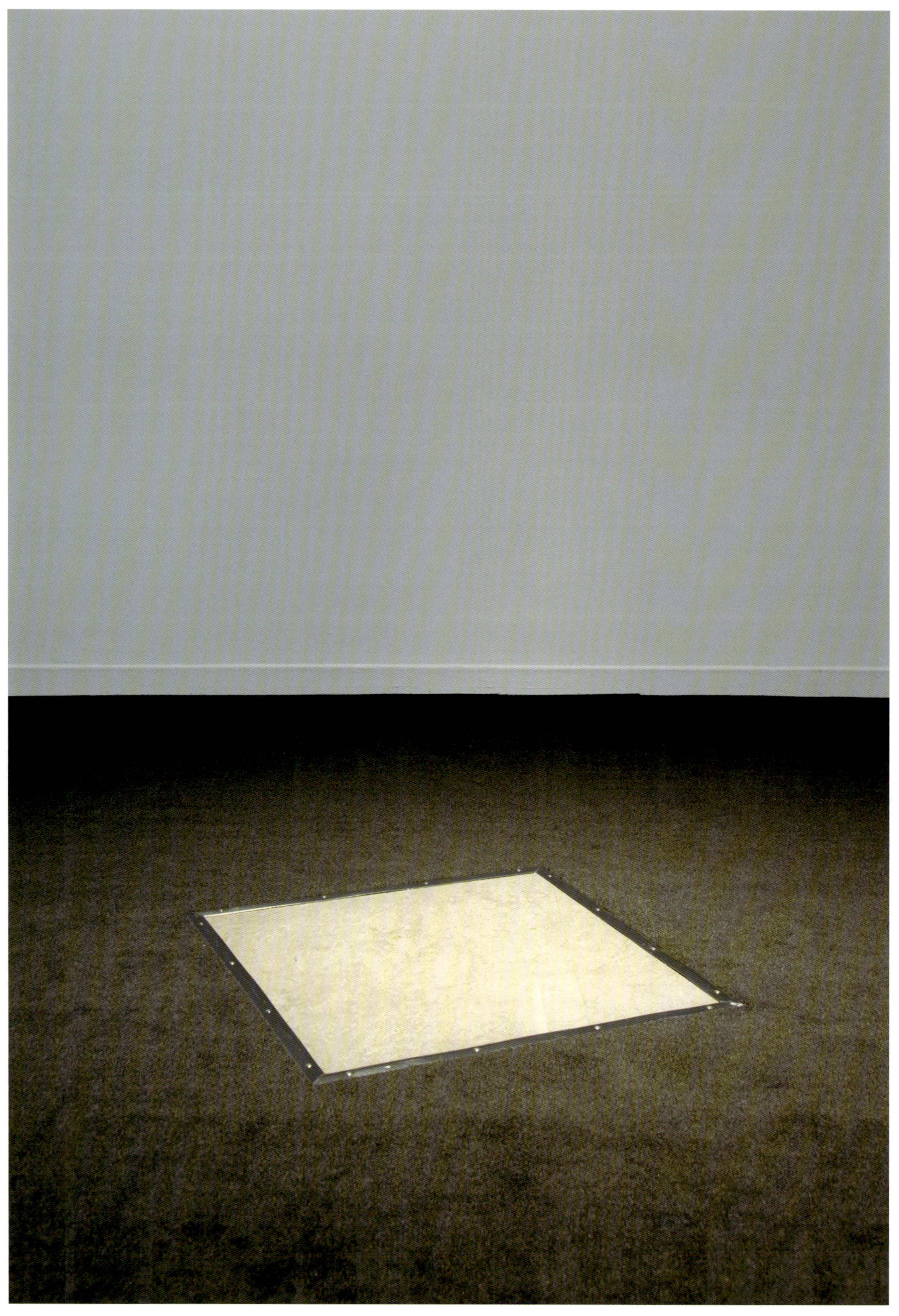

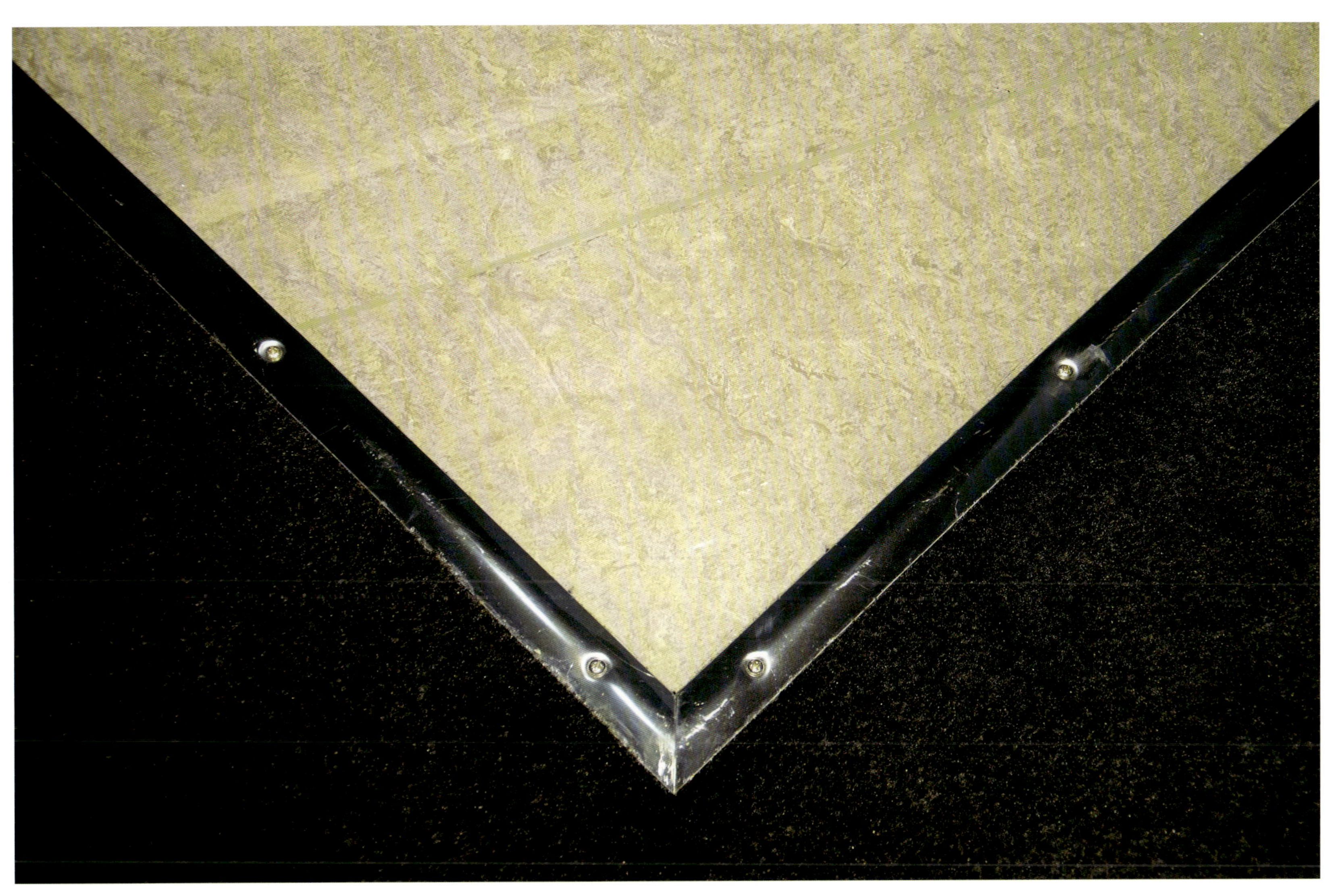

Seuils, 2004
Carpet and steel door strips, door threshold: 73 × 73 cm (standard French HLM door dimensions)
Exhibition view, Le rappel des oiseaux, FRAC Champagne-Ardenne, Reims, 2010

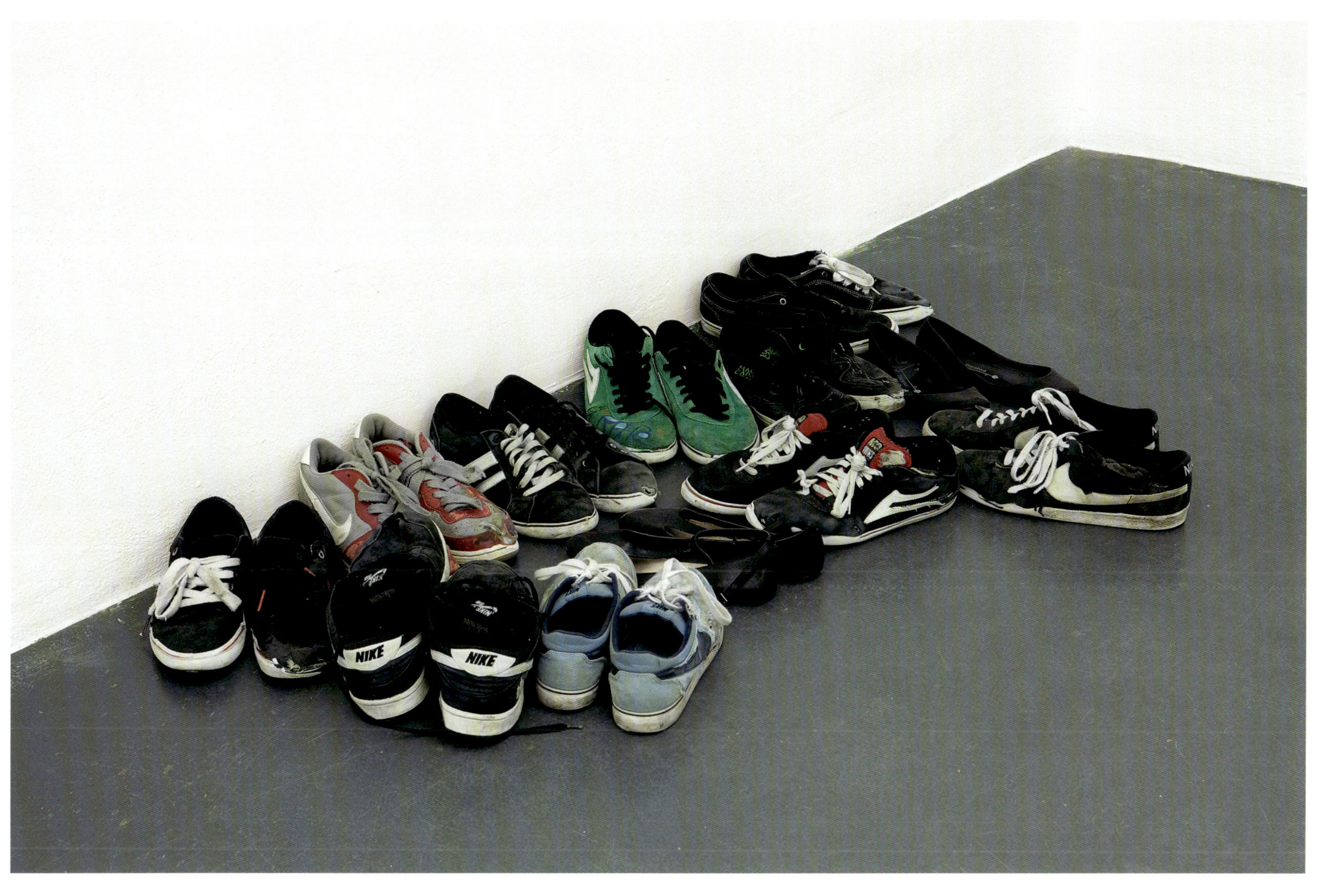

Skin, 2010
12 pairs of shoes, dimensions variable
Exhibition view, Le rappel des oiseaux,
GAMeC, Bergamo, 2010

Smoke Ring

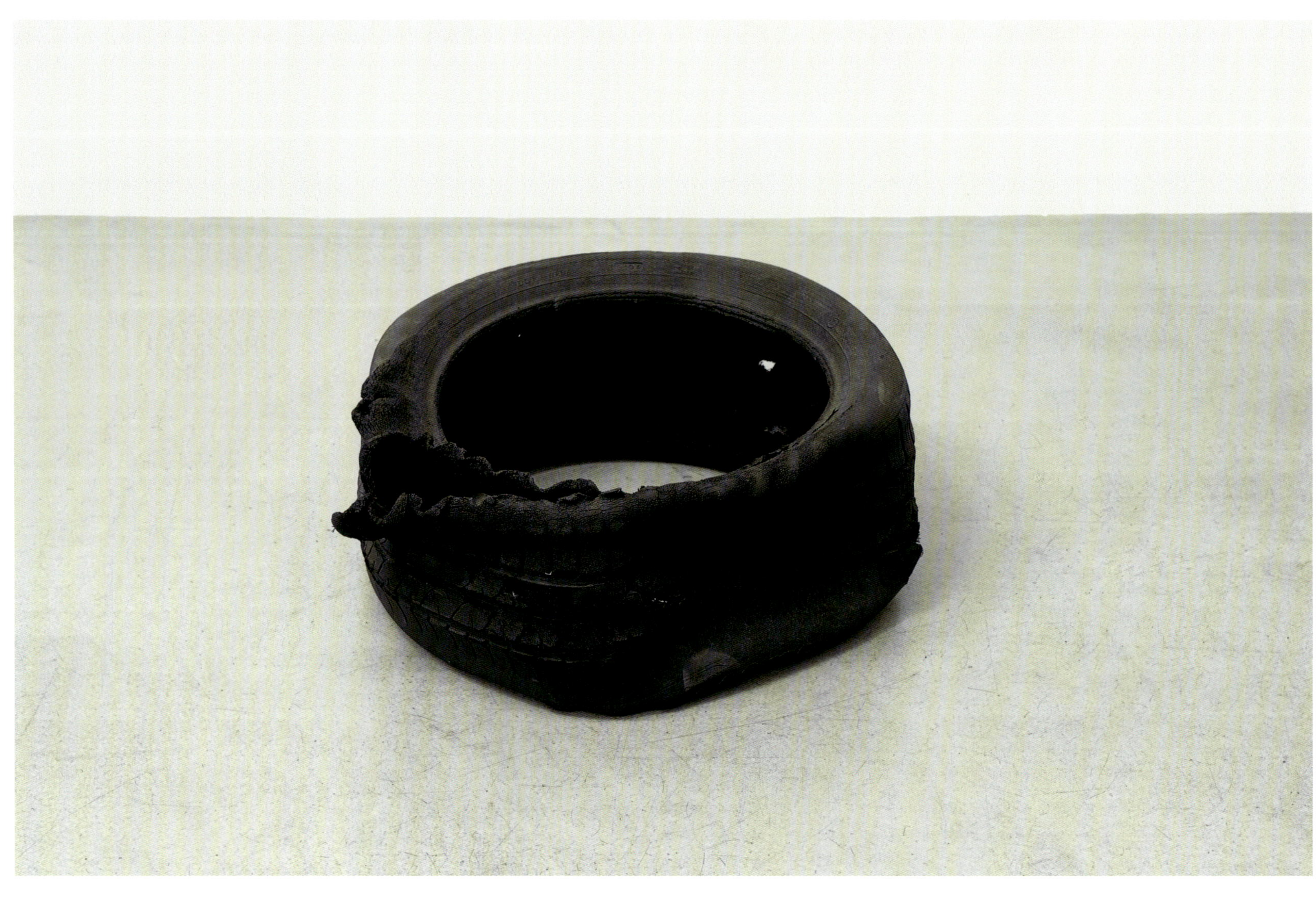

Smoke Ring I, 2008
Burned tire, 20 × 60 × 60 cm

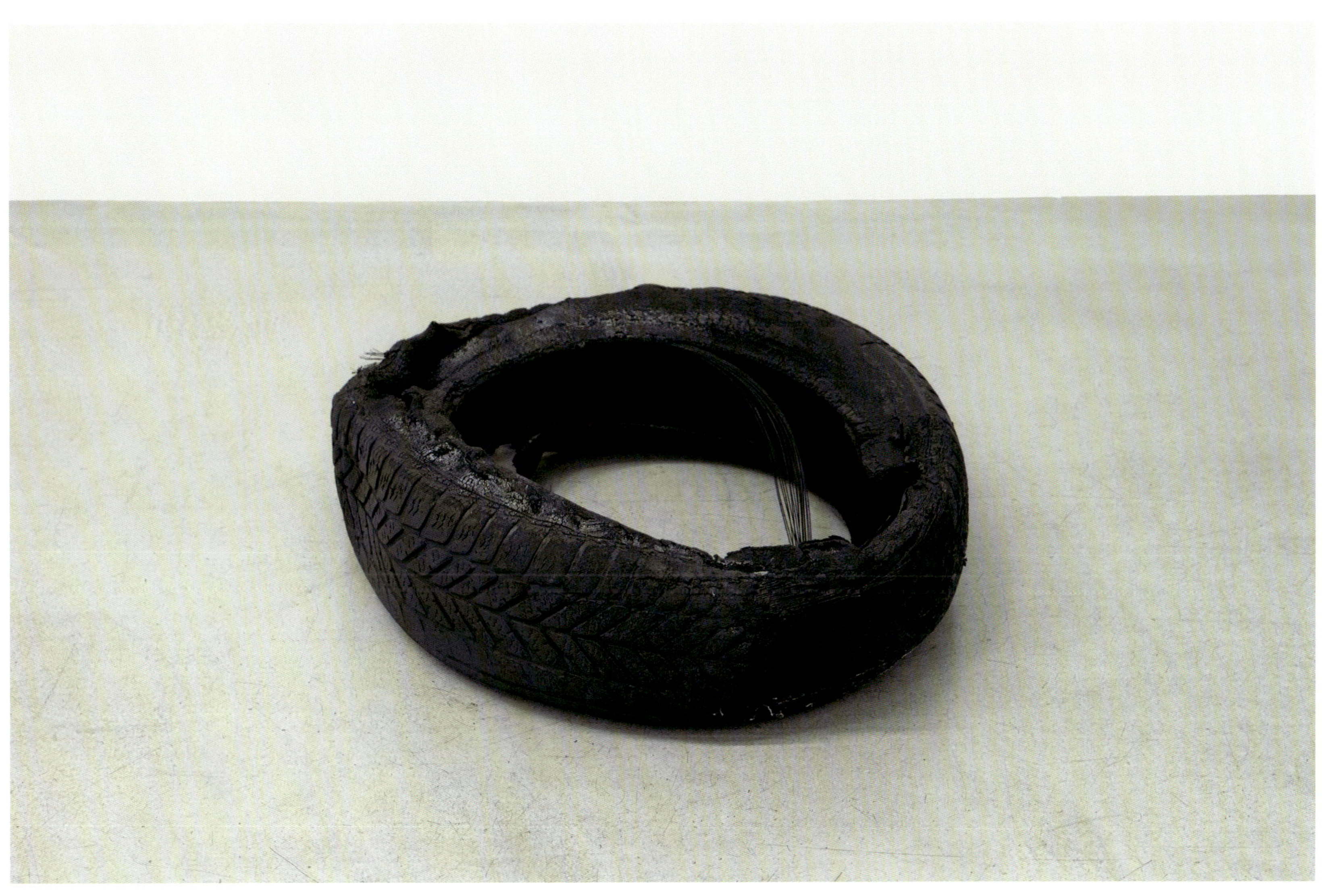

Smoke Ring VIII, 2008
Burned tire, 20 × 52 × 51 cm

Southern Night (J.T.)

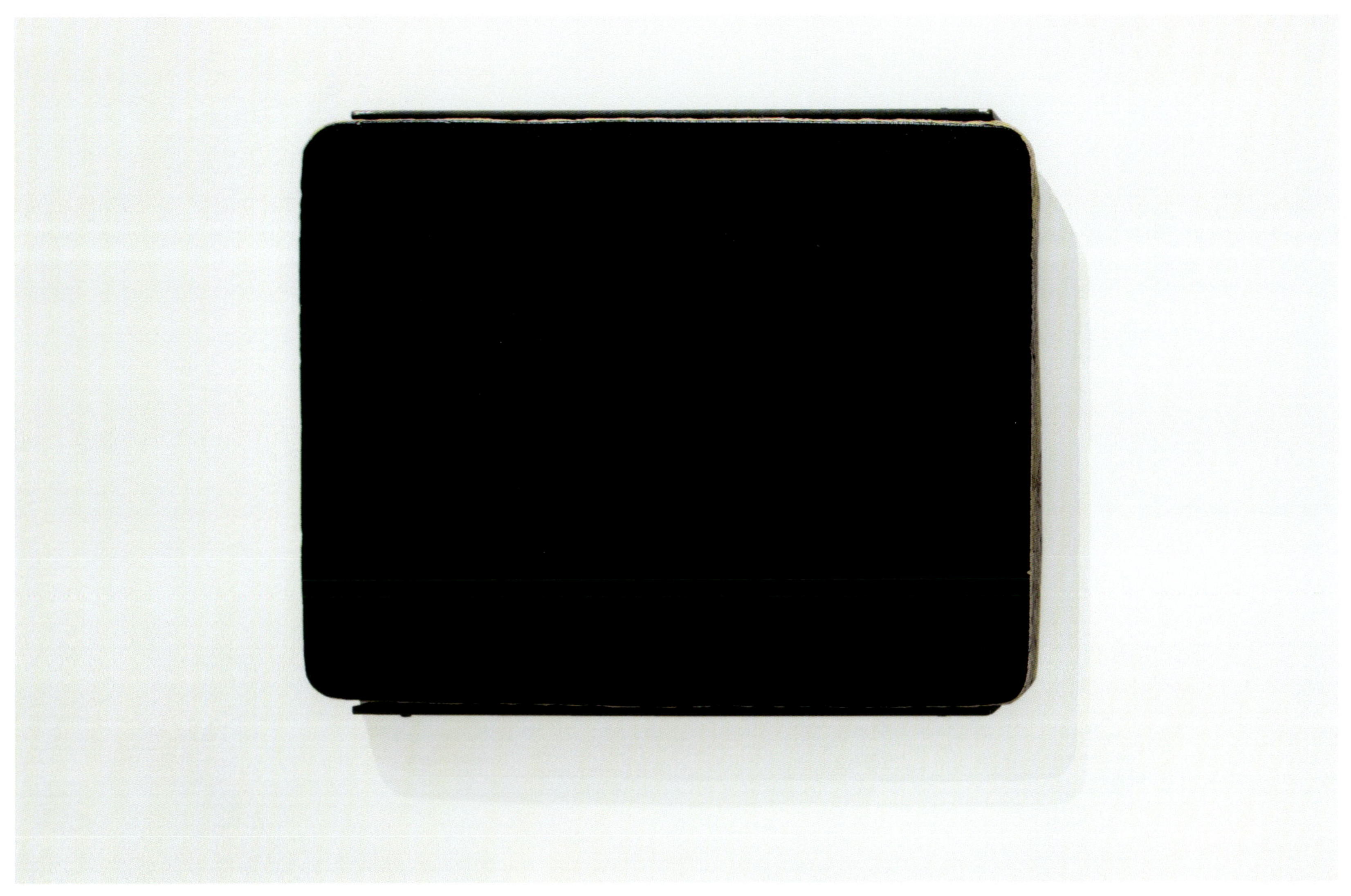

Southern Night (J.T.), 2012
Lithographic stone, printing ink, varnish,
steel angles, 30.8 × 40.7 × 5.4 cm

Speakers' Corner (Soap Box) 135

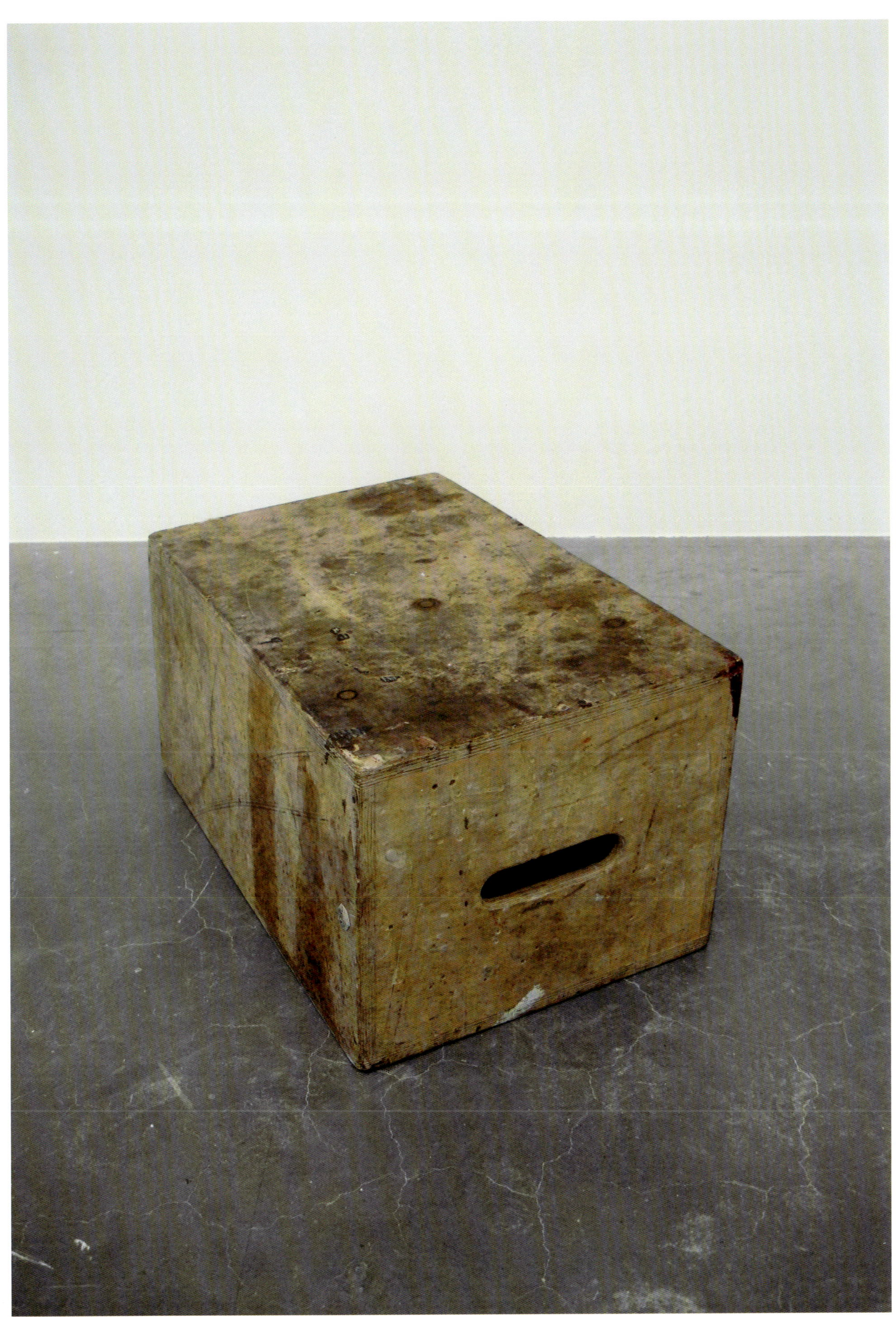

Speakers' Corner (Soap Box), 2008
Wood crate from Tate Modern
Art Handling Department,
31 × 60.5 × 38 cm
Exhibition view, Speakers' Corner,
Tate Modern, London, 2009

Still Life (Vanités)

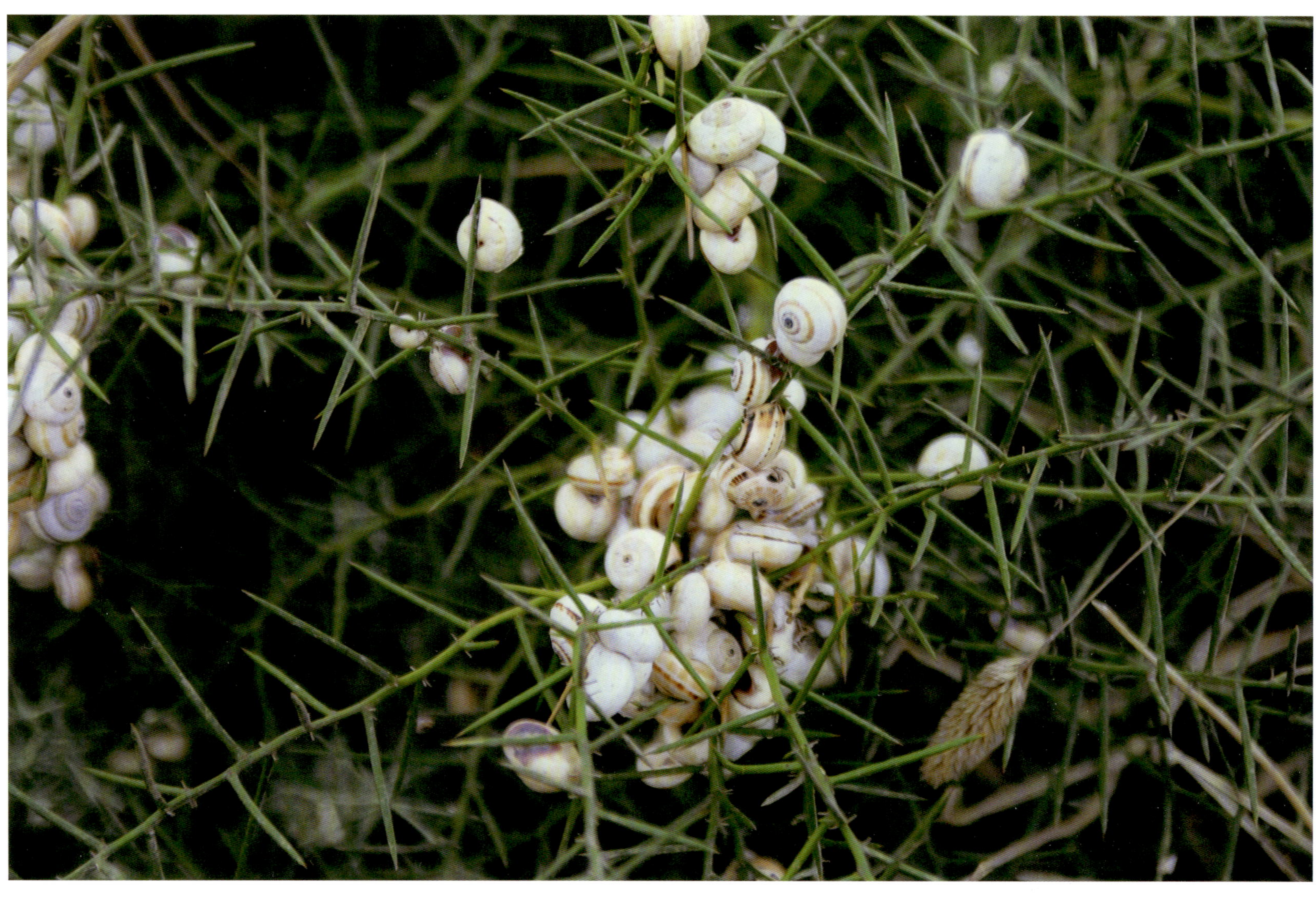

Still Life (Vanités) a, b, c, d, e, 2010
C-prints on aluminum, 26.5 × 40 cm each

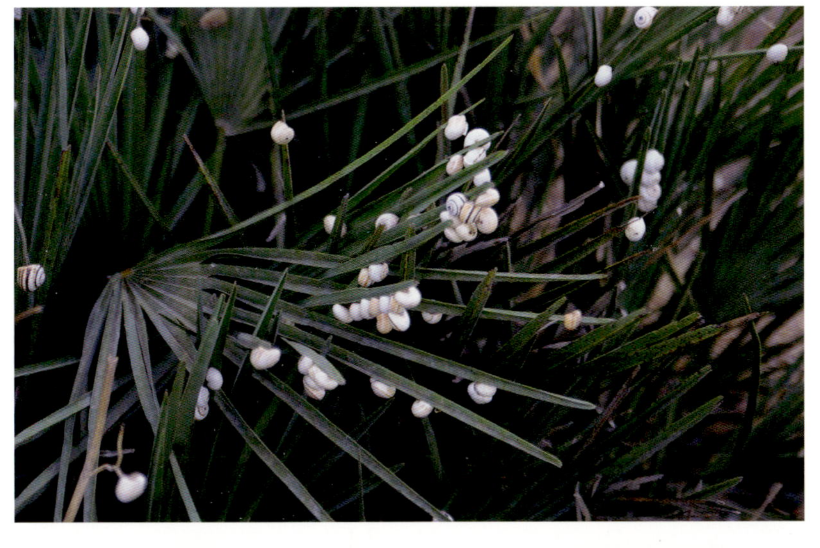

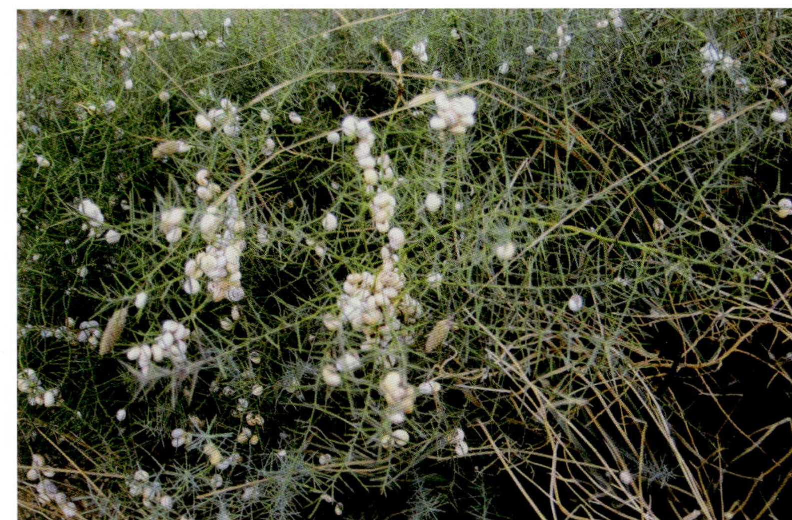

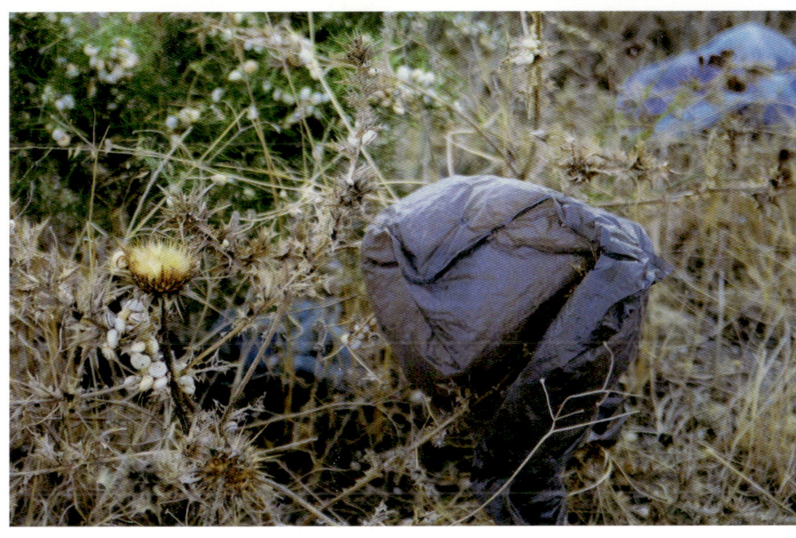

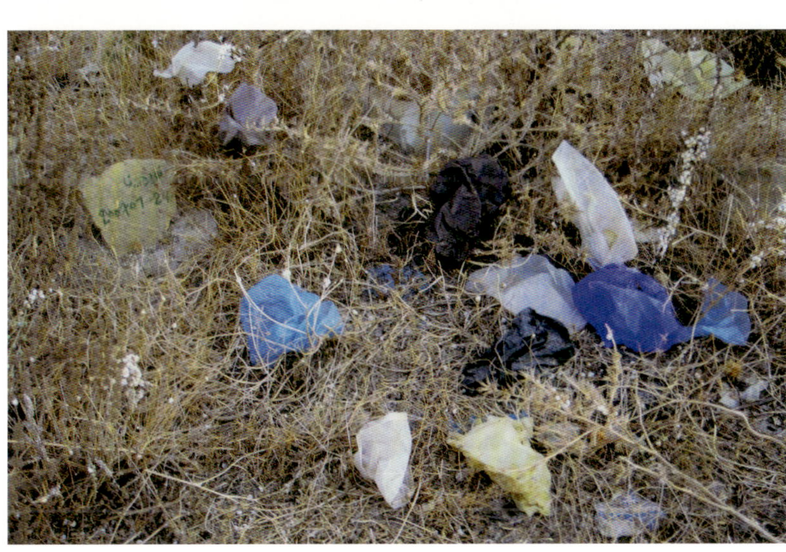

Stoning

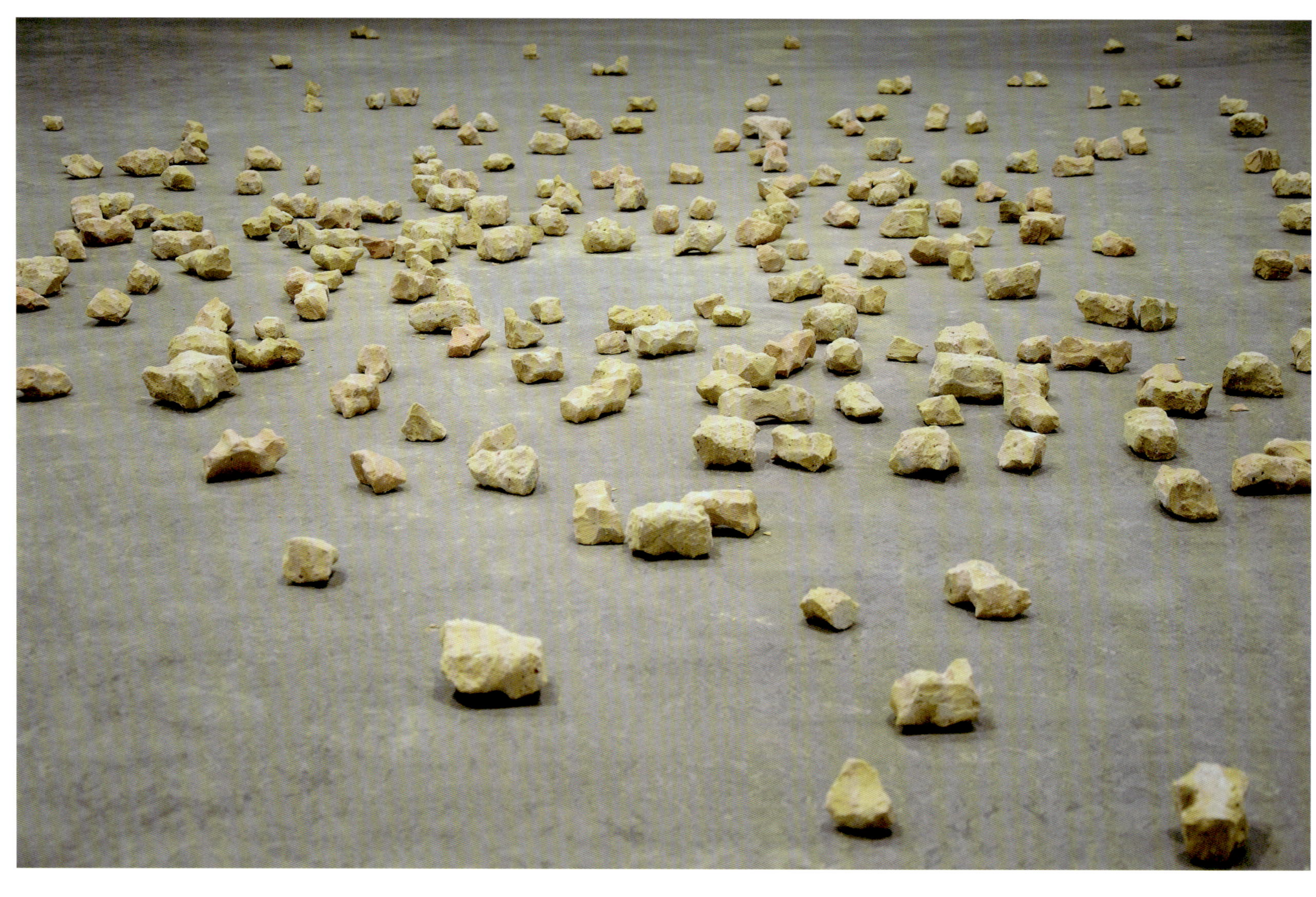

Stoning, 2010
Dressed stones from the former Boulingrin Halles market, Reims, dimensions variable

Collection FRAC Champagne-Ardenne, Reims

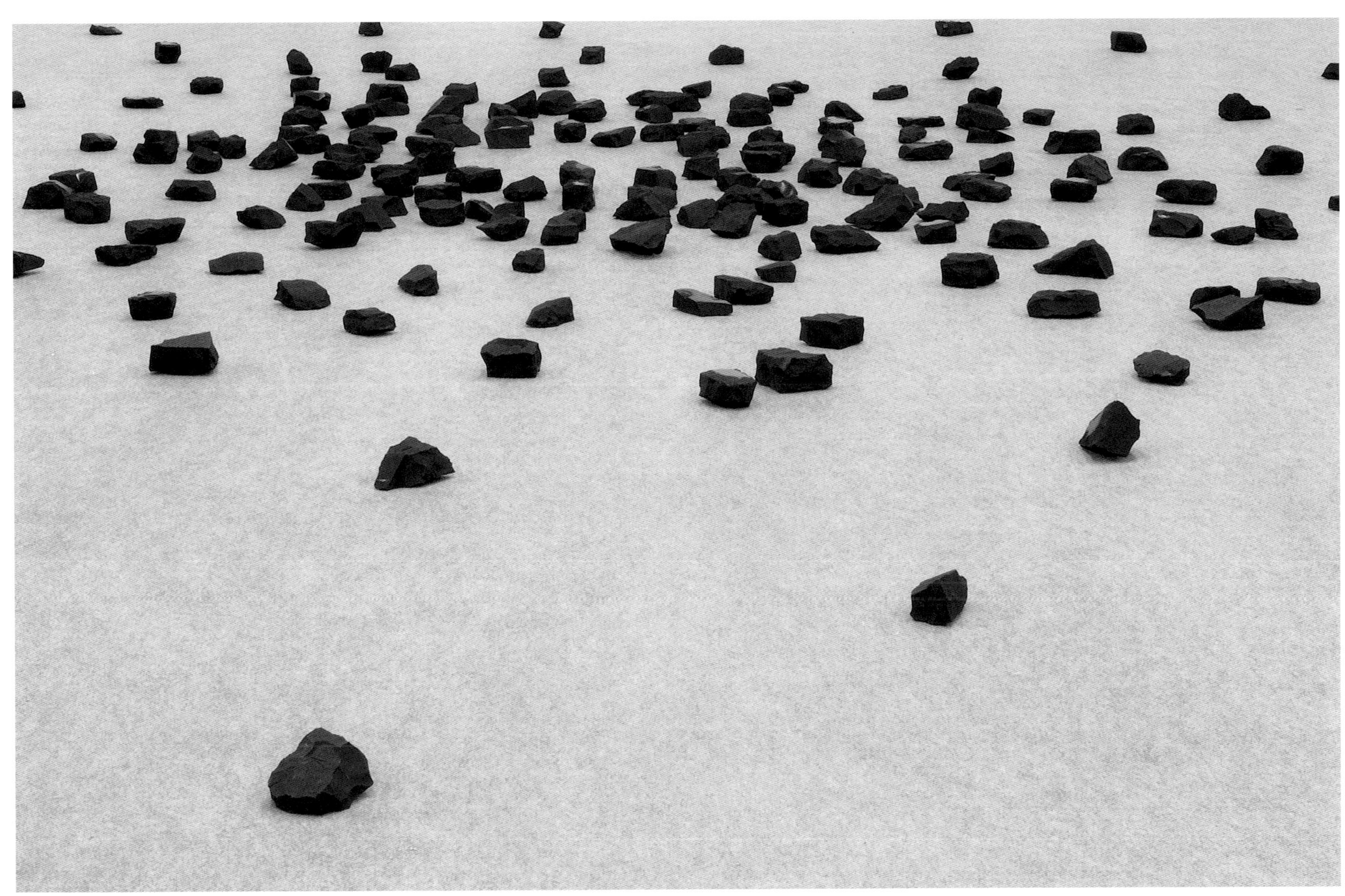

Stoning (Black Marble), 2010
Black marble, dimensions variable

Tambour

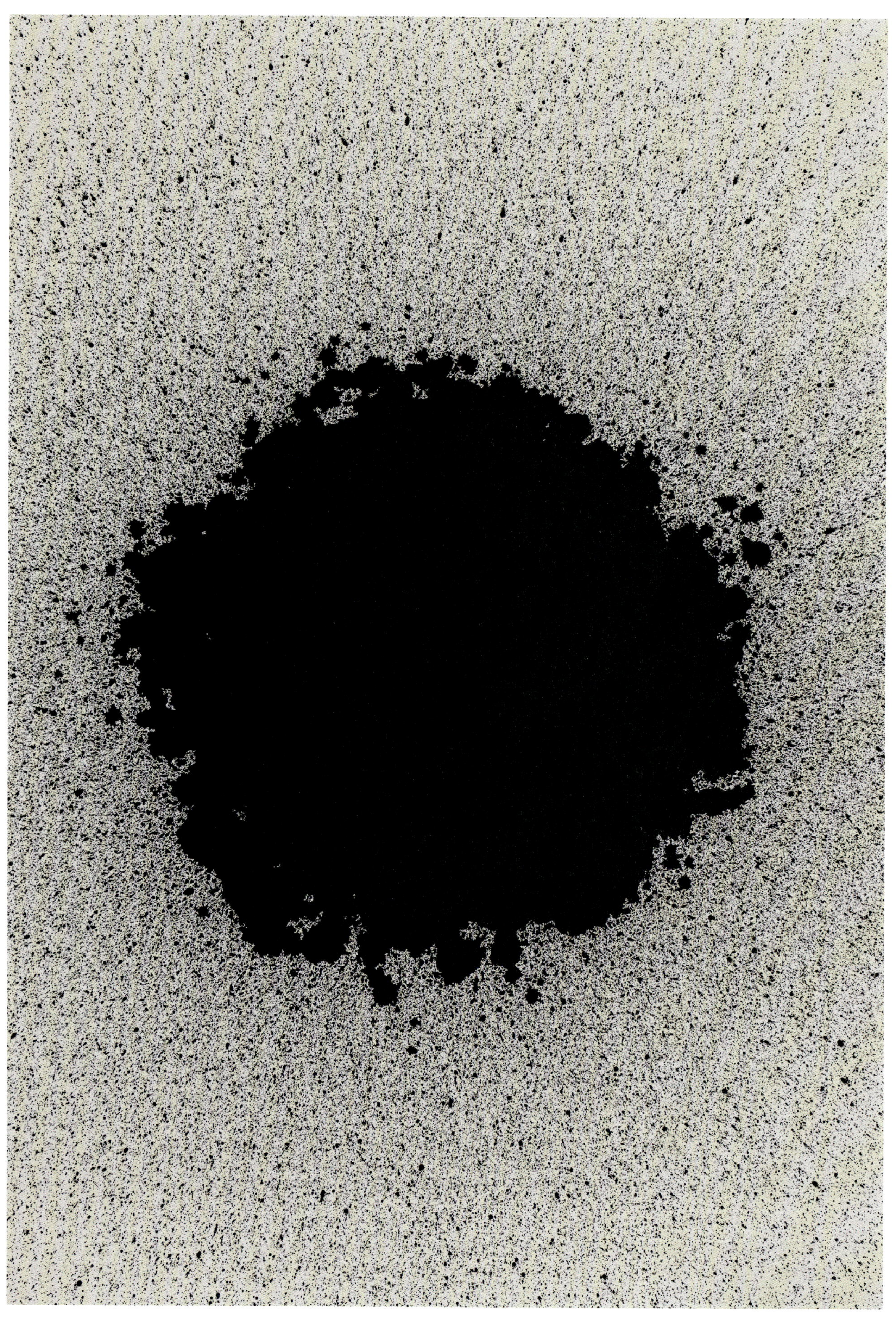

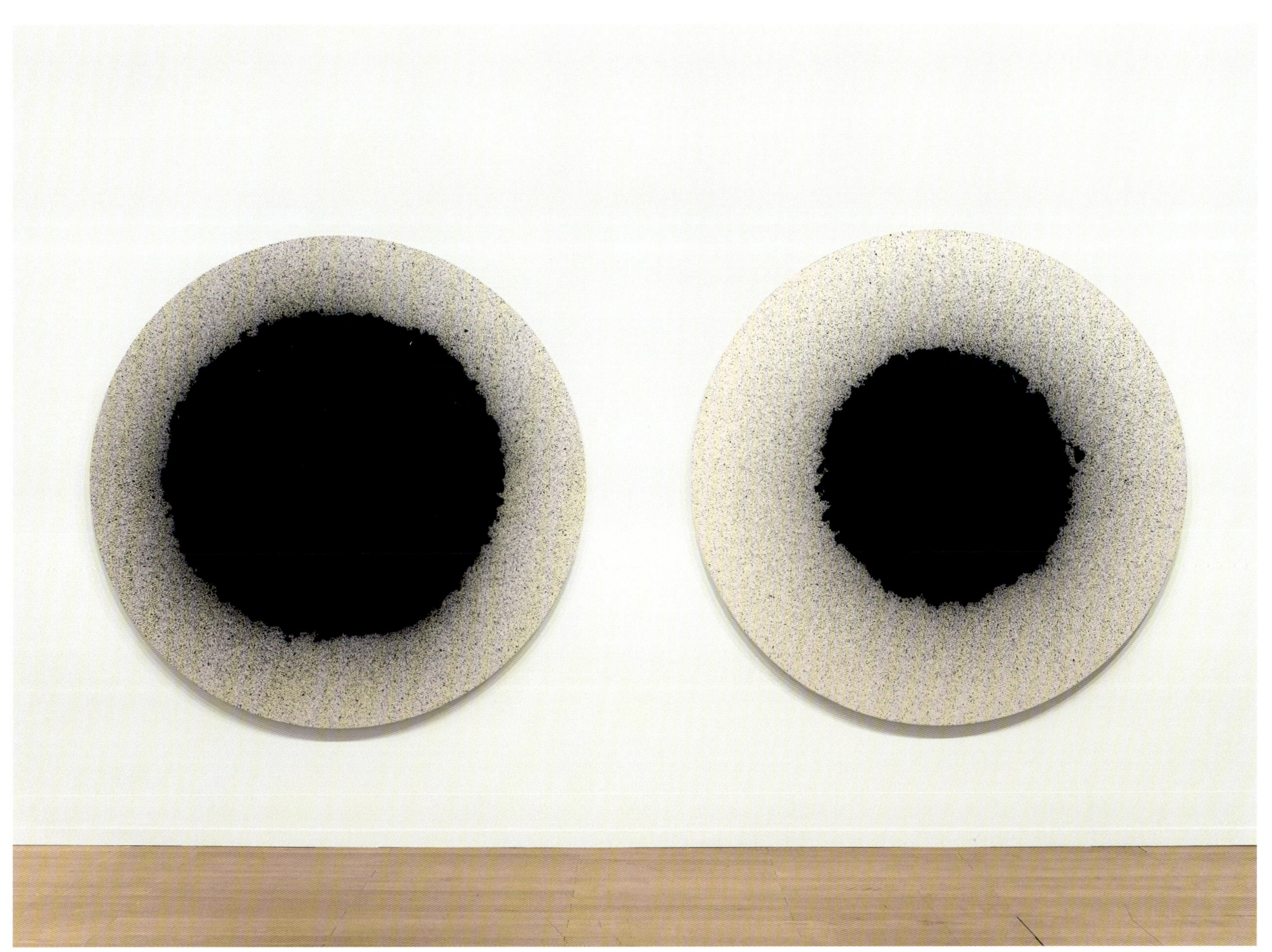

Tambour 128', and Tambour 65', 2013
(and detail)
Black India ink on canvas, ø 173 cm each
Exhibition view, Laps, Musée d'Art
contemporain, Lyon, 2013

Tkaf

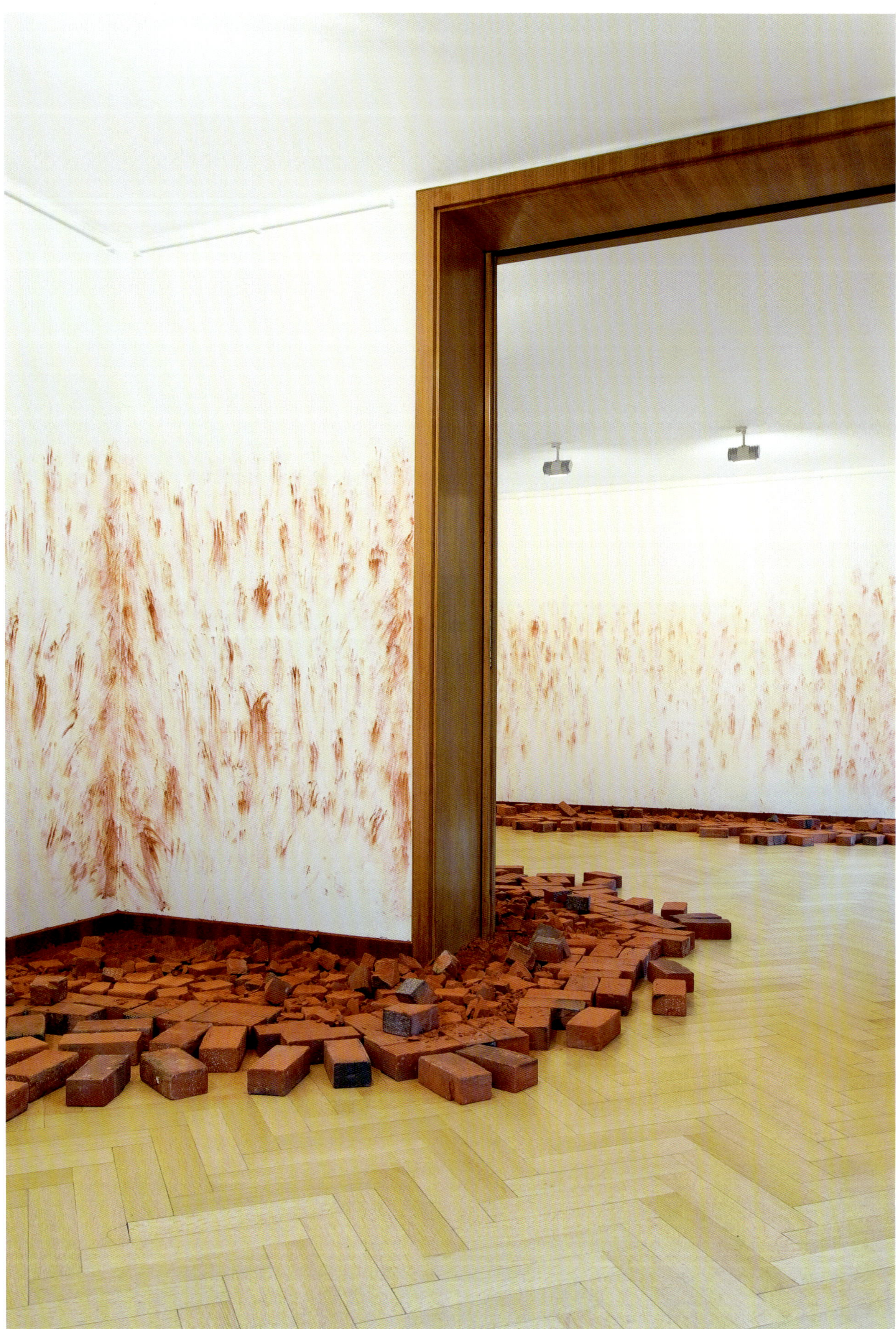

Tkaf, 2011
Bricks and sanguine pigment,
height: 2 m
Exhibition view and details,
From Threshold to Threshold,
Mies van der Rohe Haus der Esters,
Kunstmuseen, Krefeld

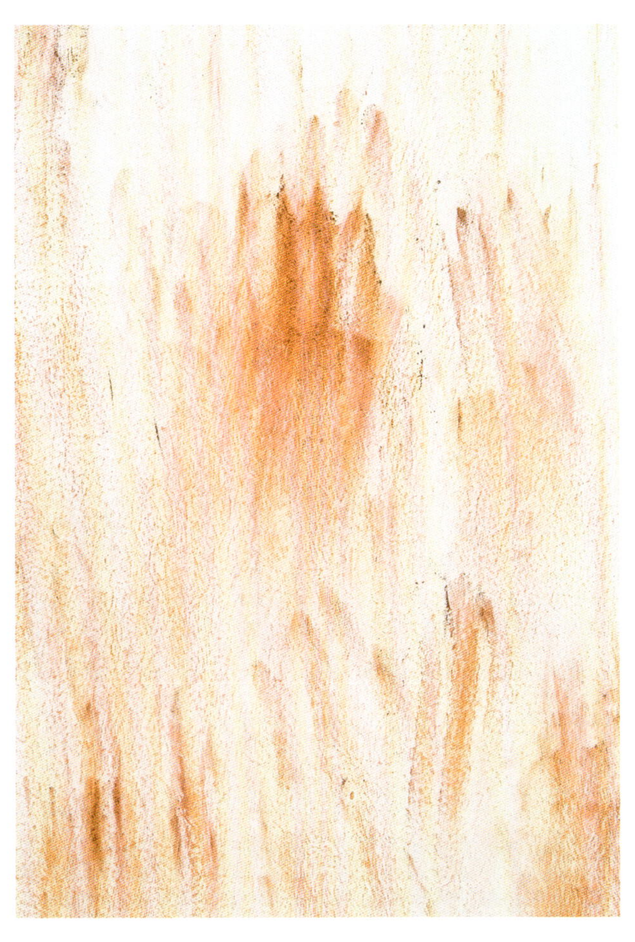

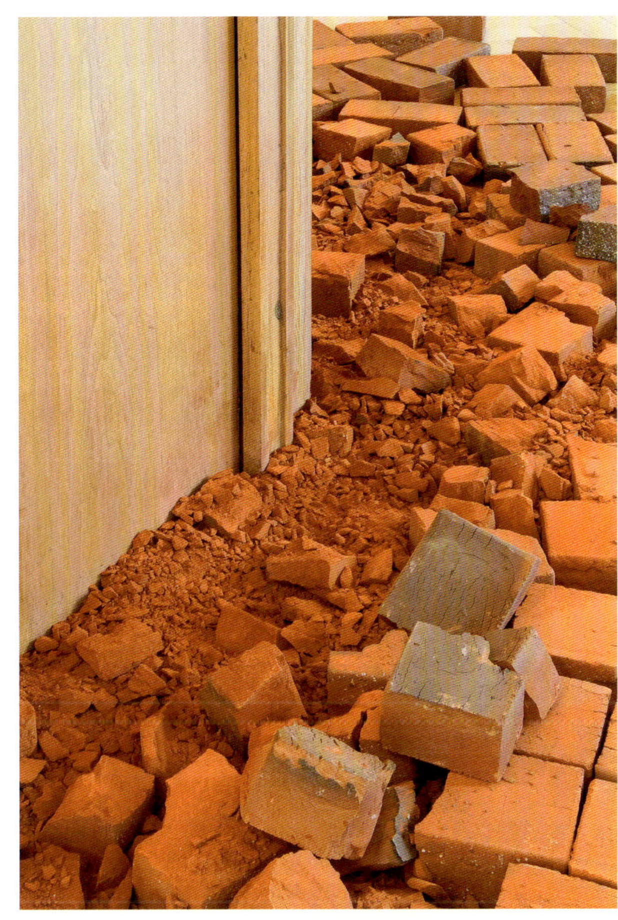

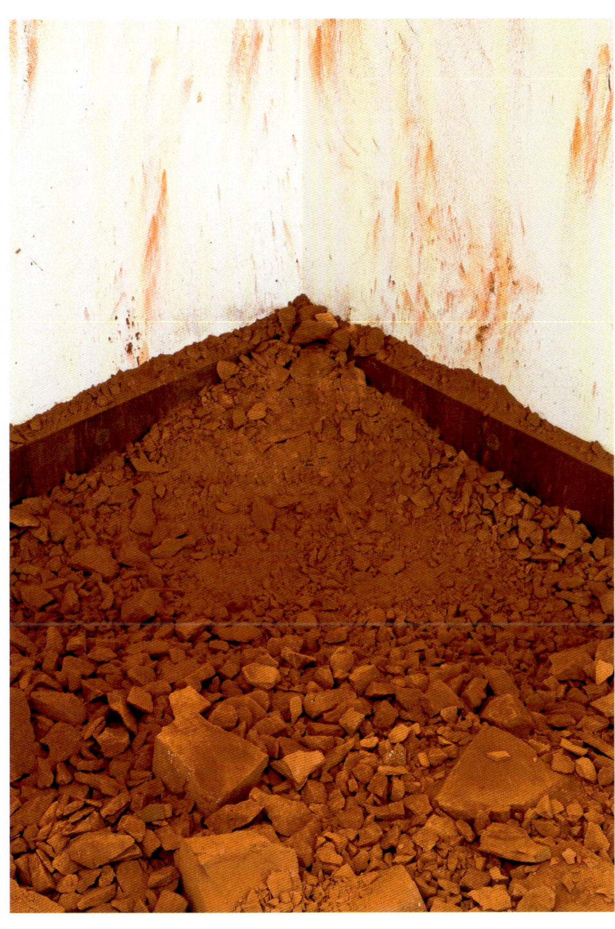

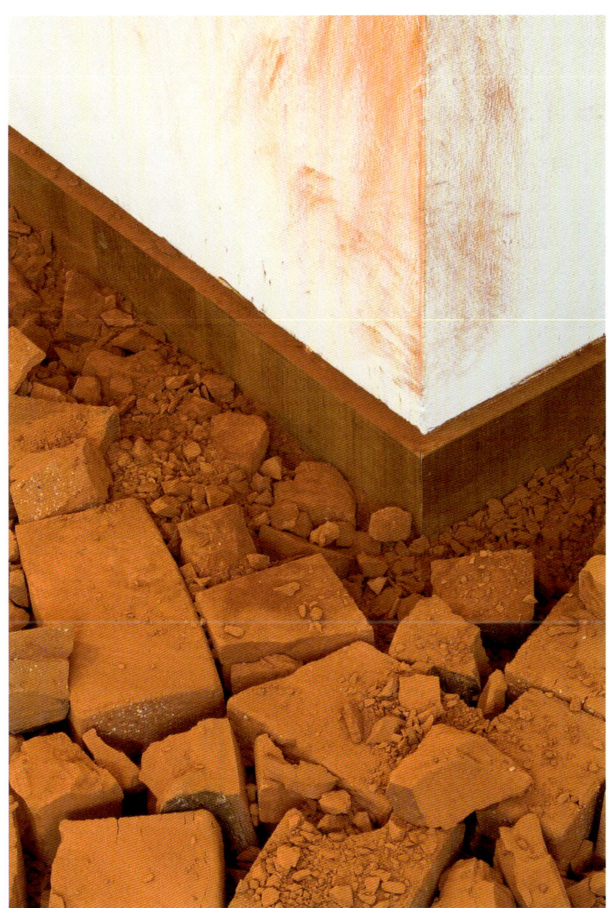

Tumbleweeds

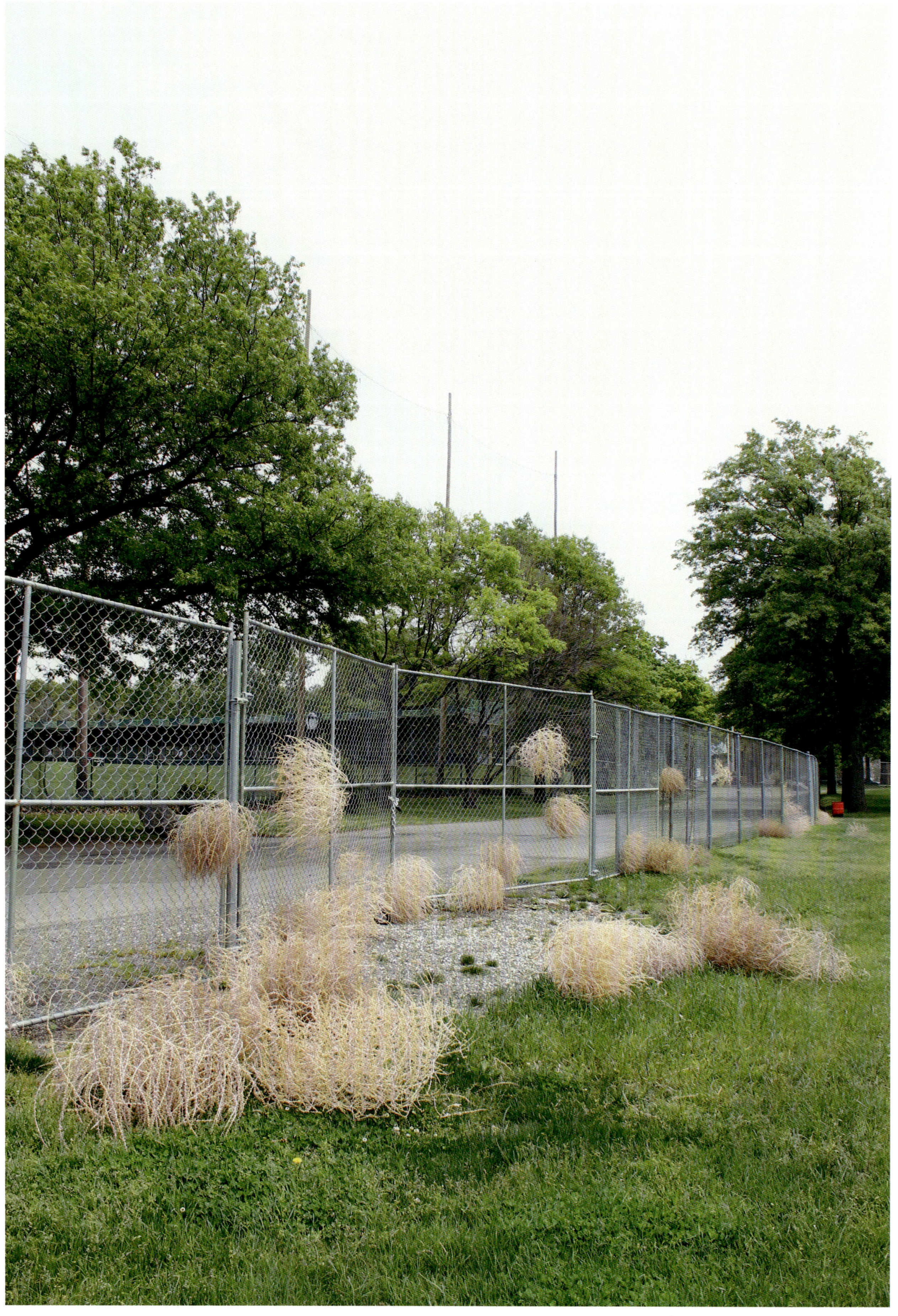

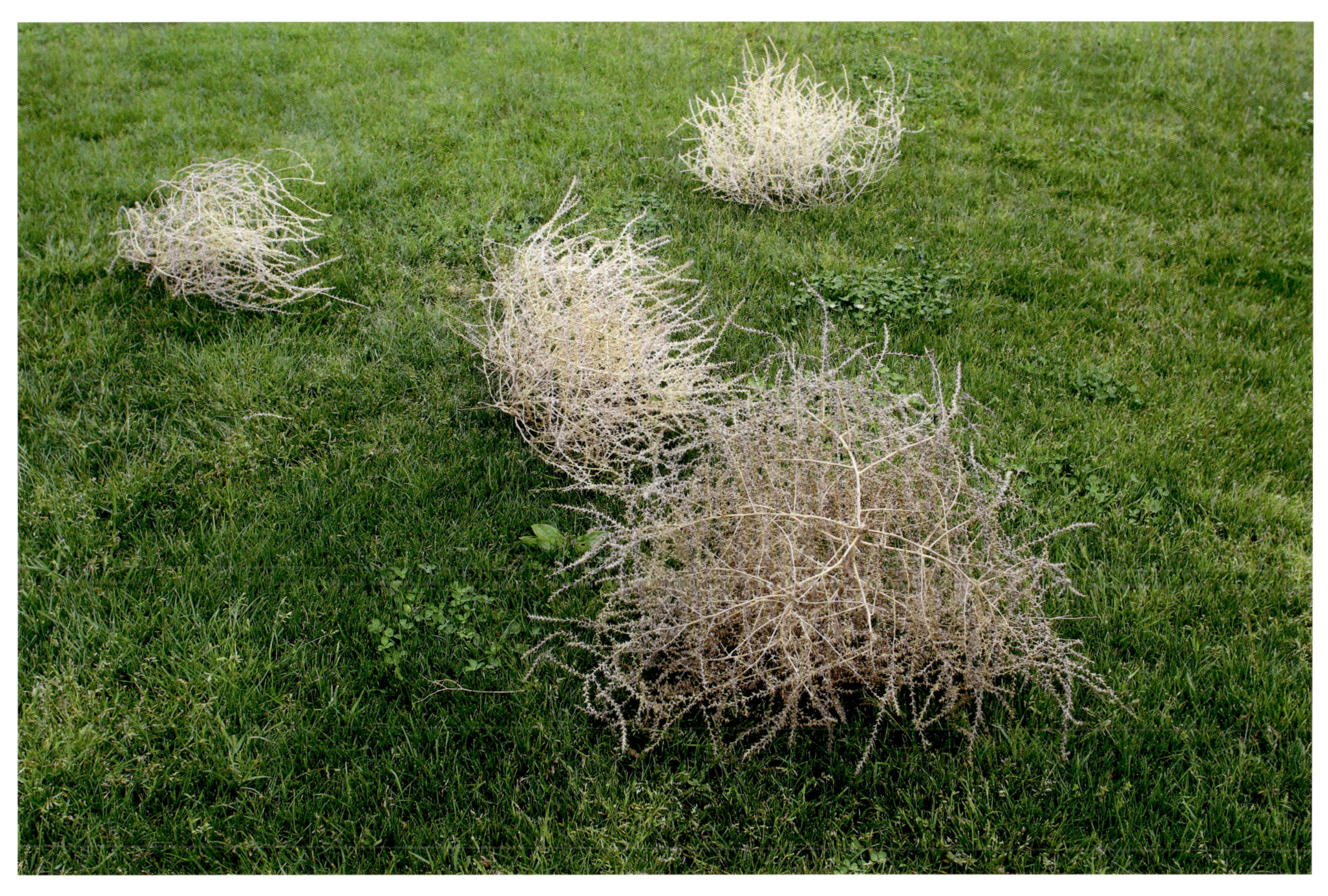

Tumbleweeds, 2012
Tumbleweed plants, dimensions variable
Installation views, Frieze Projects,
Randall's Island, New York, 2012

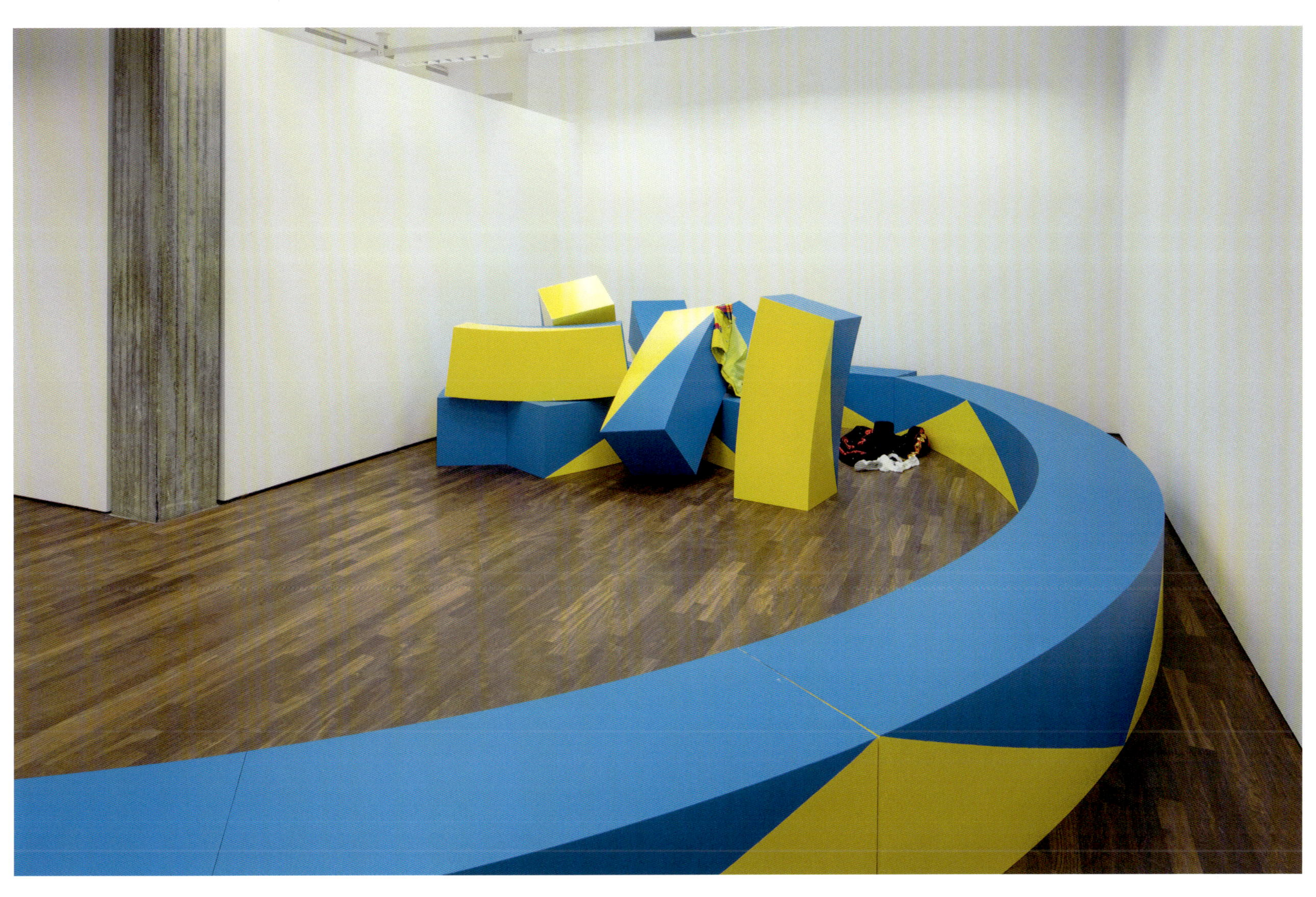

Untitled (Auguste and Clown), 2012
Circus ring, hardboard, paint, white clown costume, Auguste costume, shoes,
120 × 1000 × 1000 cm
Exhibition view, Goodbye Horses,
Kunsthaus Zürich, Zurich, 2012

Collection Kunsthaus Zürich, Zurich

Untitled (Fanfare l’Indépendante)

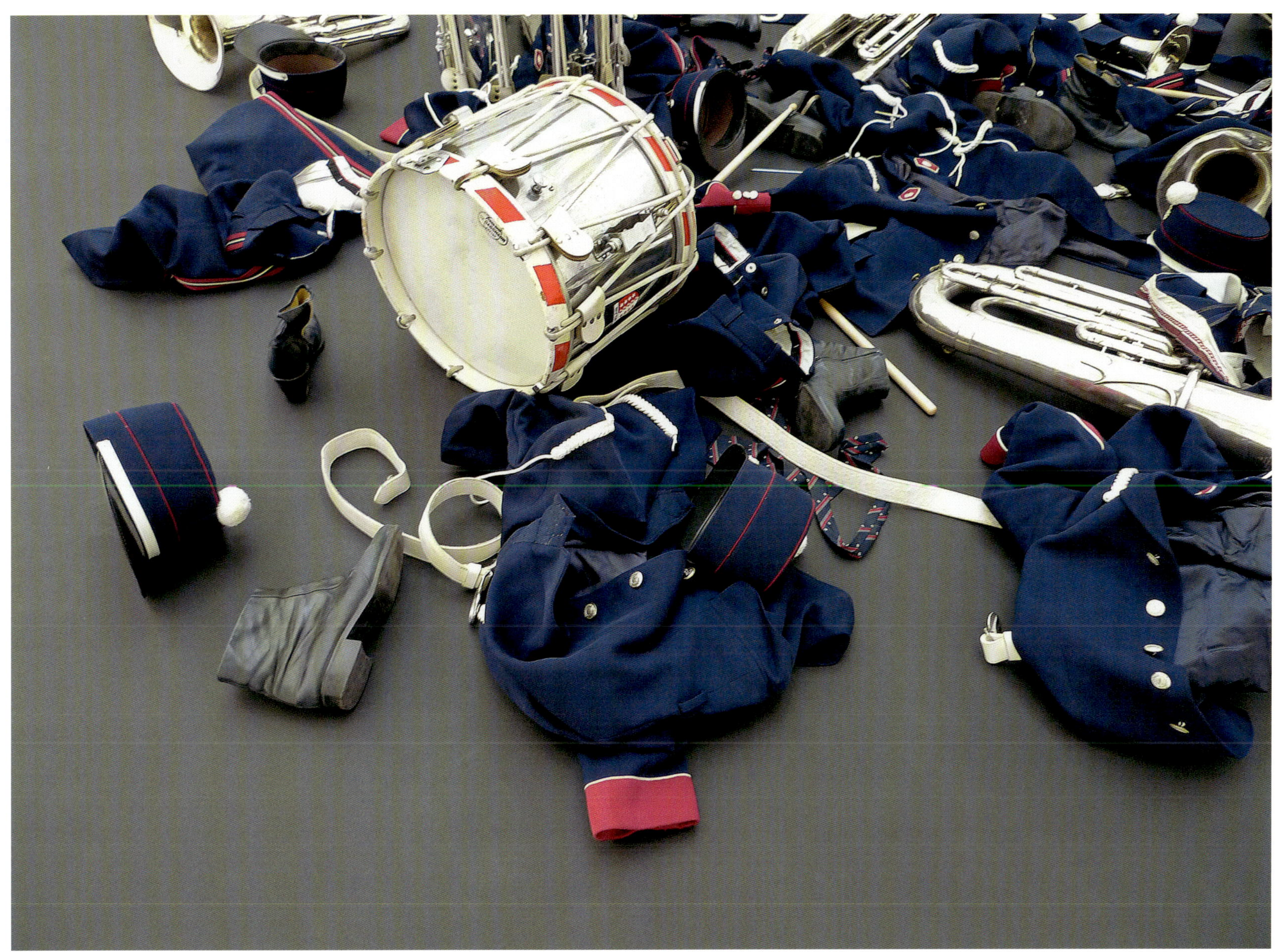

Untitled (Fanfare l’Indépendante), 2008
Costumes, shoes, hats, drums, brass instruments from the Swiss Fanfare l’Indépendante, pedestal, dimensions variable
Exhibition view, Invasion of Sound, Zacheta National Gallery of Art, Warsaw, 2009

Untitled (Sepia)

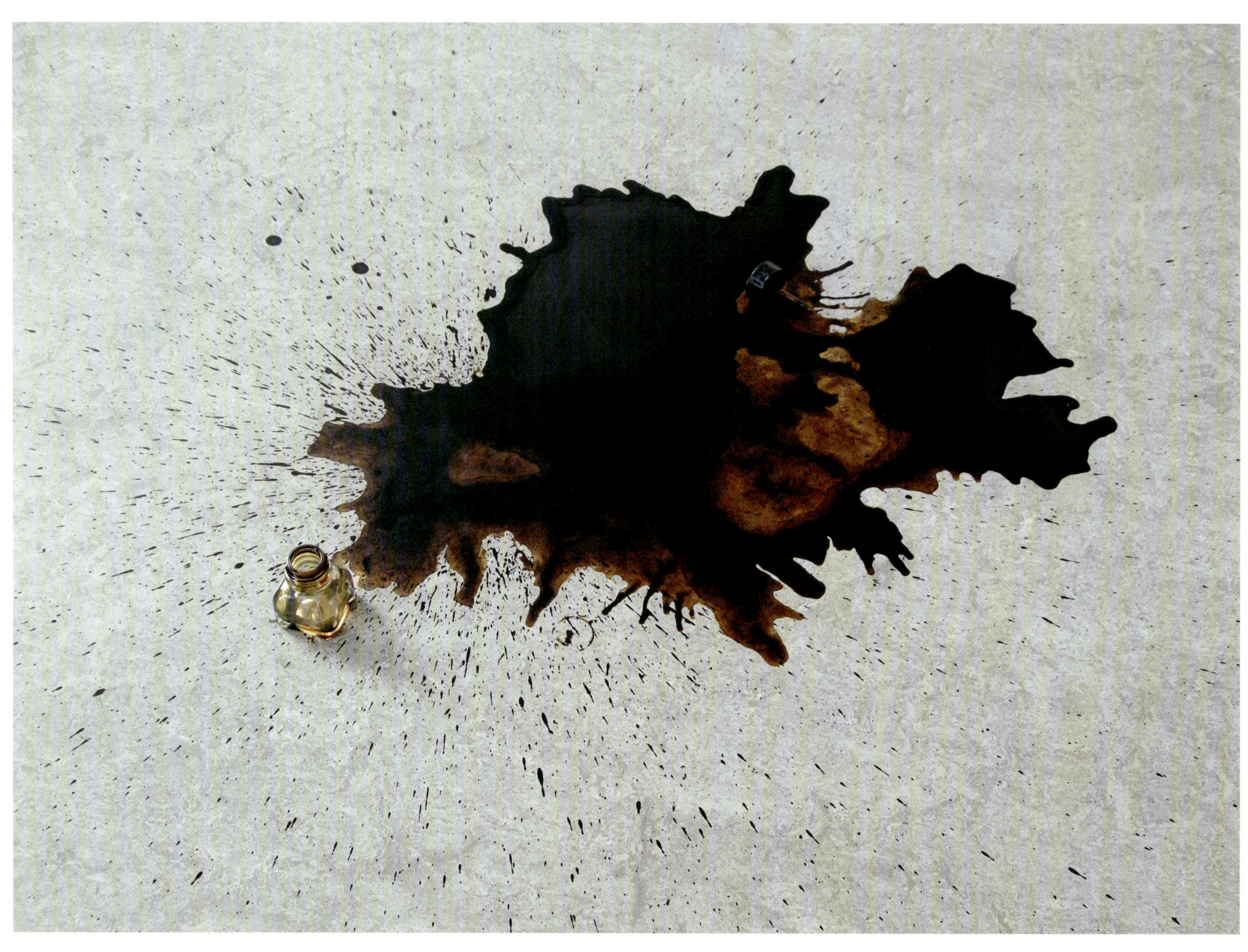

Untitled (Sepia), 2009
22 ml glass bottle, plastic top, 11 ml of sepia India ink, dimensions variable
Exhibition views, Le rappel des oiseaux, FRAC Champagne-Ardenne, Reims, 2010 (above), GAMeC, Bergamo, 2010 (right)

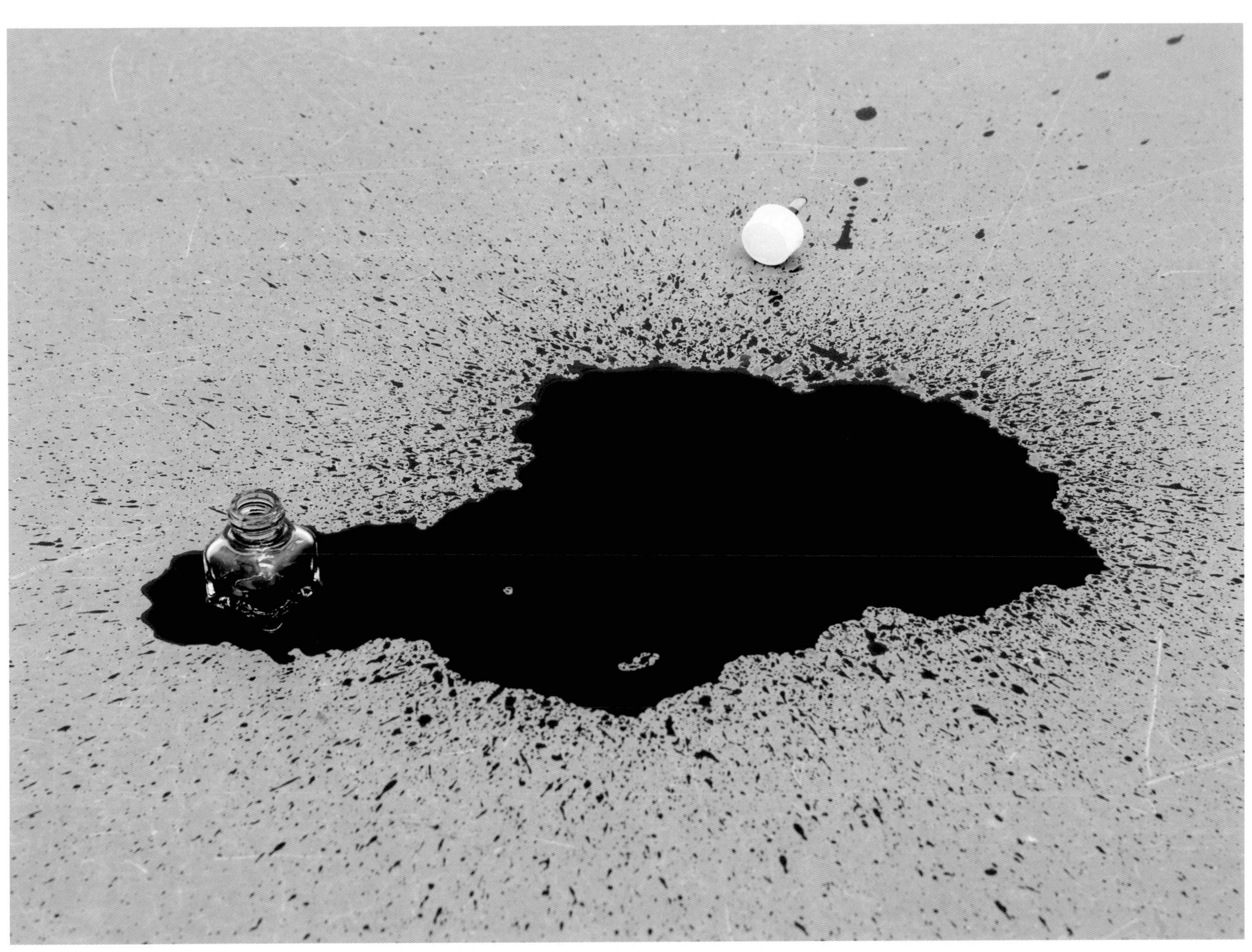

Untitled (The Sand from the Jar)

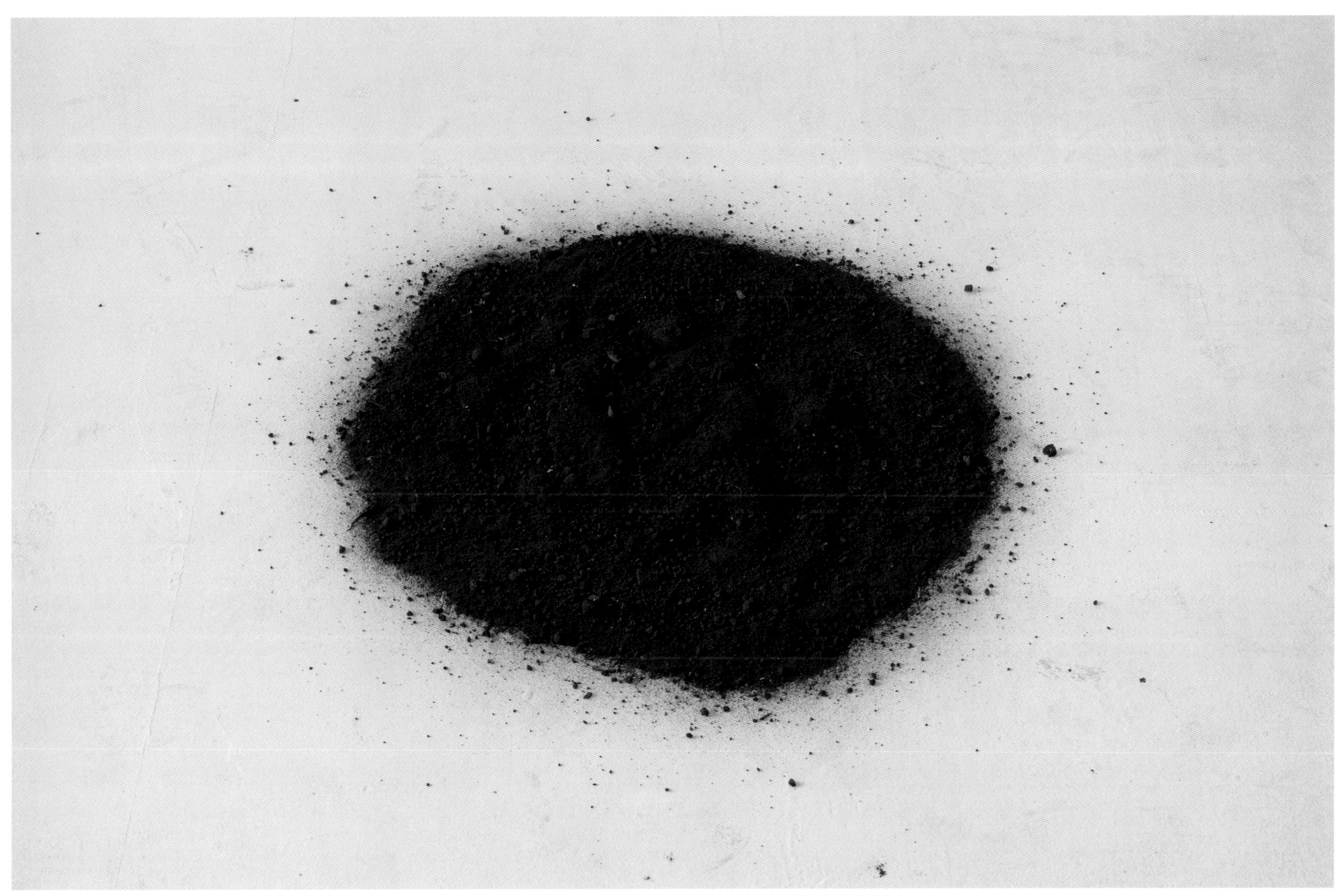

Untitled (The Sand from the Jar), 2013
Tel Aviv soil, India ink, ø 70 cm

Untitled (Two Figures and a Fauve)

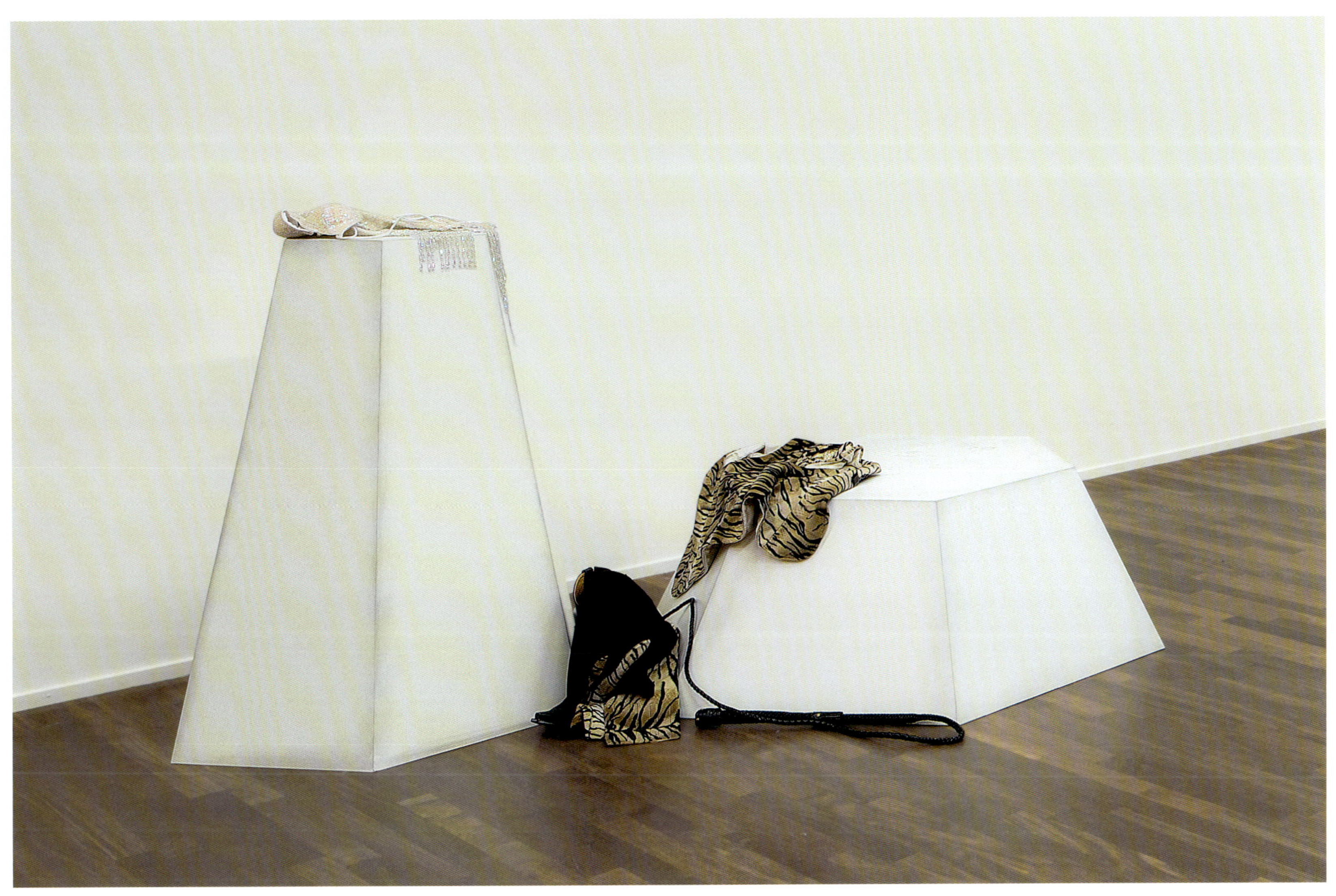

Untitled (Two Figures and a Fauve), 2012
Circus costumes, cowboy boots, stilettos, riding crop, glitter, 130 × 220 × 122 cm
Exhibition view, Goodbye Horses, Kunsthaus Zürich, Zurich, 2012

Biography

Born in 1974 in El Khnansa (Morocco), Latifa Echakhch lives and works in Martigny (Switzerland).

She graduated from the École des Beaux-Arts de Lyon in 2002, and received the Mies van der Rohe Stipondium in 2011.

She is represented by Dvir Gallery, Tel Aviv; kaufmann repetto, Milan; kamel mennour, Paris; and Galerie Eva Presenhuber, Zurich.

Selected Solo Exhibitions

2013
For Each Stencil a Revolution, Hammer Museum, Los Angeles
Laps, Musée d'Art contemporain, Lyon*
Bait, Dvir Gallery, Tel Aviv
Galerie Eva Presenhuber, Zurich

2012
Goodbye Horses, Kunsthaus Zürich, Zurich
Columbus Museum of Art, Colombus (Ohio)
Die Vögel, Portikus, Frankfurt
Dialogue: Latifa Echakhch, Kunstmuseum Liechtenstein, Vaduz
TKAF, kamel mennour, Paris*
Verso, kaufmann repetto, Milan

2011
From Threshold to Threshold, Mies van der Rohe Haus der Esters, Kunstmuseen, Krefeld
La Passion, Effigies, Fondation Louis Moret, Martigny

2010
Le rappel des oiseaux, FRAC Champagne-Ardenne, Reims; GAMeC, Bergamo
La Ronda, MACBA, Barcelona
Still life, Frame still, Fri Art, Fribourg

2009
Les sanglots longs, Kunsthalle Fridericianum, Kassel
Partitas, Bielefelder Kunstverein, Bielefeld
Movement and Complication, Swiss Institute, New York
Pendant que les champs brûlent, kamel mennour, Paris*

2008
Speakers' Corner, Tate Modern, London
Vitta Kuben, NorrlandsOperan, Umeå

2007
Il m'a fallu tant de chemins pour parvenir jusqu'à toi, Le Magasin, Grenoble

Selected Group Exhibitions

2013
Re:emerge, Towards a New Cultural Cartography, 11th Sharjah Biennial, Sharjah*
Hotel Abisso, Centre d'Art Contemporain, Geneva
EXPO 01: New York, MoMA PS1, New York*
Decorum. Tapis et tapisseries d'artistes, Musée d'Art moderne de la Ville de Paris, Paris*

2012
All Our Relations, 18th Sydney Biennial, Sydney*
Latifa Echakhch & David Maljković, Kunsthalle, Basel
The Spirit Level, Gladstone Gallery, New York

2011
ILLUMInazioni/ILLUMInations, 54th Venice Biennale, Venice
Volume!, MACBA, Barcelona
Eroi (Heroes), GAM, Turin

2010
After Architects, Kunsthalle, Basel
Leopards in the Temple, Sculpture Center, New York

2009
The Spectacle of the Everyday, 10th Biennial of Contemporary Art, Lyon
Invasion of Sound, Zacheta National Gallery of Art, Warsaw

2008
The Rest of Now, Manifesta 7, Bolzano
Shifting Identities–(Swiss) Art Today, Kunsthaus Zürich, Zurich

2007
Global Feminisms, Brooklyn Museum, New York; Davis Museum and Cultural Center, Wellesley*

2006
La Force de l'art, Grand Palais, Paris*
Strategies of Learning, Periferic 7-International Biennial for Contemporary Art, Iasi*

* Publication

Imprint

This monograph is published in conjunction with the following solo exhibitions:

- Les sanglots longs, August 29–November 15, 2009, at Kunsthalle Fridericianum, Kassel
- Partitas, September 5–October 25, 2009, at Bielefelder Kunstverein, Bielefeld
- Le rappel des oiseaux, April 4–May 23, 2010, at FRAC Champagne-Ardenne, Reims
- Le rappel des oiseaux, October 6, 2010–January 9, 2011, at GAMeC–Galleria d'Arte Moderna e Contemporanea, Bergamo

It has received the support of the following institutions:

Kunsthalle Fridericianum
Friedrichsplatz 18
34117 Kassel–Germany
www.fridericianum-kassel.de

KUNSTHALLE
FRIDERICIANUM

Artistic Director, Curator
Rein Wolfs

Curatorial Assistants
Andrea Linnenkohl, Johanna Adam

Communication
Christine Messerschmidt, Friederike Siebert

Education
Sandra Ortmann & Team

Secretary
Barbara Toopeekoff

Production
Winfried Waldeyer & Team

The body responsible for Kunsthalle Fridericianum is documenta und Museum Fridericianum Veranstaltungs-GmbH, CEO: Bernd Leifeld.

The documenta und Museum Fridericianum Veranstaltungs-GmbH is a non-profit organization owned and financed by the City of Kassel and the State of Hessen and supported by the Kulturstiftung des Bundes.

Corporate friends
Kunsthalle Fridericianum
Kasseler Sparkasse, KVG, and Städtische Werke, OKEL GmbH & Co. KG

Bielefelder Kunstverein
im Waldhof, Welle 61
33602 Bielefeld–Germany
www.bielefelder-kunstverein.de

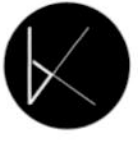

BIELEFELDER KUNSTVEREIN

Director
Thomas Thiel

Curatorial Assistant
Anna Jehle

Project Assistant
Sarah Kindermann

Visitor and Member Support
Christine Jodar

Technical Assistants
Klaus Braun, Marcus Mutz

Corporate Partners:

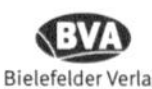

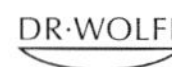

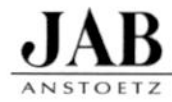

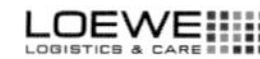

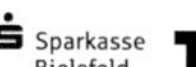

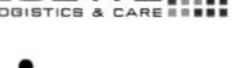

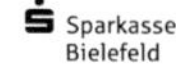

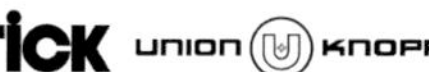

HÖRMANN

The exhibition was kindly supported by Institut français Deutschland in collaboration with the French Ministry of Culture and Communication (DGCA)

FRAC Champagne-Ardenne
1, place Museux
51100 Reims–France
www.frac-champagneardenne.org

frac
champagne-
ardenne

President
Matali Crasset

Director
Florence Derieux

Administration
Stéphanie Clément

Exhibitions and Publications
Antoine Marchand

Communication and Education
Sébastien Bourse

Publicity and Press
Isabelle Brichet

Registrar
Frédéric Nadeau

Collection
Jean-Martial Dutheil

Office
Edith Sauthier

FRAC Champagne-Ardenne receives funding from the Regional Council of Champagne-Ardenne, the Ministry of Culture and Communication, and the City of Reims.

GAMeC–Galleria d'Arte Moderna e Contemporanea, Bergamo
Associazione per la Galleria d'Arte Moderna e Contemporanea di Bergamo–onlus
Via San Tomaso, 53
24121 Bergamo–Italy
www.gamec.it

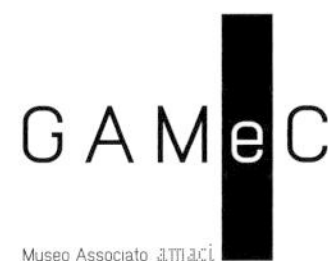

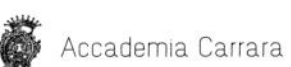

Associazione per la Galleria
d'Arte Moderna e Contemporanea
di Bergamo - Onlus

Soci Fondatori / Founding Members

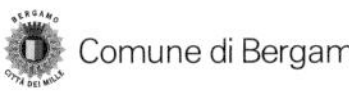

TenarisDalmine

Soci Benemeriti / Members

UBI Banca Popolare di Bergamo

Audi
BONALDI

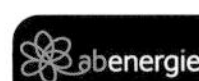

Founding Members
Comune di Bergamo
TenarisDalmine

Members
UBI–Banca Popolare di Bergamo
Bonaldi Motori
ABenergie

Board of Directors
Mario Scaglia, Chairman
Stefano Müller, Vice Chairman
Giuseppe Calvi, Giorgio Giovanni Pandini, Armando Spajani, Board Members

Auditor
Anna Venier

Legal Office
Elisabetta Racca

Board of Experts
Iwona Blazwick, Jan Hoet, Giorgio Verzotti

Director
Giacinto Di Pietrantonio

Head of Accademia Carrara and GAMeC, Director
M. Cristina Rodeschini

COO
Alessandro G. Montel

Consulting Director, Responsible for Events and Artists' Archives
Angela Fabrizia Previtali

Curators
Sara Fumagalli
Stefano Raimondi

Curator at Large
Alessandro Rabottini

GAMeCinema Curator
Daniela Vincenzi

Educational Department
Giovanna Brambilla, Manager
Clara Manella

Communication and Promotion
Manuela Blasi
Paola Colombo

Administration
Valentina Rapelli, Manager
Ilaria Trussardi

Administrative Support
Claudio Gamba
Lorella Grammatico

Booking and Ticket Office
Rachele Bellini

Latifa Echakhch's exhibition at GAMeC was part of a series in honor of Arturo Toffetti.

The exhibition has been staged with the support of Pro Helvetia, the Swiss Arts Council.

swiss arts council
prohelvetia

Thanks to the Istituto Svizzero di Roma for its precious cooperation.

Istituto Svizzero

This publication has been made possible thanks to the generous support of GAMeC Club.

This publication also received the support of the following galleries representing Latifa Echakhch:

Dvir Gallery
11 Nahum Hanavi Street
Tel Aviv 63503-Israel
www.dvirgallery.com

גלריה דביר
Dvir Gallery

kaufmann repetto
Via di Porta Tenaglia 7
20121 Milan-Italy
www.kaufmannrepetto.com

kaufmann repetto

kamel mennour
47, rue Saint-André des Arts
6, rue du Pont de Lodi
75006 Paris-France
www.kamelmennour.com

kamel mennour

Galerie Eva Presenhuber
Maag Areal
Zahnradstrasse 21
8005 Zurich-Switzerland
www.presenhuber.com

GALERIE EVA PRESENHUBER

Editor
Florence Derieux

Authors
Ben Borthwick, Florence Derieux, Alessandro Rabottini

Editorial Coordination
Clément Dirié, Antoine Marchand
With the assistance of Naima Saidi

Copyediting
Clare Manchester

Translation from the French
Simon Pleasance & Fronza Woods
(Florence Derieux)

Translation from the Italian
Catherine Bolton
(Alessandro Rabottini)

Graphic Design
Nicolas Eigenheer, Vera Kaspar

Typeface
Swiss Gothic (François Rappo)

Color Separation & Print
Musumeci S.p.A., Quart (Aosta)

Dust Jacket Image
À chaque stencil une révolution, 2013 (detail)
Exhibition view, Hammer Museum, Los Angeles, 2013
Wall installation; A4 carbon paper, glue, methylated alcohol, dimensions variable

The artist would like to thank:
Marie-Fabienne Aymon, Ami Barak, Ben Borthwick, Giovanni Carmine, Valentin Carron, Corinne Charpentier, Loulou Cherinet, Bice Curiger, Lisa Dent, Florence Derieux, Redouane Echakhch, Marie-Sophie Eiché, Maria Florut, Hou Hanru, Gauthier Herrmann, Dean Inkster, Dvir Intrator, Sébastien Janssen, Francesca Kaufmann, Bartomeu Mari i Ribas, Silvia Martin, Kamel Mennour, Han Nefkens, Thierry Ollat, Gerardo Peral, Eva Presenhuber, Alessandro Rabottini, Jean-Pierre Rehm, Chiara Repetto, Ugo Rondinone, Gabi Scardi, Shifra Shalit, Yotam Shalit-Intrator, Mats Stjernstedt, Adam Szymczyk, Hilde Teerlinck, Thomas Thiel, and Rein Wolfs.

Photo Credits
Blaise Adilon: p. 58–59, 60–61, 68–69, 101, 141; Columbus Museum of Art, Ohio: p. 53, 65, 75, 87, 99, 107, 133; Courtesy Kunstmuseum Liechtenstein, Vaduz: p. 6–7, 14–15; Courtesy Swiss Institute, New York: p. 4–5, 80–81, 108; Brian Forrest: dust jacket; Volker Döhne: p. 46–47, 71r, 142–143; Isabelle Giovacchini: p. 24, 51, 88–89, 97, 126–127, 138, 150; Nils Klinger: p. 16–17; Julie Langenegger: p. 118–119, 120–121; Mancia/Bodmer, FBM Studio, Zurich/ Kunsthaus Zürich: p. 20–21, 147, 155; Jacopo Menzani: p. 10–11, 72, 96, 129, 151; Roberto Marossi: p. 2–3; Philipp Ottendörfer: p. 95, 109; Pere Pratdesaba /Fundació Miró: p. 12–13; Helena Schlichting/ Courtesy Portikus: p. 18–19; Fabrice Seixas: p. 70l, 71l, 83; Rafael Vargas: p. 8–9; and all rights reserved for the other photographs.

Published by

JRP|Ringier
Limmatstrasse 270
CH-8005 Zurich
T + 41 (0) 43 311 27 50
F + 41 (0) 43 311 27 51
E info@ jrp-ringier.com
www.jrp-ringier.com

ISBN: 978-3-03764-200-9

JRP|Ringier books are available internationally at selected bookstores and from the following distribution partners:

Switzerland
AVA Verlagsauslieferung AG
verlagsservice@ava.ch, www.ava.ch

France
Les presses du réel
info@lespressesdureel.com,
www.lespressesdureel.com

Germany and Austria
Vice Versa Distribution
info@vice-versa-distribution.com,
www.vice-versa-distribution.com

UK and other European countries
Cornerhouse Publications
publications@cornerhouse.org,
www.cornerhouse.org/books

USA, Canada, Asia, and Australia
D.A.P./Distributed Art Publishers
dap@dapinc.com, www.artbook.com

For a list of our partner bookshops or for any general questions, please contact JRP|Ringier directly at info@jrp-ringier.com.